MW01644917

The Seven Pillars of Worship

A Systematic Study of the Principles of Biblical Worship

Wendell Warman

All Hebrew and Greek words, and their transliterations and definitions are taken from Strong's Exhaustive Concordance by James Strong, Abingdon Press, 1890. All words in bold within Scripture quotations are exclusively the author's emphasis.

Cover design by Wendell Warman
Photo by Jan Zhukov on Unsplash

Published in the United States of America
ISBN: **9798531247193**

CONTENTS

ACKNOWLEDGMENTS

I thank the heavenly Father for the mercy and grace he has given us through his only begotten Son, Jesus. I thank him for the Spirit of wisdom and revelation he gives to his children. I also thank him for the opportunity to publish this work. May it bring him glory! Lastly, I thank my dear wife and friend, Marilina, for her love and patience during a long season of writing. Her help in translating this work in Italian, along with her suggestions (several of which have also been applied to the English version) have proven invaluable. It is to you, Marilina, I dedicate this book.

Introduction

Wisdom has built her house; she has hewn her seven pillars (Prov. 9:1, ESV).

Proverbs, chapter nine, verse one is symbolic of the house of God and the seven pillars of worship. The house of God is, of course, his dwelling place, but it is also a place of spiritual encounter, a place of worship. The pillars represent seven divine principles of wisdom that collectively *define*, *express*, and *inspire* biblical worship. These principles are what give worship its *structure*, *symmetry*, and *aesthetics*. They are what constitute the divine means through which man may approach God and worship him in a way that is both acceptable and pleasing to him. They are also what set biblical worship apart from all other world religions and religious philosophies. In short, these principles are what form the main thesis of the following studies.

Our series of studies will closely examine the lives and experiences of seven prophetic men in the Old Testament: *Abel*, *Seth*, *Noah*, *Abraham*, *Isaac*, *Jacob*, and *Moses*. These seven men exemplified and embodied the very principles of biblical worship we are examining. During our studies, we will invariably point to the quintessence of each principle—the *Messiah*. Jesus is the sum total of all that God would say or reveal, regarding the subject of worship.[1]

We have added Hebrew and Greek to provide a little more insight into the meaning of specific words related to the subject of worship that might otherwise go unnoticed. But the author is by no means an expert in ancient languages; however, he does know how to find his way through a concordance and an interlinear Bible!

If you are looking for easy reading, a collection of personal stories or anecdotes, you have clearly picked up the wrong book. But if you are looking for an investigative study of worship in the Scriptures (and a lot of them!),

[1] Matt. 12:42; John 4:23-26

then you indeed hold the right book in your hands. It is our hope this study will be a great blessing to you, to the church, and to any student of the Scriptures. It is also our hope that the book might encourage, inspire, and even challenge the reader to be even more engaged in worship. Above all, may the Lord Jesus Christ be glorified by this work. He is completely worthy of all our love and devotion.

CHAPTER 1

The Pillar of Sacrifice

(The Expression of Biblical Worship)

In the course of time Cain brought to the Lord an offering of the fruit of the ground, and Abel also brought of the firstborn of his flock and of their fat portions. And the Lord had regard for Abel and his offering, but for Cain and his offering he had no regard. So Cain was very angry, and his face fell. The Lord said to Cain, "Why are you angry, and why has your face fallen? If you do well, will you not be accepted? And if you do not do well, sin is crouching at the door. Its desire is contrary to you, but you must rule over it" (Gen. 4:3-7, ESV).

If there is a singular point of encounter between biblical worship and that of ancient and many modern religions, it is the concept of sacrifice. However, the meaning, purpose, and motivation behind the expression are as divergent as the east is from the west. We may trace the origins of the ritual back to the early chronicles of history. According to the account in the book of Genesis, "in the course of time," Cain and Abel brought their sacrifices to God.[1] Cain, who worked the ground, brought an offering from his harvest. Abel, who was a shepherd, brought the fat portions of the firstborn of his flock. While their respective sacrifices reflected each man's vocation, only one moved beyond self and touched the heart of God; only one became an enduring legacy of faith and righteousness; and only one imbibed the true nature and meaning of worship.

Sacrifice—an Integral Expression of Worship

All through the Old Testament Scriptures, sacrifices were offered up as

---

[1] Heb. 11:4 uses the word, *sacrifice*, instead of *offering*.

an integral expression of worship.[2] This is perhaps nowhere more exemplified than in the story of Abraham and his exceptional offering to God. According to the account, the Lord God tested Abraham and his devotion. The Lord instructed Abraham to offer his beloved son, Isaac, on one of the mountains that he would indicate (Gen 22:2). Early the following morning, Abraham saddled up the donkey, and with two of the young servants, headed out with Isaac towards the mountains the Lord had indicated. Upon arriving at their destination, Abraham instructed the young men: "Stay here with the donkey; I and the boy will go over there and **worship** and come again to you" (Gen. 22:5 ESV). Abraham climbed the summit of the mountain, fully intending on sacrificing his beloved son as an act of worship. The Hebrew word for *worship*, שָׁחָה, *shachah*, literally means *to bow down*. From the above account, however, we understand that *shachah* sometimes signifies more than its etymology suggests. According to the account, when Abraham and Isaac arrived at the location, Abraham built an altar, bound his son, and placed him on the altar. The moment the patriarch raised his knife prepared to sacrifice his son the angel of the Lord called out to Abraham and stopped him, acknowledging that he had indeed acted in the fear of the Lord. Lifting his eyes, Abraham noticed a ram caught in a thicket. He took the ram and offered it as a burnt sacrifice in the place of his son (Gen. 22:13). This dramatic event in the life of Abraham not only identifies sacrifice with worship or bowing down, it also introduces the concept of *substitution*, which is a fundamental principle of atonement. We will discuss this later in our study.

The book of Exodus provides a further example of how sacrifice and worship are interconnected. In chapter three, during the burning-bush encounter on the mountain, God instructed Moses to gather the elders of Israel and reveal his intentions to deliver the people from Egypt and bring them to the promise land. They were to bring their petition before the king of Egypt: "The Lord, the God of the Hebrews, has met with us; and now, please let us go a three days' journey into the wilderness, **that we may sacrifice to the Lord our God**" (Exod. 3:18 ESV). In a later occasion, the Lord spoke again to Moses, instructing him to use all the signs and wonders he had been given while on the

[2] By *Old Testament sacrifices*, we mean all sacrifices recorded in the Old Testament, including those offered before the Mosaic covenant and laws were ever given.

mountain. But he also warned him of how events would unfold:

> And the Lord said to Moses, "When you go back to Egypt, see that you do before Pharaoh all the miracles that I have put in your power. But I will harden his heart, so that he will not let the people go. Then you shall say to Pharaoh, 'Thus says the Lord, Israel is my firstborn son, and I say to you, "Let my son go that he may serve me." If you refuse to let him go, behold, I will kill your firstborn son"' (Exod. 4:21-23, ESV).

In both the passages of Scripture cited above, Moses is instructed to relay a message, if not an open threat, to Pharaoh. To paraphrase: *Release your despotic control over my people, let them separate themselves from Egypt and journey into the wilderness to worship me. If you do not let my firstborn son, Israel, go, I will kill your firstborn son.* It is this journey into the wilderness to sacrifice and serve God that constitutes the principal theme in the first twelve chapters of Exodus. In these chapters, the words, *sacrifice* and *serve* are often used interchangeably, as we may note from the passages of Scripture already cited above.[3] Sacrifice and serve are among several key words that denote the inherent qualities of biblical worship: *fear*, *love*, *serve*, *bow down*, and *sacrifice* (Deut. 10:12-13; 2 Kgs. 17:25-26). Any one of these words may be used in Scripture to express the concept of worship. Whenever two or more are used together, they either convey a greater emphasis or a more comprehensive meaning of worship.

Other accounts in the Old Testament clearly identify and connect sacrifice with worship. Elkanah, father of Samuel the prophet, faithfully worshipped and sacrificed to God in Shiloh, before the tabernacle, every year (1 Sam. 1:3). In a psalm of thanksgiving, King David enjoins the people to bring an *offering* and *worship*[4] the Lord (1 Chr. 16:29). During the reign of Hezekiah, Sennacherib king of Assyria invaded Judah. The Assyrian king sent messengers to speak to the people. They challenged and mocked Hezekiah for encouraging the people to trust in God for deliverance, and for instructing them to *worship* and *sacrifice* before the altar in Jerusalem (2 Chr. 32:10-12).[5]

The connection between animal sacrifices and worship is foundational

---

[3] Exod. 3:12, 18; 4:23; 5:3, 8, 17; 7:16; 8:1, 8, 20, 25-29; 9:1, 13; 10:3, 7-8, 24-26

[4] The same Hebrew verb, שָׁחָה, *shachah*, translated *worship* in Gen. 22:5.

[5] The Hebrew verb, קָטַר, *qatar*, means *to make sacrifices smoke*. It can either refer to *incense* (Exod. 30:7, 8; 40:27) or a burnt offering (Exod. 29:13, 18, 25; Lev. 1:9). Even grain offerings were *burnt* on the fire of the altar (Lev. 2:11).

in understanding New Testament worship. In fact, numerous passages in the New Testament draw analogies from Old Testament offerings. When John the Baptist saw Jesus, walking towards him, John declared: "Behold, the Lamb of God, who takes away the sin of the world!" (John 1:29, ESV). In his letter to the Corinthians, Apostle Paul refers to Christ as our *Passover* who was sacrificed for us (1 Cor. 5:7). The letter of Hebrews observes that we have an *altar*, but the priests who serve in the tabernacle have no right to eat from it (Heb. 13:10). Just as animal sacrifices were connected to Old Testament worship, Christ's sacrifice is likewise connected to New Testament worship.

Atonement and Worship

Animal sacrifices were unquestionably an integral expression of Old Testament worship. The question that naturally follows is: *Why are sacrifices so important and necessary to biblical worship?* To answer this and other questions relating to sacrifice, we need to have a general understanding of the nature of sin and how it affected Adam and Eve's relationship with God. We also need to understand how the Lord dealt with their transgression. When Adam and Eve acquired knowledge of good and evil through their disobedience, their eyes were opened and perceptions of themselves, of one another, and of God were dramatically changed (Gen. 3:7-8). Transgression awoke within Adam and Eve such a sense of self-awareness, they felt compelled to clothe themselves with loincloths made of fig leaves. However, the moment the couple heard the Lord God, walking in the garden, fear filled their hearts and minds, and they hid themselves among the trees. The one with whom they had previously had fellowship—their Creator, Benefactor, and Law-giver—had suddenly became their Judge. When the Lord questioned Adam how he knew he was naked, if he had eaten fruit from the forbidden fruit, Adam responded by quickly pointing a finger at the woman and indirectly at God. The woman, instead, blamed the serpent for deceiving her. The Lord swiftly pronounced judgments on the serpent, the woman, and the man for their respective roles in bringing transgression into the world. Judgment was severe, but it was also tempered with mercy and hope. Though Adam and Eve did not immediately die for their transgression, the narrative infers that something else died that day: "And the Lord God made for Adam and for his wife garments of skins and clothed them" (Gen. 3:21, ESV).[6] Within this short yet significant verse are the seeds of redemption and atonement. An animal or animals had to be immolated; blood poured out on the ground; carcasses skinned; hides tanned; and garments fitted so man and the woman could properly be clothed with dignity before each other and especially before God.[7] The Lord then cast Adam and Eve out of the garden and barred them from entering, lest they eat of the fruit of the tree of life and perpetuate their fallen and sinful state forever. Fortunately, man was not barred from the presence of God. However, as the garments of skin and the expulsion from the garden intimated, he would have to approach the Lord God on different grounds. Such grounds are further illustrated in the story of Cain and Abel (Gen. 4:3-7).

When Cain and Abel brought offerings, the Lord had regard for Abel and his sacrifice, but not for Cain and his offering. God showed favor towards Abel and his sacrifice for two reasons: First, according to the book of Hebrews, Abel acted in *faith* towards God when he offered his sacrifice (Heb 11:4). Second, Abel offered "the firstborn of his flock and their fat portions." In other words, he offered God *animal sacrifices*. Faith and sacrifice are important two factors in biblical worship. When man violated God's law in the garden, his actions deeply impacted his relationship with God. First of all, transgression involved mistrust in God's character and integrity, and unbelief in his word. When the serpent first spoke to Eve, it began by questioning the veracity of God's word (Gen. 3:1). The serpent then proceeded to openly accuse God of lying and withholding knowledge from the couple. Man's transgression also denied God of his legitimate rights to rule over man and of his divine sovereignty over all knowledge. Moreover, transgression constituted a moral threat within the paradise of God. Transgression also violated man's own moral nature; it stained his conscience with guilt and subjected his mind to the flesh, that is, to self-centered thoughts and desires. Man's spiritual condition would only further exacerbate his rapport with a holy and omniscient God. Transgression clearly created formidable obstacles between God and man. But Abel's faith and sacrifice

---

[6] There is an interesting parallel between the garments of skins that God made for Adam and Eve and the skins of the burnt offering in Leviticus. According to Lev. 7:8, the priest who offered the burnt offering could keep the skins for himself.

[7] Even if the Lord God created garments, *ex nihilo*, the skins would still implicate the complex process required in making skins for garments. Moreover, Adam and Eve would have to learn the process to clothe themselves and their children in the future.

bridged the immense chasm that sin had created and elicited a favorable response from God. Through faith, Abel demonstrated confidence in God, as opposed to the unbelief and mistrust demonstrated in the garden. Through sacrifice, he acknowledged man's sinful condition, God's justice, and the need for atonement and reconciliation. Conversely, Cain's sacrifice failed to acknowledge anything but his own skills and accomplishments as a tiller of the ground. Moreover, his dejection and anger exposed a clear lack of faith in God.

The Need for "Better Sacrifices"

> "Thus it was necessary for the copies of the heavenly things to be purified with these rites, but the heavenly things themselves with better sacrifices than these" (Heb. 9:23, ESV).

Animal sacrifices have played an important role in worship from the beginning of biblical history. Abel, Noah, Abraham, Isaac, and Jacob all understood the importance of such sacrifices, long before burnt offerings were codified in the Law of Moses. As previously discussed, sacrifices acknowledged the sinful condition of man, the demands of divine justice, and the need for atonement. Sacrifices also served to celebrate the goodness of God and offer thanksgiving for his bounty. They also connected the worshipper and his family to their heritage. Through the annual sacrifice of the Passover, parents could teach their children how God delivered Israel from Egypt (Exod. 12:24-28). Despite the benefits of animal sacrifices, they were weak, ineffective, and limited in dealing with the sin problem. They clearly intimated the need for "better sacrifices."[8]

Animal sacrifices could not fully demonstrate the attributes of God. The blood of non-moral and non-spiritual creatures could hardly reveal the depths of God's love, goodness, and mercy. Better sacrifices were needed that could express the heart of God. For this very reason, Jesus Christ took on a body of flesh and blood,[9] and by offering himself as a sacrifice, he fully

---

[8] Hebrews uses the plural form, "better sacrifices," to draw a better analogy between the sacrifices required in purifying "the copies of the things in the heavens" and "the heavenly things" themselves (Heb. 9:23, HCSB). In no way should it be inferred from the verse that more than one sacrifice was offered. Indeed, the context is emphatic that Christ offered himself "once for all" (Heb. 9:12 [and also verse, 28] HCSB. cf. Heb. 7:27; 10:1).

[9] Heb. 2:14-15

revealed the grace and love of God; something animal sacrifices in themselves could hardly do (Heb. 2:9; 1 John 4:10). Nothing could possibly commend more the grace and love of God than the sacrifice of his only Son.

Animal sacrifices might impress the seriousness of sin upon the heart and mind of the worshipper, but they were limited in their ability to fully demonstrate the righteousness of God in the forgiveness of sins. Apostle Paul writes:

> God presented Christ as a sacrifice of atonement, through the shedding of his blood—to be received by faith. **He did this to demonstrate his righteousness**, because in his forbearance he had left the sins committed beforehand unpunished—**he did it to demonstrate his righteousness** at the present time, so as to be just and the one who justifies those who have faith in Jesus (Rom. 3:25-26, NIV).

The apostle mentions two times that Christ's atonement (or propitiation) *demonstrates* God's righteousness: First, by in dealing with *sins of the past*, which burnt offerings and sacrifices were ineffectual in removing; and second, by dealing with *sins of the present.* The blood of animals could not completely express the demands of the moral law and divine justice. For that reason, God had to show "forbearance" as he overlooked the sins of the past, until his righteousness could be fully manifested through the sacrifice and blood of his Son. Now, through the atonement of Christ, God can justly forgive sin and justify "those who have faith in Jesus."[10] Furthermore, faith in Jesus' blood upholds the law of God. in fact, Paul writes, "Do we, then, nullify the law by this faith? Not at all! Rather, **we uphold the law**" (Rom. 3:31, NIV). If God were to always show mercy, he would weaken the force of the law, disregard its demands for justice, and cast a dark shadow on his own holy character (our perceptions of God's divine nature and moral character greatly influence how and why we worship him). Furthermore, a law that is neither valued nor enforced by its own legislator would hardly be esteemed by those who are subject to the law. On the other hand, if God were to always execute judgment, he would certainly uphold the demands of the law, but he would also suffocate his love for the world and desire to show mercy. Indeed, God would appear to be cruel and merciless. Instead, through the atonement

[10] Faith and sacrifice have always been the soteriological thread, woven throughout biblical history.

of his Son, God has reconciled mercy and justice. He upholds the law and all that it represents, even as he shows mercy to the one who has faith in Christ's blood. In this way, the righteousness of God is fully declared.

Animal sacrifices were ineffective in dealing with sin. They could not remove sin or purify the guilty conscience of the worshippers. The letter to the Hebrews observes:

> Since the law has only a shadow of the good things to come, and not the actual form of those realities, it can never perfect the worshipers by the same sacrifices they continually offer year after year. Otherwise, wouldn't they have stopped being offered, since the worshipers, once purified, would no longer have any **consciousness of sins**? But in the sacrifices there is a reminder of sins every year. **For it is impossible for the blood of bulls and goats to take away sins** (Heb. 10:1-4, HCSB).

Under the old covenant system, the worshipper had to continually offer sacrifice for his sins. This is because sacrifices were ineffectual in removing sin and guilt; instead, they were a continual reminder of the worshipper's sins. Clearly, a better sacrifice was needed, one that could deal with sin and guilt. Christ is, indeed, that better sacrifice. Faith in Christ's blood absolves the sinner of all sin and cleanses the conscience from dead works so that he or she may truly serve and worship God (Heb. 9:14). Animal sacrifices were also extremely limited in their ability to atone for every type of sin under the old covenant. In fact, there were many sins for which there was no sacrifices or second chances, only a sentence of death.[11] Clearly, there was a need for a better sacrifice that could provide a greater range of application. In fact, John declares in his first letter: "But if we walk in the light, as he is in the light, we have fellowship with one another, **and the blood of Jesus his Son cleanses us from all sin**" (1 John 1:7, ESV). "All sin"—those two simple words are powerful and comprehensive. It means Jesus' blood cleanses us even from the sins for which there was no atonement under the old covenant.

Animal sacrifices were also limited in their ability to grant entrance into the presence of God for *all* worshippers. Under the old covenant, only the

---

[11] There were many sins under the old covenant for which there was no atonement, such as *blasphemy* (Lev. 24:16); *profaning the Sabbath* (Exod. 31:14-15); *premeditated murder* (Exod. 21:14); *offering one's children to the god, Molech* (Lev. 20:1-5); *sorcery and necromancy* (Exod. 22:18; Lev. 20:27); *cursing or striking one's father or mother* (Exod. 21:15), and *adultery* (Lev. 20:10). The list, of course, continues.

High Priest could enter the most holy place of the tabernacle and appear before the Lord, but only once a year (Heb. 9:6-7). According to Hebrews, "The Holy Spirit was making it clear that the way into the most holy place had not yet been disclosed while the first tabernacle was still standing" (Heb. 9:8, HCSB). Again, a better sacrifice was needed that could open the way to God's presence for all worshippers.

> Therefore, brothers, since we have boldness to enter the sanctuary through the blood of Jesus, by a new and living way He has opened for us through the curtain (that is, His flesh), and since we have a great high priest over the house of God, let us draw near with a true heart in full assurance of faith, our hearts sprinkled clean from an evil conscience and our bodies washed in pure water (Heb. 10:19-22, HCSB).

Through Jesus' blood, we are cleansed and even sanctified (Heb. 13:12). We may now enter with boldness into the presence of God, to worship him and offer up our prayers and petitions (Heb. 4:16).

Lastly, animal sacrifices were also limited in their ability to infuse devotion and elicit a sense of worship in the worshipper. In Psalms 51, David declares:

> Purge me with hyssop, and I shall be clean; wash me, and I shall be whiter than snow. Let me hear joy and gladness; let the bones that you have broken rejoice. Hide your face from my sins, and blot out all my iniquities.
>
> Deliver me from bloodguiltiness, O God, O God of my salvation, and my tongue will sing aloud of your righteousness. O Lord, open my lips, and my mouth will declare your praise. For you will not delight in sacrifice, or I would give it; you will not be pleased with a burnt offering. The sacrifices of God are a broken spirit; a broken and contrite heart, O God, you will not despise. (Ps. 51:7-9, 14-17, ESV)

David clearly correlates forgiveness and brokenness of spirit with praise and worship. Animal sacrifices and burnt offerings, however, are not even factored into the equation. Indeed, David's psalm somewhat diminishes the importance of sacrifice and burnt offering. This same sentiment is also expressed elsewhere in the Scriptures (1 Sam. 15:22; Ps. 40:6-8; 50:8-14; Hos. 6:6; Matt. 9:13; 12:7; Mk. 12:33). Clearly, there was a need for a better sacrifice that would delight the Lord and be an integral part of worship. Jesus Christ is indeed that better sacrifice.

Citing Psalms 40, Hebrews declares:

> Consequently, when Christ came into the world, he said, "Sacrifices and offerings you have not desired, but a body have you prepared for me; in burnt offerings and sin offerings you have taken no pleasure. Then I said, 'Behold, I have come to do your will, O God, as it is written of me in the scroll of the book'" (Heb. 10:5-7, ESV).

Moreover, Christ's sacrifice inspires and motivates the worshipper towards a greater devotion and expression of worship than animal sacrifices could ever do. The power of Christ's sacrifice excels in both virtue and in its ability to capture the hearts and minds of those who contemplate him. Apostle Paul, for example, wholly devoted himself to Christ, because of Christ's love and extraordinary sacrifice:

> "I have been crucified with Christ; it is no longer I who live, but Christ lives in me; and the *life* which I now live in the flesh I live by faith in the Son of God, **who loved me and gave Himself for me**" (Gal. 2:20, NKJV).[12]

The Nature of Christ's Sacrifice

In the book of Leviticus, the Lord provided specific instructions to his people, regarding the various types of sacrifice and offerings that could be offered.[13] The priests were given detailed procedures how they were to prepare each offering for the altar. They were also given special directions, regarding the blood of sacrifices. The priests were to sprinkle the blood of *burnt offerings*, *peace offerings* and *trespass offering* on the sides of the altar (if the burnt offering were a bird, the priest would wring off the head and drain the blood on the side of the altar).[14] The blood of the *sin offering* was treated a little differently. The high priest was to take blood of the sacrificial bull and bring it into the tabernacle. He then dipped his finger in the blood and sprinkled it seven times in front of the veil. Then he applied some of the blood on the horns of the altar of incense. The rest of the blood was poured out at the foot of the altar before the entrance of the tent of meeting (Lev. 4:7).[15] The blood of a sacrifice had a particular importance; it is what affected

[12] 2 Cor. 5:14-15; Eph. 5:1-2; Phil. 2:5-8

[13] *Burnt Offering*, Lev. 1:3-17; 6:8-13; *Grain Offering*, Lev. 2:1-16; 6:14-23; *Peace Offering*, Lev. 3:1-17; 7:11-18, 28-34; *Sin Offering*, Lev. 4:1-35; 6:24-30; *Trespass Offering*, Lev. 5:1-19; 6:1-7; 7:1-7; *Drink Offerings*, Lev. 23:13, 18, 37.

[14] Lev. 1:5, 11, 15; 3:2, 8, 12; 5:9; 7:2

[15] Lev. 4:5-7, 16-18

the atonement: "For the life of the flesh is in the blood, and I have given it for you on the altar to make atonement for your souls, for it is the blood that makes atonement by the life" (Lev. 17:11, ESV).

The most that could be said of these sacrificial victims is that they were ceremonially clean and without physical defect.[16] Incontrovertibly, Christ's sacrifice was infinitely more valuable, more effective, and more extensive than any sacrifice or burnt offering. First and foremost, his sacrifice was infinitely more valuable because of the dignity of his person—Jesus was the Son of God and the Messiah.[17] Second, as a sacrifice, Christ was holy and blameless, without any *moral* defect, which is of infinitely more worth to God than an animal without any *physical* defect. Peter testifies to the virtue of Christ's character as he bore our sins on the cross:

> He committed no sin, neither was deceit found in his mouth. When he was reviled, he did not revile in return; when he suffered, he did not threaten, but continued entrusting himself to him who judges justly. He himself bore our sins in his body on the tree… (1 Peter 2:22-24, ESV).

Third, Christ *willingly* chose to lay down his life on our behalf. Sacrificial victims had no choice in the matter. Jesus said to his disciples:

> "Therefore My Father loves Me, because I lay down My life that I may take it again. No one takes it from Me, but I lay it down of Myself. I have power to lay it down, and I have power to take it again. This command I have received from My Father" (John 10:17-18, NKJV).

Because Christ *chose* to lay down his life, he was neither victim nor martyr, but the perfect sacrifice.

Fourth, Christ's atonement not only entailed the shedding of his blood on the cross; it fully embraced unimaginable *suffering*. Jesus underwent a tremendous ordeal of spiritual and physical suffering, even before he was barbarously nailed to a cross of wood. Sacrificial animals were never tortured or abused before or during their immolation. The gospel of Matthew paints a detailed and portentous portrait of Christ's sufferings. According to the account, Jesus was betrayed by a friend; he was forsaken by his disciples; and later, one of his closest disciples denied three times that he knew him. Jesus

---

[16] Lev. 1:1-17; Deut. 17:1

[17] Matt. 16:16; 27:54; 1 Cor. 1:9, 23; Fil. 2:5-11; Eb. 1:1-5

was falsely accused and deprived of justice; he was mocked and abused by the leaders of his people and delivered to the Roman governor, Pontius Pilate. Though he was innocent, at the pleading of a mob, Pilate released Barabbas, a criminal, and then had Jesus scourged. Jesus was mocked by a whole battalion of Roman soldiers before being forced to carry his own cross to the place of crucifixion. When they arrived at the place called, Golgotha, the soldiers offered Jesus, drugged wine, which he refused to drink. The soldiers removed the Lord's garments, nailed him to a cross, and lifted him up for all to see. "And over his head they put the charge against him, which read, 'This is Jesus, the King of the Jews'" (Matt. 27:37, ESV). But the litany of torture did not stop there. He was ridiculed by the people; mocked by the priests, scribes, and elders; and reviled by the thieves who were crucified with him. As Jesus bore our sins,[18] he felt the intense anguish of being abandoned by God before expiring: "And about the ninth hour Jesus cried out with a loud voice, saying, 'Eli, Eli, lema sabachthani?' that is, 'My God, my God, why have you forsaken me?'" (Matt. 27:46, ESV). God treated his own Son as though he were incarnation of sin—our sin. Paul writes: "For our sake he made him to be sin who knew no sin, so that in him we might become the righteousness of God" (2 Cor. 5:21, ESV). When we speak of the precious blood of Jesus, we must also consider the mental, spiritual, and physical sufferings that Christ underwent—something that the victims of animal sacrifice never had to experience.

Sacrifice in New Testament Worship

> "Therefore he had to be made like his brothers in every respect, so that he might become a merciful and faithful high priest in the service of God, to make propitiation for the sins of the people" (Heb. 2:17, ESV).

Christ's sacrifice thoroughly dealt with the sin and guilt problem. Worshipers no longer need burnt offerings and sacrifices; nor do they need a priesthood of men who can mediate such offerings. Christ has become both "high priest" and the "propitiation." The only thing we need is faith in Jesus' blood to receive forgiveness of sin from God. Through faith, Christ's sacrifice becomes a propitiation or atonement for our sins. Moreover, we avail ourselves through faith of all the blessings and benefits of Christ's sufferings and sacrifice. Since Christ's sacrifice and propitiation have

---

[18] 1 Peter 2:24

rendered the blood of animals and the Levitical priesthood redundant, and since sacrifice is an integral part of worship, it is only natural to ask: *What further role does sacrifice have in New Testament worship?* The question is particularly relevant, considering that not all Old Testament sacrifices were expiatory in nature.

Christ's sacrifice has become the new *paradigm* of worship. Jesus not only offered himself as a sacrifice for our redemption; he also modeled a pattern of virtue and worship for his disciples to follow. Most believers have no problems in relating Christ's sacrifice to the subject of redemption. However, some might have difficulty in seeing Jesus' sufferings as an act of worship. If we are to accept the full meaning of Christ's humanity, we must allow that his sacrifice was also an expression of worship and devotion to God. In fact, all biblical expressions of worship and devotion are clearly identified in Christ. *Is worship singing hymns to God?* Christ sang hymns with his disciples, at the end of the meal, before going to Gethsemane. *Is worship kneeling or prostrating oneself before God in prayer?* Christ knelt down and he prostrated himself, even with his face to the ground as he prayed to the Father with unfathomable intensity.[19] *Is worship submitting to the will God?* Christ prayed fervently, regarding the cup of suffering that was set before him and the will of the Father (Matt. 26:39). *Is worship invoking the name of God?* Christ called on the name of God as he hung on the cross (Matt. 27:46). *Is worship surrendering oneself to God?* Christ cried out with a loud voice and committed his spirit to the Father before breathing his last breath (Luke 23:46). And more relevant to our present study: *Is worship offering sacrifice to God?* Apostle Paul writes that Christ "gave himself up for us, **a fragrant offering and sacrifice to God**" (Eph. 5:2, ESV). It is impossible to understand the role or place of sacrifice in New Testament worship without considering the example and pattern of Jesus Christ. In fact, he is the divine paradigm of worship.

Perhaps no place in the New Testament better portrays how Christ's sacrifice dramatically changed the way biblical worship is currently understood and expressed than the book of Revelation. In chapter four, in John's vision of the throne room, he sees twenty-four elders, dressed in royal and priestly attire, and sitting on thrones around the throne of God. He also sees four living creatures, standing like sentries at each side of the throne:

---

[19] Matt. 26:39; Mk. 14:35; Luke 22:41

> And the four living creatures, each of them with six wings, are full of eyes all around and within, and day and night they never cease to say, "Holy, holy, holy, is the Lord God Almighty, who was and is and is to come!" (Rev. 4:8, ESV).

Whenever the creatures raise their voices in praise, the twenty-four elders fall down before the throne and worship God. Casting down their crowns, they reply:

> "Worthy are you, our Lord and God, to receive glory and honor and power, for you created all things, and by your will they existed and were created" (Rev. 4:11, ESV).

John understands this to be a pattern or frequency of worship that continues unabated, day and night. In the following chapter, the pattern is suddenly interrupted. John sees a sealed scroll in the hand of the one who is seated on the throne. He then hears a question that grips the core of his being: "Who is worthy to open the scroll and break its seals?" (Rev. 5:2, ESV). Because the answer is not forth coming, John begins to weep, until one of the elders offers him comforting words: "Weep no more; behold, the Lion of the tribe of Judah, the Root of David, has conquered, so that he can open the scroll and its seven seals" (Rev. 5:5, ESV). Suddenly, John sees the most awesome and tremendous of all visions:

> "And between the throne and the four living creatures and among the elders I saw a Lamb standing, as though it had been slain, with seven horns and with seven eyes, which are the seven spirits of God sent out into all the earth" (Rev. 5:6, ESV).

John obviously understood the Lamb had been slain from the deadly wounds it still bore. Its unique physical features, the seven horns and seven eyes, are symbols of divine attributes—*omnipotence* and *omniscience*. John continues to gaze at the Lamb as it took the scroll from the hand of God:

> And when he had taken the scroll, the four living creatures and the twenty-four elders fell down before the Lamb, each holding a harp, and golden bowls full of incense, which are the prayers of the saints. And they sang a new song, saying, "Worthy are you to take the scroll and to open its seals, for you were slain, and by your blood you ransomed people for God from every tribe and language and people and nation, and you have made them a kingdom and

> priests to our God, and they shall reign on the earth." Then I looked, and I heard around the throne and the living creatures and the elders the voice of many angels, numbering myriads of myriads and thousands of thousands, saying with a loud voice, "Worthy is the Lamb who was slain, to receive power and wealth and wisdom and might and honor and glory and blessing!" And I heard every creature in heaven and on earth and under the earth and in the sea, and all that is in them, saying, "To him who sits on the throne and to the Lamb be blessing and honor and glory and might forever and ever!" And the four living creatures said, "Amen!" and the elders fell down and worshiped. (Rev. 5:8-14, ESV).

John observes one of the most stunning and poignant displays of worship in all the Scriptures. After the Lamb receives the scroll, the four living creatures and the twenty-four elders prostrate before the Lamb and sing a new song. All of a sudden, the elders and creatures are surrounded by an immense sea of angelic hosts who raise their voices and proclaim the praises of the Lamb. And like a mighty tidal wave, worship rises and surges to the furthest reaches of creation, until every creature also declares the praises of the Lamb and of the one who sits on the throne. When the living creatures give their full assent, the twenty-four elders fall down again and worship. The sudden revelation of the Lamb dramatically changes the former pattern of worship. The Lamb that had been slain becomes the *inspiration* and *catalyst* that compels the hosts of heaven and all of creation to worship the Lamb and the one who sits on the throne. The vision is, of course, a symbolic representation of Christ's sacrifice and the new paradigm of worship. His sufferings, death, and resurrection are the absolute focus and center piece of New Testament worship. Not only faith, but New Testament rites, observances, and expressions spiritually connect us to Christ's sacrifice, such as water baptism, the Lord's Supper, hymnody, prayer, etc.[20]

---

[20] Though we have lost early century songs, some Bible scholars believe portions of early hymns are actually cited in some of the New Testament epistles or letters. For example, Joshua W Jipp, assistant professor at Trinity Evangelical Divinity School writes: "Most biblical scholars use the method of form criticism—looking for clues that suggest a biblical passage had an earlier use than its current literary location—to locate hymns that have found their way into the New Testament compositions. These include: parallel statements, vocabulary that is distinctive to the author, the frequent use of pronouns, and elevated prose. If one uses these critical criteria, one will likely conclude that such passages

Christ's sacrifice has also initiated a new order of priesthood. When the four living creatures and the twenty-four elders fall down before the Lamb, they sing a new song:

> "Worthy[21] are you to take the scroll and to open its seals, for you were slain, and by your blood you ransomed people for God from every tribe and language and people and nation, and you have made them a kingdom and priests to our God, and they shall reign on the earth" (Rev. 5:9-10, ESV).

Redemption and priesthood are both fruit of the precious blood of the Lamb. Under the old covenant, the blood of sacrifice played an important role in consecrating Aaron and his sons as priests (Exod. 29:19-21). Their primary vocation was to serve God and offer sacrifice on behalf of the people. The new order of priesthood, established through the blood of Jesus, also offers sacrifices to God. The sacrifices of this new priesthood, however, have nothing to do with atonement or propitiation. They are, exclusively, sacrifices of praise and worship. Apostle Peter explains:

> As you come to him, a living stone rejected by men but in the sight of God chosen and precious, you yourselves like living stones are being built up as a spiritual house, **to be a holy priesthood, to offer spiritual sacrifices** acceptable to God through Jesus Christ. For it stands in Scripture: "Behold, I am laying in Zion a stone, a cornerstone chosen and precious, and whoever believes in him will not be put to shame" (1 Peter 2:4-6, ESV).

According to Peter, as a "holy priesthood," believers serve God by offering him "spiritual sacrifices." *But what exactly are these sacrifices?* We would like to offer three suggestions. First of all, spiritual sacrifices relate to the

---

as Phil 2:5-11, Col 1:15-20, 1Tim 3:16, Heb 1:1-3, and 1Pet 2:21-25 may very well have had earlier literary lives as actual hymns sung by early Christian communities." Jipp, Joshua W. "Hymns in the New Testament," *Bible Odyssey*, https://www.bibleodyssey.org/en/passages/related-articles/hymns-in-the-new-testament. A significant feature of these suggested texts is that all of them, except for 1 Timothy 3:16, use key words and concepts that directly point to Jesus Christ's sacrifice. Even if we do not accept the theory that these texts possibly represented early church hymnody, they unquestionably denote New Testament doctrine. Moreover, biblical teaching always finds its way into church hymns, poetry, and art. We should not think it any different in the first century church.

[21] *Worship* in English is etymologically related to the words, *worth* and *worthiness*.

excellencies or praises of God. Continuing the theme of a new priesthood, Peter writes: "But you are a chosen race, **a royal priesthood**, a holy nation, a people for his own possession, **that you may proclaim the excellencies of him** who called you out of darkness into his marvelous light" (1 Peter 2:9, ESV). The letter to the Hebrews similarly exhorts us: "Through him then let us continually offer up **a sacrifice of praise to God**, that is, **the fruit of lips** that acknowledge his name" (Heb. 13:15, ESV). Secondly, spiritual sacrifices are related to sanctification or holiness. The Apostle Paul writes: "Therefore, brothers, by the mercies of God, I urge you to present your bodies as a living sacrifice, holy and pleasing to God; this is your spiritual worship" (Rom. 12:1, HCSB). Thirdly, spiritual sacrifices also connote a deeper meaning, one that is well defined by Christ's own example. Before Jesus ever carried his cross through the crowded streets of Jerusalem, he had already offered his life to God that previous evening. The synoptic gospels record an important event that took place, immediately after Jesus and his disciples had departed from the room where they had shared the Passover:

> Then Jesus went with them to a place called Gethsemane, and he said to his disciples, "Sit here, while I go over there and pray." And taking with him Peter and the two sons of Zebedee, he began to be sorrowful and troubled. Then he said to them, "My soul is very sorrowful, even to death; remain here, and watch with me." And going a little farther he fell on his face and prayed, saying, "**My Father, if it be possible, let this cup pass from me; nevertheless, not as I will, but as you will**" (Matt. 26:36-40, ESV).

The gospel of Matthew relates that Jesus prayed the same prayer, three times. Christ prayed with such intensity because he knew his hour had come. The will of God was the absolute focus of his petition. Christ's Gethsemane experience is highly suggestive of the meaning of spiritual sacrifice. It relates to the giving of ourselves to God and surrendering to his will. An excellent example of this is found in the second letter of Corinthians, where Apostle Paul writes of the churches of Macedonia and their participation in giving towards the needs of other believers, despite their own extreme poverty:

> We want you to know, brothers, about the grace of God that has been given among the churches of Macedonia, for in a severe test of affliction, their abundance of joy and their extreme poverty have overflowed in a wealth of generosity on their part. For they

> gave according to their means, as I can testify, and beyond their means, of their own accord, begging us earnestly for the favor of taking part in the relief of the saints— and this, not as we expected, **but they gave themselves first to the Lord and then by the will of God to us** (2 Cor. 8:1-5, ESV).

Before any actions were taken, any collections taken up, or any material sacrifices made; the churches of Macedonia had *first* given themselves to the Lord and then to Paul and his colleagues, "by the will of God." The concept of offering ourselves to God is both implicit and explicit in New Testament teaching.[22] Giving ourselves to God to do his will *is* a spiritual sacrifice. And as we stated at the beginning of our study, sacrifice is, unquestionably, an integral expression of biblical worship.

[22] Matt. 20:28; 22:21; Rom. 6:13; 12:1; 2 Cor. 5:14-15; Gal. 2:20

CHAPTER 2

The Pillar of the Prophet

(The Authority of Biblical Worship)

Part One

"And I will put enmity between you and the woman, and between your offspring and hers; he will **crush your head***, and you will strike his heel" (Gen. 3:15, NIV).*

*And Adam knew his wife again, and she bore a son and called his name Seth, for she said, "***God has appointed for me another offspring instead of Abel***, for Cain killed him." To Seth also a son was born, and he called his name Enosh. At that time people began to call upon the name of the Lord (Gen. 4:25-26, ESV).*

"Touch not my anointed ones, do my prophets no harm!" (1 Chron. 16:22, ESV)

The prophetic anointing is the *authority* of biblical worship. It has always been God's way of *revealing* to men the *dynamics* of worship, answering such questions as *why*, *how*, *when*, and *where* God is to be worshipped. It has also been the means through which the Lord disclosed how worship was to be *structured* and *organized* among his people (e.g., the tabernacle, the priesthood, the altar, the various types of sacrifice, sacred music, the temple, etc.). Men under the prophetic anointing have even impacted the way whole generations have worshipped the Lord. Our study will discuss four prophetic movements that have helped forge and define biblical worship: *Prophetic Paradigms*; *Prophetic Transitions*; *Prophetic Reformations*; and *Prophetic Restorations*. Before we continue, a word of caution is warranted: The four movements serve to facilitate our study of the prophet and the prophetic anointing. It is not our intention to pigeonhole any prophet in a particular category. In fact, our study will show that some of the prophets of God represented more than one movement.

Our study begins with the story of Seth, the son of Adam and Eve. According to the Genesis account, when Eve gave birth to her third son, she called him, *Seth*, for she said, "God has **appointed** for me **another offspring**[1] instead of Abel, for Cain killed him."[2] Seth's name means, *appointed*; it comes from the Hebrew verb, שִׁית, *shith*, *to put*, *set*.[3] Evidently, more was involved in the story of Cain and Abel than appears at first blush. We may *infer* from Eve's words the Lord not only regarded Abel and his sacrifice, but he also *appointed* him to be the offspring, according to the prophetic promise spoken to the serpent in the garden:

> "And I will put enmity between you and the woman, and between your offspring and hers; he will crush your head, and you will strike his heel" (Gen 3:15, NIV).

Abel's faith and sacrifice effectively dealt the first severe bruise to the serpent's head. Abel's actions become even more significant when we understand that the prophetic anointing was on him. In fact, the Lord Jesus referred to Abel as a prophet:

> "Therefore also the Wisdom of God said, 'I will send them prophets and apostles, some of whom they will kill and persecute,' So that the blood of all the prophets, shed from the foundation of the world, may be charged against this generation, from the blood of Abel to the blood of Zechariah, who perished between the altar and the sanctuary. Yes, I tell you, it will be required of this generation" (Luke 11:49-51, ESV).

When Abel worshipped God with "the firstborn of his flock and of their fat portions" (Gen. 4:4, ESV), his actions were prophetic on two accounts: First, Abel established a *prophetic paradigm* of worship that would be followed by future generations. Second, his sacrifice also spoke prophetically of the sacrifice of Jesus

---

[1] Offspring, seed, descendent, come from the same Hebrew word: זֶרַע, zara, a sowing, seed, offspring.

[2] I must give credit to where credit is due. Several years ago, I first learned about the biblical theme of the *appointed offspring* and its continuity throughout Scripture in a course of Old Testament Survey from a Global University. Needless to say, the course made a lasting impression on me. The theme of the appointed offspring plays an important role in our study.

[3] Note that שִׁית, *shith* is the same verb used in Gen. 3:15, "And **I will put** enmity between you and the woman, and between your offspring and hers…" (NIV).

Christ, "the Lamb of God, who takes away the sin of the world!" (John 1:29, ESV). The Scriptures recognize Abel as a prophet, a righteous man, a man of faith, and a worshipper of God —the very qualities that define and even intensify the enmity between the woman and serpent's offspring. Indeed, Cain murdered his brother, Abel, and metaphorically speaking, he continues to do so. When Seth was born, he effectively became the appointed offspring in place of his brother, Abel. This view is strongly supported by the fact that Seth became the patriarch of a lineage noted for godly and prophetic men,[4] and from whence would also come the Messiah.[5] As the appointed offspring, Seth was a prophet of God, for inherent to the appointment is also the *prophetic anointing.*

Prophetic Paradigms[6]

> "To Seth also a son was born, and he called his name Enosh. At that time people began to call upon the name of the Lord" (Gen. 4:26, ESV).

Concerning the life of Seth, Scripture provides us with little background information. Nonetheless, a remarkable event occurred during his lifetime, important enough to be recorded in the Scriptures. When Seth's son, *Enosh*, was born, "people began to call upon the name of the Lord." This noted event occurred in the 105th year of Seth's life. We are not informed of what exactly had transpired that suddenly moved men towards such a spiritual and significant direction. The statement simply identifies this new paradigm with the birth of Enosh. Perhaps *fatherhood* became an important catalyst or milestone in Seth's prophetic calling. Having a son was certainly vital in fulfilling the prophetic promise of Gen 3:15. Perhaps the birth of Enosh gave people grounds for hope and faith in this promise of God. While we may only speculate, one thing is certain; the birth of Enosh marked an unprecedented event in early biblical history. Men began to worship God and identify themselves with him in a way that had not been done before. This sudden spiritual movement among men was somehow related to the appointed offspring and the prophetic anointing. This new *prophetic paradigm* dealt another severe blow to the serpent's head, drawing a clearer and more

---

[4] Gen. 5:3-32

[5] Luke 3:23-37

[6] *Prophetic paradigm* refers to a new *model*, *example*, or *form* of worship, initiated through prophetic anointing. For example: Abel expressed faith in God and offered the first acceptable sacrifice. Abel's faith and sacrifice served as a model and criteria of worship in Biblical history. In Seth's day, people began to call upon the name of the Lord. This also became a normal characteristic of Biblical worship.

defined line of demarcation between the offspring of the woman and that of the serpent.

The Legacy of Seth

The descendants of Seth represent a lineage of godly and prophetic men who carried on his legacy and also that of the *appointed offspring*. The longevity of each firstborn among Seth's descendants may very well suggest a prophetic purpose in their role as leader and head of their families (Gen. 5:1-32). Conversely, nothing is said of longevity in Cain's genealogy (Gen. 4:17-22). Among Seth's genealogy, the Scriptures specifically speak of three descendants who demonstrated a notable prophetic anointing: *Enoch*, *Lamech*, and *Noah*.[7] Each one of these men prophesied of future events that would dramatically impact biblical history. But of the three, Noah would especially be remembered for an unprecedented global event.

The Last Prophet and Patriarch of the Ancient World

> By faith Noah, being warned by God concerning events as yet unseen, in reverent fear constructed an ark for the saving of his household. By this he condemned the world and became an heir of the righteousness that comes by faith (Heb. 11:7, ESV).

Noah was indeed the last prophet and patriarch of the ancient world.[8] He was instrumental in bringing about a prophetic paradigm that would affect how God would be worshipped in a new, post-diluvial world. God warned Noah of a coming flood and instructed to build an ark. Fearing the Lord, Noah obeyed his voice and, by faith, built a massive ship on dry ground. His ark eventually saved him, his household, and all the animals that God brought to the vessel made of gopher wood and pitch. After the floodwaters had abated, and Noah disembarked from the ark, he celebrated the goodness and mercy of God by worshipping him with extravagant sacrifices: "Then Noah built an altar to the Lord and took some of every clean animal and some of every clean bird and offered burnt offerings on the altar" (Gen. 8:20, ESV).

Noah's extravagant act of worship gave occasion to God to fulfill the promise he had made to Noah to make a *covenant* with him. The covenant—a solemn promise and agreement—would affect Noah, his *offspring*, all the

---

[7] Heb. 11:5; Jude 1:14-15; Gen. 5:28-29; 9:25-27

[8] 2 Peter 2:5

animals that came forth from the ark, and even the earth.[9] God promised to never again destroy the earth with a flood. The Lord placed his bow in the clouds to remind him of the covenant and as a sign for all future generations. The covenant clearly demonstrated the Lord's mercy and patience, but it also revealed his willingness to bind himself in a unique agreement with the offspring of the woman. We will have much more to say about the subject of covenant in a future chapter, but suffice to say, the first time the word, *covenant*, appears in Scripture is found in the story of Noah. The Noahic Covenant established a new paradigm in worship. God would continue to operate through the prophetic anointing and the offspring of the woman, but he would do so within the context of covenant.

The Appointed Offspring in the New World

Noah was indeed a prophet of God, but the prophetic anointing did not end with the flood or with the establishing of a covenant. In later years of his life, he prophesied concerning the descendants of his three sons, Shem, Japheth, and Ham, with special regard to *Canaan*, the son of Ham. The book of Genesis relays both Noah's words and the circumstances leading up to the prophecy. Noah had become inebriated with wine made from the very vineyard he had planted, and he lay naked in his tent. When Ham saw the nakedness of his father, he went and reported it to his brothers. Shem and Japheth took a garment, and placing it on their shoulders, walked backwards so as not to see their father's nakedness, and covered him. When Noah awoke from his drunkenness, he realized what Ham had done, and he spoke:

> He said, "Cursed be Canaan; a servant of servants shall he be to his brothers." He also said, "Blessed be the Lord, the God of Shem; and let Canaan be his servant. May God enlarge Japheth, and let him dwell in the tents of Shem, and let Canaan be his servant" (Gen. 9:25-27, ESV).

Noah's words were more than a spontaneous reaction to Ham's sinful deed. He spoke prophetically of future generations. But more importantly, *Shem* was singled out as the appointed offspring among his brothers and their future progenies. Moreover, the prophetic curse and blessing that Noah spoke respectively over Canaan and Shem and their descendants, clearly points to the perennial enmity between the offspring of the woman and that

---

[9] Gen. 6:18-20; 9:9-17

of the serpent.[10] Though the flood had destroyed the ancient world, the waters were unable to eradicate the seed of the serpent and the spiritual enmity. Both found their way into the new world.

The Patriarchal Prophet

While prophets and the prophetic anointing have existed since the foundation of the world, we encounter the word, *prophet*, for the first time in the story of Abraham. According to Genesis, chapter twenty, Abimelech, king of Gerar, had taken Sarah, Abraham's wife, into his household, thinking she was his sister. But the Lord severely warned the king in a dream that he was as good as a dead man for having taken the wife of another man. But Abimelech explained that he had been misled by the couple, and that he had acted in innocence and with integrity:

> And God said to him in a dream, "Yes, I know that you did this in the integrity of your heart. For I also withheld you from sinning against Me; therefore I did not let you touch her. **Now therefore, restore the man's wife; for he *is* a prophet, and he will pray for you and you shall live**. But if you do not restore *her,* know that you shall surely die, you and all who *are* yours" (Gen. 20:6-7, NKJV).

In the above passage, the Lord himself specifically calls Abraham a *prophet.*[11] As a descendant of Shem,[12] Abraham was called by God to continue the prophetic legacy. And as a prophet, Abraham would bring about a paradigm

---

[10] Lev. 18:1-30; 20:1-27; Deut. 12:29-31; 18:9-14; 20:17-18. This spiritual enmity becomes even more apparent when we compare and confront the moral character and worship practices of the appointed offspring and those of the descendants of Canaan. From the writings of Moses, it appears that the Canaanites and other neighboring nations in the land of Canaan were involved in all types of sexual promiscuity, including incest, homosexuality, and bestiality; idolatry and sacrificing children to the god, Molech; divination, and sorcery; and other abominable acts.

[11] Abraham's offspring, Isaac, and grandson, Jacob, were also patriarchal prophets (Gen. 26:2-5, 24-25; 27:27-29, 39-40; 28:3-4, 12-18; 31:11-13; 32:1-2, 24-30; 33:20; 35:1, 7, 9-15). Both Isaac and Jacob are referred in the Scriptures as prophets (1 Chr. 16:19-22, Ps. 105:15). Both Isaac and Jacob heard the voice of God and received divine guidance and confirmation of the covenant promises; both spoke prophetically to their offspring, and both made altars and worshipped God in the promise land.

[12] Gen. 11:10-26

in worship that would dramatically impact his offspring and future generations. God spoke to Abraham (or Abram as he was called in his earlier years) and commanded him to leave his country and relatives, and head for a land that the Lord would show him. The Lord promised to bless him and make of him a great nation, and to protect him from all his adversaries. When Abraham arrived in the land of Canaan, "the Lord appeared to Abram and said, 'To your offspring I will give this land.' So he built there an altar to the Lord, who had appeared to him" (Gen. 12:7, ESV). The destiny of the appointed offspring and the worship of Yahweh thus became indissolubly linked with Abraham's offspring and the promise land.

A Prophetic Sacrifice

In due season, the Lord God visited Sarah and gave her the ability to bear a child in her old age, just as he had promised. Abraham and Sarah called him, Isaac. Several years had gone by, the Lord commanded Abraham to go to the land of Moriah and offer up his son as a burnt offering, on a mountain that he would show him. Early the next morning, Abraham packed up the donkey and headed out with Isaac and two young men.

> On the third day Abraham lifted up his eyes and saw the place from afar. Then Abraham said to his young men, "Stay here with the donkey; **I and the boy will go over there and worship and come again to you**." And Abraham took the wood of the burnt offering and laid it on Isaac his son. And he took in his hand the fire and the knife. So they went both of them together (Gen. 22:4-6, ESV).

When Abraham and Isaac arrived at the location, Abraham bound his son and prepared to offer him as a burnt sacrifice. But the angel of the Lord intervened and stopped him: "Do not lay your hand on the boy or do anything to him, **for now I know that you fear God**, seeing you have not withheld your son, your only son, from me" (Gen. 22:12, ESV). Abraham noticed a ram, caught in the nearby thickets. Recognizing that God had provided a *substitution*, Abraham offered the ram "instead of his son" (Gen. 22:13, ESV). The angel of the Lord spoke once again:

> "By myself I have sworn, declares the Lord, because you have done this and have not withheld your son, your only son, I will surely bless you, and I will surely multiply your offspring as the stars of heaven and as the sand that is on the seashore. And your offspring shall

> possess the gate of his enemies, and in your offspring shall all the nations of the earth be blessed, **because you have obeyed my voice**" (Gen. 22:16-18, ESV).

Abraham had offered to God the best of himself—his "only begotten" (Heb. 11:17, NKJV). Even though the angel of the Lord prevented him from plunging the knife, the mere fact that Abraham actually attempted to offer his son was certainly prophetic of another sacrifice that would take place many generations later: Jesus Christ, God's "only begotten Son" (John 3:16, KJV). Abraham not only believed the promises of God, he also obeyed his voice; therefore, the Lord swore Abraham would be greatly blessed, his offspring would be multiplied like the stars and sand. "And your offspring shall **possess the gate of his enemies**, and in your offspring shall all the nations of the earth be blessed, because you have obeyed my voice." There is a certain affinity between the promise of possessing the gates of the enemy and the ancient Edenic prophecy, concerning the crushing of the head of the serpent.

The Prophet of the Burning Bush

Moses had been pastoring the flocks of his father-in-law, Jethro in the western part of the wilderness when he came to Mount Horeb. Suddenly, he espied a burning bush not far away. Wanting to get a closer look, he made his way toward the unusual phenomenon. "When the Lord saw that he turned aside to look, God called to him from the midst of the bush and said, 'Moses, Moses!' And he said, 'Here I am'" (Exod. 3:4, NASB). Moses' simple response was the beginning of a prophetic calling and singular relationship with the Lord. Indeed, Moses would become one of the most important prophets in Israel's history. Like Abel, Seth, Noah, and Abraham, he would be instrumental in bringing about a unique and pivotal paradigm that would impact present and future generations of worshippers. Because of his calling and relationship with God, a unique prophetic mantle rested on Moses. It is written of him: "And there has not arisen a prophet since in Israel like Moses, **whom the Lord knew face to face**" (Deut. 34:10, ESV). Moses' calling and prophetic anointing would remain unparalleled in history until the coming of the Messiah. God powerfully used Moses to lead his people out of Egypt and into the wilderness, where they were to sacrifice and worship God at the foot of Mount Horeb.[13] It was on this mountain—the very place where Moses had first encountered the burning bush—the Lord God made a covenant with his people, Israel. This covenant would single them out from among all other nations:

> "'Now therefore, if you will indeed obey my voice and keep my covenant, you shall be **my treasured possession** among all peoples, for all the earth is mine; and you shall be to me a kingdom of priests and a holy nation.' These are the words that you shall speak to the people of Israel" (Exod. 19:5-6, ESV).

The covenant, particularly the Ten Commandments, provided explicit boundaries of worship and a clear delineation of godly character. The laws and regulations of the covenant even provided the people with health and social codes of conduct. But also relevant to our studies, the covenant extensively regulated every detail and aspect of the construction of the tabernacle and the manufacturing of all things pertaining to worship, the Levitical priesthood and their various services, the various types of offerings and sacrifices, the holidays and their functions and many other important details.[14] In essence, through the prophetic leadership of Moses, the Lord initiated a monumental paradigm of worship among his people. Because of the laws and covenant mediated through him, and because of his unprecedented role as prophet, Moses would become the standard by which every other prophet would be evaluated and judged, including the Messiah.[15]

Prophetic Transitions

Samuel served the Lord as a priest and he served the people of Israel as a prophet (1 Sam. 3:1, 20). We may define Samuel as a *prophet of transition.* He helped facilitate political and spiritual changes in Israel that would greatly impact its national identity and culture. Samuel was also instrumental in restoring the faith and devotion of God's people.[16] Samuel served as Israel's last acting judge-leader. Under his prophetic oversight, Israel's political structure transitioned from judgeship to kingship. Samuel anointed Saul to be king over Israel. In later years, Samuel presided over another important

---

[13] Exod. 3:1, 12; 19:11 (Mount Horeb or Mount Sinai)

[14] Exod. 23:10-17; 25:8-40; 27:1-19; 28:1-43; 29:1-46; 30:1, 17-21, 30; 40:12-15; Lev. 23:1-44; Nu. 3:5-39

[15] Deut. 13:1-5; 18:15-22; Acts 3:22; 7:37

[16] We will discuss prophetic restoration in the following chapter.

change in national leadership—the anointing of David, son of Jesse. As king, David would spearhead a *prophetic reformation* within Israel's worship culture. Through David, the theme of the promised offspring and future Messianic kingdom would become more defined.

According to the Scriptures, when the prophet Samuel had become aged, he made his sons judges over Israel. But the people were displeased with them, because they did not act like their father; instead, they took advantage of their position for illicit gain, even ignoring justice (1 Sam. 8:3). The elders of Israel came to Samuel and requested a king. "They said to him, 'Look, you are old, and your sons do not follow your example. Therefore, appoint a king to judge us the same as all the other nations have'" (1 Sam. 8:5, HCSB). Samuel attempted to dissuade the people by letting them know all that what would happen to them under a kingship, but to no avail. The people insisted on having a king who would judge them and lead them in battle like other nations (1 Sam. 8:19-20). With the Lord's guidance, Samuel anointed Saul as their first king. But Saul demonstrated a tremendous lack of faith in God. He also failed to recognize the spiritual boundaries of his own authority. According to the account, Samuel had instructed Saul to go to Gilgal and wait seven days for him to come. He would then come and offer burnt offerings and sacrifices. He would also give further instructions, regarding that which Saul and the people were to do. At the head of an ill-equipped army, Saul went to Gilgal, just as Samuel had instructed him. But the people were fearful of the Philistines, who were encamped in Michmash and ready to do battle. Some of the men who followed Saul deserted the ranks. This, of course, unsettled the king. On the seventh day, Samuel had still not arrived; Saul decided to take matters into his own hands and offer the burnt offering himself. But no sooner had he finished when Samuel showed up.

> And Samuel asked, "What have you done?" Saul answered, "When I saw that the troops were deserting me and you didn't come within the appointed days and the Philistines were gathering at Michmash, I thought: The Philistines will now descend on me at Gilgal, and I haven't sought the Lord's favor. **So I forced myself to offer the burnt offering**" (1 Sam. 13:11-12, HCSB).

Samuel reproved Saul for not fully obeying the word of the Lord. His failure had compromised the permanency of his kingship and that of his offspring. In fact, Samuel informed Saul that the Lord has sought out another man according to his own heart who would rule over his people (1 Sam. 13:14).

The Lord, however, did not completely reject Saul as king until the second time he failed to obey the word of the Lord. Not only did he fail miserably, but he also allowed the people who were with him to transgress the word of the Lord. Through the prophet Samuel, the Lord had instructed Saul to destroy the Amalekite people and all they possessed, sparing nothing. The Lord judged the Amalekites because of the hostility they had shown towards his people, as they journeyed in the wilderness toward the land of Canaan.[17] But Saul allowed the people to spare some of the flock and cattle; Saul also spared the life of Agag, king of Amalek. When Samuel questioned him, concerning the bleating and lowing of the animals he could hear, Saul reasoned that the people had saved the best of the flock and cattle to offer them as sacrifices to the Lord. The prophet reproved him for his disobedience, but Saul insisted that he had obeyed the voice of the Lord.

> Then Samuel said: Does the Lord take pleasure in burnt offerings and sacrifices as much as in obeying the Lord? Look: to obey is better than sacrifice, to pay attention is better than the fat of rams. For rebellion is like the sin of divination, and defiance is like wickedness and idolatry. Because you have rejected the word of the Lord, He has rejected you as king (1 Sam. 15:22-23, HCSB).

Samuel's words reveal the importance of both hearing and obeying the Lord's voice. Expressions of worship (i.e., burnt offerings and sacrifices, bowing down, prostrating, etc.) are meaningless without faith and obedience; both are evidence of the fear of the Lord. Regrettably, Saul's lack of faith and inability to follow through the Lord's directives caused him to further drift away from God and spiritually spiral downward. In fact, the book of Samuel recounts that Saul ordered the slaughter of the priests of the Lord; he accused them of being complicit in helping David escape his hand. On another occasion, Saul even sought out the help of a medium. Saul clearly had no regard for the Lord, for his word, or for genuine worship.

The Lord sent the prophet Samuel to the house of Jesse in Bethlehem, to anoint one of his sons to be king over his people. The Lord chose David, the youngest of Jesse's sons. When Samuel anointed the young lad, a powerful anointing came upon him.[18] David was not only a skillful shepherd in keeping his father's flock; he also knew how to minister to God with harp

---

[17] Exod. 17:8-16;1 Sam. 15:2-3

[18] 1 Sam. 16:11-13; Ps. 89:20

and song. Soon enough, David would grow up to become a mighty warrior, an accomplished psalmist, and the keeper of the Lord's flock. Time and again, he would prove himself to be a man after God's own heart. This is not to say he was perfect; he would certainly make terrible and unconscionable decisions during his reign, but he would also repent and learn from them. Under his leadership, Israel's territories and political dominance would grow and extend well beyond the borders of the original conquest. Jerusalem would also become the nation's capital, and the ark of the covenant would be brought to the city. Under David's reign, the character of national worship would also be reformed. But before we get too far ahead of ourselves, let us recall where the story all began. The Lord raised up the prophet Samuel to oversee a political and spiritual transition in Israel that would eventually pave the way for the Davidic Kingdom, the reformation of national worship, and the construction of a temple in Jerusalem.

Prophetic Reformations

The Scriptures recount the various stories of David as a shepherd boy, giant-slayer, mighty warrior, harpist, psalmist, and king. But what some perhaps overlook is that David was also a prophet of God. As king, David wisely conferred with his prophets, Gad and Nathan; however, a powerful prophetic anointing also rested on him. Through his leadership, and with the assistance of Gad and Nathan, David initiated powerful reformation in Israel's political and spiritual culture.

Not long after the tribes were consolidated under his rule, David and his men moved against the Jebusites in Jerusalem, to take control of the city. They encountered strong resistance, but eventually took control of the city and made it a stronghold for David—a center, not only of political life, but of spiritual life as well. David consulted with his army leaders to move the ark of the covenant from Abinadab's house to Jerusalem. Unfortunately, David and his men followed the example of the Philistines and transported the ark on a new cart. According to the account, Abinadab's two sons, Uzzah and Ahio, led the oxen-drawn cart towards the city, with Ahio in the front, and Uzzah walking behind. The people continued to celebrate the Lord with both song and instruments as the procession proceeded towards Jerusalem. But then, tragedy struck. When they reached the threshing floor of a certain Nacon, the oxen suddenly stumbled. In quick response, Uzzah reached for the ark to keep it from tipping over or falling off the cart. The Lord, in his fierce wrath, immediately struck down Uzzah for touching the ark. David was upset with the Lord, perplexed at Uzzah's untimely death. "And David was afraid of the Lord that day, and he said, **'How can the ark of the Lord come to me?'"** (2 Sam. 6:9, ESV). David was afraid to bring the ark to Jerusalem, so the ark was brought to the house of Obed-edom and placed under his care. When David has informed that the house of Obed-edom and all he had was being greatly blessed, he decided to make another attempt to bring the ark to Jerusalem. His decision, however, included important and substantial changes:

> Then David summoned the priests Zadok and Abiathar, and the Levites Uriel, Asaiah, Joel, Shemaiah, Eliel, and Amminadab, and said to them, "You are the heads of the fathers' houses of the Levites. Consecrate yourselves, you and your brothers, so that you may bring up the ark of the Lord, the God of Israel, to the place that I have prepared for it. **Because you did not carry it the first time, the Lord our God broke out against us, because we did not seek him according to the rule**. So the priests and the Levites consecrated themselves to bring up the ark of the Lord, the God of Israel. And the Levites carried the ark of God on their shoulders with the poles, **as Moses had commanded according to the word of the Lord**" (1 Chr. 15:11-15, ESV).

David commanded the leaders of the Levites to organize their singers and musicians, to offer up praise and worship during the procession. He also pitched in the city a special tent for the ark. As the Levites carried the ark, their brothers made a loud and joyful sound to the Lord and offered sacrifices along the way. When the ark was placed in the tent, even more sacrifices were offered. In occasion of the festivities, David also distributed food to all the people. Celebrations, however, did not end that day: "Then he [David] appointed some of the Levites as ministers before the ark of the Lord, to invoke, to thank, and to praise the Lord, the God of Israel" (1 Chr. 16:4, ESV). The whole episode of the carrying of the ark in an atmosphere of joyous music, and the establishing of a continual worship service in the tent created a new precedent in worship, one that would eventually transition to the temple. This by no means suggests Israel was formerly without songs of praise and worship. Moses and other people of God had composed psalms and hymns to God. In fact, the Levites, who had been called to partake in the procession of the ark, already knew how to sing songs of praise and play musical instruments unto the Lord. David simply took praise and worship music to a whole new level. He incorporated songs and instruments in the daily services of both the tabernacle of the Lord in Gibeon and the tent in Jerusalem.[19] This new reform, however, was not without *prophetic guidance and input*. Even though David was himself a prophet, as aforementioned, he took counsel with his prophets. Indeed, Gad the seer and Nathan the prophet played an important role in organizing and promoting the worship of Yahweh in Jerusalem. The second book of Chronicles recounts that some three-hundred years later, when King Hezekiah sought to restore worship in the temple and among God's people, he looked back to the precedent and directives that were established under the prophetic leadership of David, Gad, and Nathan (Even Asaph the seer and his contributions are mentioned.):

> And he stationed the Levites in the house of the Lord with cymbals, harps, and lyres, according to the commandment of David and of Gad the king's seer and of Nathan the prophet, for the commandment was from the Lord through his prophets. The Levites stood with the instruments of David, and the priests with the trumpets. Then Hezekiah commanded that the burnt offering be offered on the altar. And when the burnt offering began, the song to the Lord began also, and the trumpets, accompanied by the instruments of David king of Israel. The whole assembly worshiped, and the singers sang, and the trumpeters sounded. All this continued until the burnt offering was finished. When the offering was finished, the king and all who were present with him bowed themselves and worshiped. And Hezekiah the king and the officials commanded the Levites to sing praises to the Lord with the words of David and of Asaph the seer. And they sang praises with gladness, and they bowed down and worshiped (2 Chr. 29:25-30, ESV).

The House of the Lord and the House of David

The ark of the covenant had successfully been brought to Jerusalem and placed in the special tent that David had set up for it. Worship services were organized and ongoing in both the tabernacle of the Lord in Gibeon and the tent in Jerusalem where the ark of the covenant was placed. David had also settled into his new home with his family. But it was not long before he began to sense the impropriety of the ark being kept in a tent while he dwelt in a

---

[19] 1 Chr. 16:37-42

house of cedar. David conferred with the prophet Nathan, concerning his desire to build a house for the Lord. Nathan approved of the king's intentions, but that same night, the word of the Lord came to the prophet. In one of the most powerful prophetic utterances in Old Testament Scripture, Nathan revealed the Lord's intentions to build an enduring house for David; moreover, his offspring would build a house for the Lord:

> "When your days are fulfilled to walk with your fathers, **I will raise up your offspring after you, one of your own sons, and I will establish his kingdom**. He shall build a house for me, and I will establish his throne forever. I will be to him a father, and he shall be to me a son. I will not take my steadfast love from him, as I took it from him who was before you, but I will confirm him in my house and in my kingdom forever, and his throne shall be established forever'" (1 Chr. 17:11-14, ESV).

Nathan's words greatly affected the king. Overwhelmed, David went into the tent of the ark and sat before the Lord (2 Sam. 7:18). He expressed his wonderment, worship, and gratitude for all the Lord was going to do for him. While Nathan's prophecy possessed predictive, revelational, and even corrective elements,[20] David's response demonstrated one of the most important functions or purposes of the prophetic anointing in both the Old and New Testament periods: To inspire praise and worship among God's people. Through the prophetic anointing, the Lord established the Davidic covenant.[21] : He would raise up an offspring who would build his house and whose throne the Lord would establish forever. Through biblical hindsight we understand that God was preparing the way for the very offspring who would one day crush the serpent's head—the Messiah.

We should note that David's desire to build a dwelling place for the Lord was not entirely without a prophetic reference. Centuries before Nathan had ever given his prophetic word, God had already spoken by the mouth of his prophet and servant, Moses, that he would choose a specific location of worship: "But you shall seek the place where the Lord your God chooses, out of all your tribes, to put His name for His dwelling place; and there you shall go" (Deut. 12:5, NKJV). The tabernacle of the Lord had been on the move for almost forty years in the wilderness. When the children of Israel

---

[20] 1 Chr. 17:4; 8-14

[21] 2 Chr. 7:18; 13:5; 21:7; Ps. 89:3; Isa. 55:3; Jer. 33:20-21, 25-26

moved into the promise land, the tabernacle continued to move from place to place.[22] In fact, the Lord said to David through Nathan the prophet: "For I have not lived in a house since the day I brought up Israel to this day, but I have gone from tent to tent and from dwelling to dwelling" (1 Chr. 17:5, ESV). According to the first book of Samuel, when the ark of the covenant was captured by the Philistines and then returned to Israel, it never made its way back to the tabernacle; instead, it was kept in private homes.[23] David's intentions—and clearly those of God as revealed by Nathan's prophecy—was not merely to *restore* the old pattern of tabernacle worship, but to *reform* it by consolidating the kingdom and national worship in the same location—*Jerusalem*; organizing the priesthood and the order of praise and worship before the altar and the ark; and making preparations for the construction of the Lord's house. This later, of course, would have to await another prophetic revelation, regarding the location of the temple.

Real-Estate Agents of the Lord

David's military campaigns met with continual success. He managed to subdue the Philistines and Moabites. He defeated King Hadadezer of Zobah and his military forces near the Euphrates and subjected the Arameans of Damascus to tribute. He also placed garrisons in Edom, subjecting the people to his rule. David also defeated the Syrians beyond the river and Ammonites. The first book of Chronicles reports twice that wherever David went, the Lord gave him the victory (1 Chr. 18:6, 13). Under his leadership Israel's borders, defenses, and wealth continued to increase. This is why it is so inconceivable that David would take a census of his people for military purposes. Some Bible scholars view the census as an act of pride, while others see it as a lack of faith. Regardless of how one interprets the event, the census was considered an act of evil that greatly angered the Lord and aroused his wrath. When David realized he had committed a terrible sin in taking the census, he asked God to remove his iniquity:

> **And the Lord spoke to Gad, David's seer**, saying, "Go and say to David, 'Thus says the Lord, Three things I offer you; choose one of them, that I may do it to you.'" So Gad came to David and said to him, "Thus says the Lord, 'Choose what you will: either three years of

---

[22] Josh. 18:1, *Shiloh*; 1 Chr. 16:39; 21:29, *Gibeon*

[23] 1 Sam. 7:1-2, the house of Abinadab; and 2 Sam. 6:10-11, the house of Obed-Edom.

> famine, or three months of devastation by your foes while the sword of your enemies overtakes you, or else three days of the sword of the Lord, pestilence on the land, with the angel of the Lord destroying throughout all the territory of Israel.' Now decide what answer I shall return to him who sent me" (1 Chr. 21:9-12, ESV).

After hearing Gad, the seer and the options that were presented him, David threw himself upon the mercies of the Lord, rather than falling into the hands of man. The Lord sent his angel with a sword to strike the land. Pestilence decimated some 70,000 men of Israel.

> And God sent the angel to Jerusalem to destroy it, but as he was about to destroy it, the Lord saw, and he relented from the calamity. And he said to the angel who was working destruction, "It is enough; now stay your hand." And the angel of the Lord was standing by the threshing floor of Ornan the Jebusite. And David lifted his eyes and saw the angel of the Lord standing between earth and heaven, and in his hand a drawn sword stretched out over Jerusalem. Then David and the elders, clothed in sackcloth, fell upon their faces (1 Chr. 21:15-16, ESV).

When David saw the angel and imminent destruction, he was deeply grieved for his sin. He pleaded for mercy and interceded for the city and for its inhabitants, asking God to punish him and his family for his own wickedness, and not the people.

> Now the angel of the Lord had commanded Gad to say to David that David should go up and raise an altar to the Lord on the threshing floor of Ornan the Jebusite. So David went up at Gad's word, which he had spoken in the name of the Lord (1 Chr. 21:18-19, ESV).

David purchased the land, the oxen, and the wood of threshing sledges from Ornan:

> And David built there an altar to the Lord and presented burnt offerings and peace offerings and called on the Lord, and the Lord answered him with fire from heaven upon the altar of burnt offering. Then the Lord commanded the angel, and he put his sword back into its sheath. At that time, when David saw that the Lord had answered him at the threshing floor of Ornan the Jebusite, he sacrificed there (1 Chr. 21:26-28, ESV).

According to the account, David could not go to the tabernacle in the high place at Gibeon to seek God before the altar of burnt offering, for he feared the sword of the Lord's judgment that had been prevailing throughout the land (1 Chr. 21:30). David's sacrifice and altar stayed the wrath of God and became one of the most singular altars in biblical history—a place where numerous generations would gather to worship the Lord. "Then David said, 'Here shall be the house of the Lord God and here the altar of burnt offering for Israel'" (1 Chr. 22:1, ESV).

Prophetic Song and Music

Prophetic anointing played a particularly important role in the Davidic kingdom. Nathan the prophet had revealed the word of the Lord to David, concerning the house of David and the house of the Lord. Gad the seer had not only been instrumental in revealing God's anger because of the census, but also the place where David should build an altar to stay divine wrath that loomed over Jerusalem. David understood the altar to also be the location of the future temple. David greatly esteemed the prophetic anointing. In fact, he appointed seers[24] or prophets and their brothers to minister to the Lord in song and music, in both the tabernacle of the Lord in Gibeon and the tent set up in Jerusalem.[25] He even made sure that prophetic singing would be integrated in the future house of the Lord:

> Moreover, David and the commanders of the army set apart for the service some of the sons of Asaph and of Heman and of Jeduthun, who were to **prophesy**[26] with lyres, harps and cymbals; and the number of those who performed their service was: Of the sons of Asaph: Zaccur, Joseph, Nethaniah and Asharelah; the sons of Asaph were under the direction of Asaph, who **prophesied**[27] under the direction of the king. Of Jeduthun, the sons of Jeduthun: Gedaliah, Zeri, Jeshaiah, Shimei, Hashabiah and Mattithiah, six, under the direction of their father Jeduthun with the harp, who **prophesied**[28] in giving thanks and praising the Lord. Of Heman,

---

[24] 1 Sam. 9:9. A seer is another term for prophet.

[25] 1 Chr. 16:4-7, 37-42; 25:1-3, 5; 2 Chr. 29:30; 35:15. Asaph, Jeduthun (Ethan?), and Heman were called *seers.*

[26] נָבִיא, nabi: a spokesman, speaker, prophet.

[27] נָבָא, naba, to prophesy.

[28] Ibid.

> the sons of Heman: Bukkiah, Mattaniah, Uzziel, Shebuel and Jerimoth, Hananiah, Hanani, Eliathah, Giddalti and Romamti-ezer, Joshbekashah, Mallothi, Hothir, Mahazioth. All these were the sons of Heman the king's seer to exalt him according to the words of God, for God gave fourteen sons and three daughters to Heman. All these were under the direction of their father to sing in the house of the Lord, with cymbals, harps and lyres, for the service of the house of God. **Asaph, Jeduthun and Heman were under the direction of the king** (1 Chr. 25:1-6, NASB).[29]

To prophesy, within context of the above passage of Scripture, is to sing and compose music under the influence and inspiration of the prophetic anointing. We often associate prophesying with the prophet who declares the word of the Lord and speaks of future events; but it is also to praise the Lord and offer him thanksgiving with the authority of heaven. In fact, many of the prophets in the Old Testament were also composers of songs and works of praise and worship (e.g., Exod. 15:1-20; 1 Sam. 10:5-6; 2 Sam. 2:1-51; Judg. 4:4; 5:1-31; Ps. 1-150; Is. 26:1-21; Hab. 3:1-19, etc.). Prophetic songs and prayers also find their way in the New Testament (Luke 1:46-55, 67-80; Rev. 5:9-14; 15:3-4). Prophetic songs also find their way in the New Testament.

---

[29] 1 Chr. 23:1-6. David organizes the Levites for the service in the future house of God.

CHAPTER 3

The Pillar of the Prophet

(The Authority of Biblical Worship)

Part Two

"But those things which God foretold by the mouth of all His prophets, that the Christ would suffer, He has thus fulfilled. Repent therefore and be converted, that your sins may be blotted out, so that times of refreshing may come from the presence of the Lord, and that He may send Jesus Christ, who was preached to you before, whom heaven must receive until ***the times of restoration of all things****, which God has spoken by the mouth of all His holy prophets since the world began. For Moses truly said to the fathers, 'The Lord your God will raise up for you a Prophet like me from your brethren. Him you shall hear in all things, whatever He says to you. And it shall be that every soul who will not hear that Prophet shall be utterly destroyed from among the people.' Yes, and all the prophets, from Samuel and those who follow, as many as have spoken, have also foretold these days" (Acts 3:18-24, NKJV).*

The Prophets of Restoration

Peter and John had gone to the temple at the time of the afternoon prayer when they encountered a man who had been lame from birth, begging at the gate called, *Beautiful* (Acts 3:2). The lame man thought he would certainly receive alms from the two men; instead, he received healing in the name of Jesus Christ of Nazareth. The unexpected healing quickly drew a large crowd, providing the apostles with an audience and the opportunity to preach the gospel. Peter addressed the crowd, explaining that the man had been healed through faith in the name of Jesus. God was glorifying his servant, Jesus, whom the people had put to death, but God had raised from the dead. Though they had done it ignorantly, Peter assured his listeners that Christ had actually fulfilled that which God had foretold by his prophets. In Peter's message that follows, the prophets assume a conspicuous and important role. This was partly to explain the miraculous healing, and partly because of the people's shared heritage with the prophets (Acts 3:25). Peter reminded them that the prophets spoke of the Messiah's sufferings and of the present days of grace, and that Moses spoke of a coming prophet who would be like him. But more relevant to our present study, the prophets also spoke of the *restoration* that would take place when the Messiah comes again. Restoration, in its fullest Biblical meaning, is always initiated by the prophetic anointing. In fact, it is Jesus, the *Prophet* and the *Anointed One*, who introduces the *spiritual* restoration and who also ushers in the *eschatological* restoration. Wherefore, Peter firmly exhorted the people:

> "Repent therefore and be converted, that your sins may be blotted out, so that times of refreshing may come from the presence of the Lord, and that He may send Jesus Christ, who was preached to you before, whom heaven must receive until **the times of restoration of all things**, which God has spoken by the mouth of all His holy prophets since the world began" (Acts 3:19-21, NKJV).

The prophets, indeed, spoke extensively on the subject of restoration, both spiritual and eschatological. But equally important, they labored in their own days to restore the people of God and covenant worship. This, because restoration is the heart and deep longing of the prophetic anointing.

The Prophet Samuel

We have already referred to Samuel as a *prophet of transition*, but he was also a *prophet of restoration.* According to the first book of Samuel, Israel had lost a major battle with the Philistines. The ark of the covenant had been captured, and Hophni and Phinehas, the sons of Eli the High Priest, perished in the conflict. At the news that the ark had been captured by the Philistines, Eli fell back from his chair and broke his neck. The Philistines eventually sent the ark back to Israel, but it was never returned to the tabernacle of the Lord; it was placed in the house of Abinadab. Almost twenty years had gone by when the people began to sense the loss of their spiritual identity and heritage. Moreover, they also felt oppressed by the Philistines. As a true prophet, Samuel sought to restore the people's faith in their God, but first, he had to purge the land of false deities and all their objects of devotion:

> And Samuel said to all the house of Israel, "If you are returning to the Lord with all your heart, then put away the foreign gods and the Ashtaroth from among you and direct your heart to the Lord and serve him only, and he will deliver you out of the hand of the Philistines" (1 Sam. 7:3, ESV).

The people responded to Samuel's exhortation; they destroyed their images of Baal and Ashtaroth and worshipped only the Lord. Samuel further instructed the people to gather at Mizpah where he would intercede for them. At the appointed time, the people gathered together and fasted and confessed their sins. They also drew water and poured it out before the Lord. Some believe this unprecedented act symbolizes the pouring out of the heart before the Lord (Job 3:24; Ps. 22:14; Lam. 2:19); but perhaps it symbolizes their acknowledgment of how fleeting and ephemeral life is and that only the Lord could redeem it (2 Sam. 14:14). Either way, the people repented and returned to the Lord. Mizpah became a place of spiritual restoration. The gathering at Mizpah also confirmed Samuel as Israel's judge (1 Sam. 7:6).

When the Philistines heard that the people of Israel had gathered together, they marched out against them. In a state of panic, the men of Israel pleaded with Samuel to continue praying for them. Samuel offered a sacrifice to God and cried out to the Lord. Samuel himself recounts in his book how the Lord miraculously delivered Israel from the Philistines. The Lord never intended for his people to become victims of fear, slavery, and oppression. But victory, peace, and security had always been contingent upon their faithfulness to covenantal worship. In fact, it is axiomatic that when the Lord is the sole object of his people's devotion, he will fight their battles and lead them into victory. Conversely, when his people drift away from true worship and devotion, they leave the door open and unguarded, allowing the enemy to enter and make incursions into their lives. This is one of the reasons why the prophetic anointing is so important; it restores the foundation and principles of biblical worship.

The Prophet Elijah

Elijah the Tishbite entered the scene during the reign of King Ahab (1 Kgs. 17:1). Signs and wonders accompanied his prophetic ministry. Because of Ahab's great wickedness, and the evil he brought to the land, Elijah informed the king there would be neither dew nor rain, except at his word. However, before the dew and rain could return, covenantal worship needed to be restored to the people of God. Three years passed without rain when Obadiah, the overseer of Ahab's house, received a visit from Elijah, who had been absent from the scene up until that moment. Obadiah feared the Lord; in fact, he had hidden a hundred prophets in caves, even providing them with bread and water, to protect them from the murderous hand of Jezebel, Ahab's wife. Elijah directed Obadiah to inform Ahab that he had come. Obadiah did as Elijah asked and informed the king. When Ahab encountered Elijah, the king accused the prophet of being the cause of the people's trouble. But Elijah countered that Ahab and his father's house were the indeed source of all of Israel's troubles. Ahab's fathers had turned their backs on the commandments of the Lord and Ahab himself followed the Baals. Elijah directed Ahab to gather the people and all the prophets of Baal and Asherah and meet with him on Mount Carmel. Ahab followed Elijah's instructions. When the men of Israel and the prophets of Baal arrived at Mount Carmel, they found themselves before an unusual challenge:

> Elijah came near to all the people and said, "How long *will* you hesitate between two opinions? If the Lord is God, follow Him; but if Baal, follow him." But the people did not answer him a word. Then Elijah said to the people, "I alone am left a prophet of the Lord, but Baal's prophets are 450 men. Now let them give us two oxen; and let them choose one ox for themselves and cut it up, and place it on the wood, but put no fire *under it*; and I will prepare the other ox and lay it on the wood, and I will not put a fire *under it*. Then you call on the name of your god, and I will call on the name of the Lord, and the God who answers by fire, He is God." And all the people said, "That is a good idea" (1 Kgs. 18:21-24, NASB).

The future of Israel hung in the balance between two opinions. Elijah sought to tip the scales of the people's opinion in favor of the God of Israel. The prophets of Baal took the challenge, made an altar and prepared their sacrifice. From morning until noon, they danced about the altar, calling upon the name of Baal. Elijah taunted them mercilessly because Baal did not respond to their cries. More determined than ever, the prophets of Baal shouted louder and slashed themselves with swords and spears until they were bleeding profusely. They continued to prophesy until evening, but Baal did not utter a word. Elijah then called the people to himself: "And he repaired the altar of the Lord which had been torn down" (1 Kgs. 18:30, NASB).[1] Elijah rebuilt the altar with twelve stones that represented the twelve tribes of Israel. He further dug a trench around the altar and arranged the wood and pieces of ox. When the altar and sacrifice were prepared, Elijah ordered that pitchers of water (twelve to be precise) be poured over the sacrifice until the altar was drenched and the trench filled with water.

> At the time of the offering of the *evening* sacrifice, Elijah the prophet came near and said, "O Lord, the God of Abraham, Isaac and Israel, today let it be known that You are God in Israel and that I am Your servant and I have done all these things at Your word. Answer me, O Lord, answer me, that this people may know that You, O Lord, are God, and *that* You have turned their heart back again" (1 Kgs. 18:36-37, NASB).

Fire suddenly came down and consumed the drenched sacrifice, wood, and stones, even the very dust that settled on the altar. The fire also totally evaporated all the water that filled the trench. "When all the people saw it, they fell on their faces; and they said, 'The Lord, He is God; the Lord, He is God'" (1 Kgs. 18:39, NASB). Elijah commanded the people to seize the false prophets and bring them to the brook Kishon, where he executed them.

Through Ahab's weak leadership and Jezebel's wicked influence, wickedness and idolatry flooded the kingdom of Israel, provoking the judgment of God, a severe drought throughout the land. Only when the

---

[1] The connection between restoration and the prophetic anointing is beautifully illustrated in the fifteenth chapter of 2 Chronicles. According to the account, the Spirit of the Lord had come upon the prophet Azariah, who went out to meet King Asa after a major battle and victory. Azariah exhorted the king and the people of Judah and Benjamin to seek the Lord and not forsake him; the prophet further encouraged Asa to persevere in the work he had begun, because it would surely be rewarded (2 Chr. 15:1-7). Inspired and strengthened by the prophet's words, Asa continued to eradicate idolatry from Judah, Benjamin, and the cities of Ephraim that he had taken. He even disposed his mother, Maacah, from being queen, because of the vile image she had made for Asherah. Asa repaired the altar of the Lord and gathered the people of Judah and Benjamin, and those from the tribes of Ephraim, Manasseh, and Simeon who dwelt among them. They gathered in Jerusalem on the third month (i.e., the Feast of Weeks) and sacrificed to the Lord numerous oxen and sheep from the spoils they had taken after the battle (2 Chr. 14:14-15; 15:8-11). The occasion prompted a powerful revival of devotion among the people. The account also notes that the land of Judah subsequently enjoyed many years of peace (2 Chr. 15:15, 19).

altar of the Lord was repaired, and worship restored could the desperately needed rain return once again. In fact, after Elijah had executed the prophets of Baal, he climbed the summit of Carmel and prayed seven times for rain until a small and promising cloud appeared over the distant sea. Elijah proved unequivocally that he was a prophet of restoration. Historically, the restoration was short-lived; nonetheless, it revealed the heart of God, and one of the primary objectives of the prophetic anointing. According to the prophet Malachi, Elijah would once again play a prominent role in restoring God's people, before the coming day of the Lord (Mal. 4:5; Matt. 17:11-13; Luke 1:17).

The Prophet Amos

The prophet Amos prophesied and warned of the severe judgments that would befall Judah and the house of Israel: *Judah*, because they despised God's law and disregarded his statutes; they also allowed themselves to be deceived by the same gods their forefathers had followed; *Israel*, because, among other things, they perverted justice, profaned the Lord's name, and even silenced his prophets.[2] Despite all the judgments that would surely befall the two kingdoms, the prophet also spoke of a coming day of restoration:

> "In that day I will raise up the booth of David that is fallen and repair its breaches, and raise up its ruins and rebuild it as in the days of old, that they may possess the remnant of Edom and all the nations who are called by my name," declares the Lord who does this. "Behold, the days are coming," declares the Lord, "when the plowman shall overtake the reaper and the treader of grapes him who sows the seed; the mountains shall drip sweet wine, and all the hills shall flow with it. I will restore the fortunes of my people Israel, and they shall rebuild the ruined cities and inhabit them; they shall plant vineyards and drink their wine, and they shall make gardens and eat their fruit. I will plant them on their land, and they shall never again be uprooted out of the land that I have given them," says the Lord your God (Amos 9:11-15, ESV).

According to Amos, the restoration of Israel, its land, and former prosperity begins with the raising and reparation of the booth of David. *What is the booth of David and how does it integrate with the restoration of worship?*

---

[2] Amos 2:6-16

Bible commentators generally understand the booth of David to represent the weakened and fallen state of the house of David. The Davidic dynasty had indeed fallen into a spiritually decrepit condition, compared to the early days of David's reign. Ironically, the golden age of the kingdom already began to tarnish under Solomon's reign, because of his disregard of the covenant and his brazen idolatry.[3] The kingdom continued to diminish in glory and power under several of Solomon's successors, especially Manasseh, because of their unabated idolatry.[4] Others believe the booth of David relates to the tent that David had erected for the ark of the covenant in Jerusalem (this was also once my view). Under David's leadership, the tent had become a place of genuine praise and worship, not to mention, prophetic music. Eventually, the ark, the tent of meeting and all its furnishings,[5] and the priesthood, along with those in charge of praise and worship, were all transferred to the temple once it was built. Unfortunately, worship in the temple gradually dwindled as the kings and people of Judah compromised with idolatry and other pagan practices. According to this view, the raising up of David's booth represents the restoration of the genuine praise and worship that took place in the simplicity of the tent David had set up.

While there is merit in both these interpretations, there is yet another possible meaning. The booth of David symbolically relates to both the *Davidic lineage* and the *Feast of Booths.* The Feast of Booths was one of three principal feasts that Israel was supposed to celebrate every year.[6] The feast commemorated the Lord who had caused the people of Israel to live in booths or huts during their journey in the wilderness.

> "You shall celebrate it as a feast to the Lord for seven days in the year. It is a statute forever throughout your generations; you shall celebrate it in the seventh month. You shall dwell in booths for seven days. All native Israelites shall dwell in booths, that your generations may know that I made the people of Israel dwell in booths when I brought them out of the land of Egypt: I am the Lord your God" (Lev. 23:41-43, ESV).

The feast was to be celebrated for seven days and with a special series of

---

[3] 1 Kgs. 11:4-13
[4] 2 Kgs. 23:26-27
[5] 1 Kgs. 8:4; 2 Chron. 5:4-5
[6] Lev. 23:34; Deut. 16:16

burnt offerings, drink offerings, and grain offerings (Num. 29:12-38). It was to be a joyous occasion in which the people were to celebrate the blessings of God for the harvest and for the labor of their hands. Because the feast took place at the end of the year during the final harvest, it was also referred to as the *Feast of Ingathering* (Exod. 23:16). Incidentally, the feast also related to another important event—the dedication of Solomon's temple.[7]

The prophet Amos identifies the house of David with the Feast of Booths. David's booth had fallen, not because the descendants of David had merely failed to observe a particular feast; indeed, the Feast of Booths had not been observed since the days of Joshua, son of Nun, until after the Jewish exiles had returned to their homeland (Neh. 8:17). Instead, the booth had fallen because the kings of Judah no longer worshipped God according to the covenant. Moreover, they failed to connect themselves to their spiritual heritage (As we already mentioned, the Feast of Booths represented the dwellings of the Israelites during their journey in the wilderness). Though history bears witness to a few extraordinary exceptions, by far and large, most of David's descendants, including most of their subjects, had fallen into the snare of idolatry. For this reason, the house and kingdom of David lay in a state of spiritual ruin. Thus, the raising and repairing of the booth is emblematic of the restoration of both the Davidic kingdom and covenantal worship. There are good reasons that support such an interpretation. First of all, Amos did not use either the Hebrew word for *tent* (אֹהֶל, *ohel*)[8] or *tabernacle* (מִשְׁכָּן, *michkan*)[9]; instead, he uses the word, *booth* (סֻכָּה, *sukkah*), the same word used in Lev. 23:34 for the Feast of *Booths*. Secondly, the passage in Amos is Messianic and eschatological in nature. In the New Testament, we find that the booth of David was indeed raised and repaired with the coming of the Messiah. In fact, James, one of the elders of the church in Jerusalem, interpreted the inclusion of the Gentiles in God's grace as the fulfillment of Amos's prophecy (Acts 15:16-18).[10] The general context of Amos, chapter nine, is also eschatological; it refers to the restoration of Israel[11]—an event that did not take place in the first century, but still awaits the second coming of the Lord, when he will restore all things. Third, according to the prophet

---

[7] 1 Kgs. 8:2, 65-66; 2 Chron. 5:3; 7:8-10

[8] 2 Sam. 6:17

[9] Exod. 25:9

[10] Apparently, there is only one Greek word used in the New Testament for *tent*, *tabernacle*, or *booth*: σκηνή, *skéné*.

[11] Amos 9:14

Zechariah, the Feast of Booths is also an eschatological event that will take place *after* the Lord has defeated the nations that come against Jerusalem, and *after* his feet are standing on the Mount of Olives (Zech 14:1-4):

> Then it will come about that any who are left of all the nations that went against Jerusalem will go up from year to year to **worship the King**, the Lord of hosts, and to celebrate the **Feast of Booths**. And it will be that whichever of the families of the earth does not go up to Jerusalem to **worship the King**, the Lord of hosts, there will be no rain on them. If the family of Egypt does not go up or enter, then no *rain will fall* on them; it will be the plague with which the Lord smites the nations who do not go up to celebrate the **Feast of Booths**. This will be the punishment of Egypt, and the punishment of all the nations who do not go up to celebrate the **Feast of Booths** (Zech. 14:16-19, NASB).

According to the prophecy, the Feast of Booths will be celebrated after the restoration of Israel. Even those who remain of the nations will come to Jerusalem and celebrate the feast. It is noteworthy that Zechariah mentions the Feast of Booths three times in his prophecy. And, according to the context, worship is an integral part of the feast.

The Prophets Haggai and Zechariah

Like the prophet Amos, the prophets Haggai and Zechariah were also prophets of restoration. Both men were instrumental in encouraging the reconstruction and restoration of the temple, which had been destroyed by the Chaldeans. Concerning these two prophets, Ezra writes:

> Now Haggai the prophet and Zechariah the prophet, a descendant of Iddo, prophesied to the Jews in Judah and Jerusalem in the name of the God of Israel, who was over them. Then Zerubbabel son of Shealtiel and Joshua son of Jozadak set to work to rebuild the house of God in Jerusalem. And the prophets of God were with them, supporting them (Ezra 5:1-2, NIV).

The Lord spoke through the prophet Haggai to Zerubbabel, the governor of Judah, and Joshua the son of Jozadak, the High Priest, that the people had put off rebuilding the temple long enough. They were stricken with poverty, drought, scarce harvests, and the loss of crops and livestock, because they were more interested in their own homes than the house of

God. The Lord commanded the people: "Go up into the mountains and bring down timber and build my house, so that I may take pleasure in it and be honored,' says the Lord" (Hag. 1:8, NIV). Encouraged by the Lord's prophet, the people began to build the house of God. Haggai also prophesied of the extraordinary glory of the house (more so than the previous house) and of the peace the Lord would give in that place (Hag. 2:9).

The prophet Zechariah prophesied that the relationship between God and his people would be restored if they would indeed return to the Lord and not walk in the ways of their forefathers (Zech. 1:1-4). Zechariah records, in one of his first visions, a conversation between the Angel of the Lord and the Lord of Hosts, concerning the restoration of the city:

> Then the Angel of the Lord responded, "How long, Lord of Hosts, will You withhold mercy from Jerusalem and the cities of Judah that You have been angry with these 70 years?" The Lord replied with kind and comforting words to the angel who was speaking with me. So the angel who was speaking with me said, "Proclaim: The Lord of Hosts says: I am extremely jealous for Jerusalem and Zion. I am fiercely angry with the nations that are at ease, for I was a little angry, but they made it worse. **Therefore, this is what the Lord says: In mercy, I have returned to Jerusalem; My house will be rebuilt within it"—this is the declaration of the Lord of Hosts—"and a measuring line will be stretched out over Jerusalem.** "Proclaim further: This is what the Lord of Hosts says: My cities will again overflow with prosperity; the Lord will once more comfort Zion and again choose Jerusalem" (Zech. 1:12-17, HCSB).

Zechariah hears the Lord declare that he has redirected his attention towards Jerusalem. His house will be rebuilt, and the cities of Judah will "again overflow with prosperity." However, the prophet also declares that the restoration of the temple is not only dependent upon the Lord's favor; it is also contingent upon the people's obedience to the Lord (Zech. 6:15).

The Prophet Malachi

> "Since the days of your fathers, you have turned from My statutes; you have not kept them. Return to Me, and I will return to you," says the Lord of Hosts" (Mal. 3:7, HCSB).

The prophet Malachi was another one of Judah's noted prophets of restoration. He prophesied during the post-exilic period. Many of the exiles had successfully returned to their land from Persia. They had rebuilt their homes, and perhaps some of the towns and villages scattered throughout Judea. The temple had been rebuilt, as well as the walls of Jerusalem. The Levites and their priestly duties were reorganized, the altar set up, and sacrifices, reinstated. Yet despite all the apparent *progress*, there was still a need of spiritual restoration among the people themselves. Often, a restorative process begins by first diagnosing the cause of declension, and then by providing the necessary cure or solution. This is where the prophet Malachi enters the story. As a prophetic diagnostician, Malachi exposed a series of transgressions and wrong attitudes among the priesthood and people. The priests were dishonoring God by offering him an inferior and second-rate worship: sick and defective sacrificial animals (1:7- 8). The priests had lost their sense of awe and fear of the Lord. They also failed in their duty to teach the people the fear of the Lord and knowledge of God; instead, because they had strayed from the way, they caused many to stumble. They did not keep the ways of the Lord but showed partiality in their instruction (2:4-9).

Malachi certainly showed no partiality towards those who were profaning the altar and covering their garments in violence by marrying foreign women and divorcing the wives of their youth. They were violating the spirit of the covenant by neglecting their moral and spiritual duties towards their wives and children (2:13-16). They were also negligent in their covenantal duties towards the house of God, namely, offering tithes and contributions of their harvests (3:8-12). The prophet also exposed wrong attitudes and harsh words that were being spoken against the Lord (2:17; 3:13-15). In contrast to the behavior and attitudes of the priesthood and of the people of Judah, the prophet also speaks of another group of people who distinguish themselves before the Lord: "At that time those who feared the Lord spoke to one another. The Lord took notice and listened. So a book of remembrance was written before Him for those who feared Yahweh and had high regard for His name" (Mal. 3:16, HCSB). Though many in Judah had allowed the moral lines to become blurred, the Lord declares through his prophet that he will show a clear distinction between the righteous and the wicked, and between those who serve God and those who serve themselves (3:18).

At the heart of Malachi's message is an unmistakable and urgent desire to *restore* worship, moral character of his people, and the blessings of a covenant relationship with God. His oracles clearly reach far beyond his own generation, foretelling of a future spiritual restoration, the coming of the Lord, and of the messenger who would go before the Lord:

> "**See, I am going to send My messenger, and he will clear the way before Me**. Then the Lord you seek will suddenly come to His temple, the Messenger of the covenant you desire—see, He is coming," says the Lord of Hosts. But who can endure the day of His coming? And who will be able to stand when He appears? For He will be like a refiner's fire and like cleansing lye. He will be like a refiner and purifier of silver; He will purify the sons of Levi and refine them like gold and silver. **Then they will present offerings to the Lord in righteousness. And the offerings of Judah and Jerusalem will please the Lord as in days of old and years gone by**.
>
> "Look, I am going to send you Elijah the prophet before the great and awesome Day of the Lord comes. And he will turn the hearts of fathers to their children and the hearts of children to their fathers. *Otherwise*, I will come and strike the land with a curse" (Mal. 3:1-4; 4:5-6, HCSB).

Samuel, Elijah, Amos, Haggai, Zechariah, and Malachi are only a few examples of the prophetic voices of restoration. What more could be said of all the other prophets: Some actively sought to restore covenant worship among God's people; some foretold of the restoration of Jerusalem, the temple, and the cities of Judah; some prophesied the Lord would gather the exiles and restore them to their land[12] (Some of the prophets even ministered among the Gentile nations).[13] Yet, in one way or another, all of them pointed towards "the times of restoration of all things" (Acts 3:21, NKJV). Restoration is the common thread that unites all of the prophets, because at the heart of God and the prophetic anointing is the desire to restore and not destroy.

---

[12] Jer. 29:14; Ez. 39:25; Hos. 6:11; Joel 3:1; Amos 9:14; Zeph. 3:20
[13] 1 Kgs. 17:8-24; 2 Kgs. 6:18-23; 8:7-15; Jonah 1:1-2; 3:1-10

The Greatest Prophet of Restoration and Transition

> "Do not be afraid, Zacharias, for your prayer is heard; and your wife Elizabeth will bear you a son, and you shall call his name John. And you will have joy and gladness, and many will rejoice at his birth. For he will be great in the sight of the Lord, and shall drink neither wine nor strong drink. He will also be filled with the Holy Spirit, even from his mother's womb. And he will turn many of the children of Israel to the Lord their God. He will also go before Him in the spirit and power of Elijah, 'to turn the hearts of the fathers to the children,' and the disobedient to the wisdom of the just, to make ready a people prepared for the Lord" (Luke 1:13-17, NKJV).

Zacharias was fulfilling his priestly duties before the altar of incense, when suddenly an angel of God appeared before him. The angel spoke to Zacharias and foretold of a future son he and his wife, Elisabeth, would have. His son would be called, *John*, and he would be a prophet of God. The angel also spelled out the prophetic nature of John's ministry: It would be *restorative*, because he would "turn many of the children of Israel to the Lord their God." It would also be *transitional*, because he would go before the Messiah "in the spirit and power of Elijah, 'to turn the hearts of the fathers to the children,' and the disobedient to the wisdom of the just, to make ready a people prepared for the Lord."[14]

John began his ministry in the regions of the Jordan River, "preaching a baptism of repentance for the remission of sins" (Luke 3:3, NKJV). John was dressed in camel's hair and a leather belt. He lived off the land, eating locust and wild honey. Despite such eccentricities, he spearheaded a powerful movement of God. People came to him from Jerusalem, Judea, and the regions surrounding the Jordan. Though he did no sign or miracle, John inspired a spirit of repentance and reconciliation. He stirred the hearts of the people with his message and raised their hopes and expectations. In fact, the people wondered whether he might even be the coming Messiah. But John set the record straight:

> "I indeed baptize you with water; but One mightier than I is coming, whose sandal strap I am not worthy to loose. He will baptize you with the Holy Spirit and fire. His winnowing fan *is* in His hand, and He will thoroughly clean out His threshing

[14] Mal. 4:5-6. The angel paraphrases the prophet Malachi's words.

> floor, and gather the wheat into His barn; but the chaff He will burn with unquenchable fire" (Luke 3:16-17, NKJV).

One day as John was baptizing the people, Jesus also came to him to be baptized. When Jesus came up out of the water, the Holy Spirit descended upon him in the form of a dove, and a voice spoke from heaven: "This is My beloved Son, in whom I am well pleased" (Matt. 3:17, NKJV). John bore witness that Jesus was the one who would baptize in the Holy Spirit and that he was the Son of God (John 3:32-33).

The gospel of John records that while Jesus was in the region of Judea, his disciples were baptizing the people. Not far away, John the Baptist also baptizing the people (John 3:22-23). It became obvious that people were gravitating towards Jesus. In fact, an argument arose between John's disciples and some of the Jews, concerning purification (i.e., baptism). They asked John why all the people were going to Jesus. Most likely, the Jews who questioned John had only seen competition and rivalry between Jewish religious factions. They did not understand the *transitional* nature of John's ministry.

> John responded, "No one can receive a single thing unless it's given to him from heaven. You yourselves can testify that I said, 'I am not the Messiah, but I've been sent ahead of Him.' He who has the bride is the groom. But the groom's friend, who stands by and listens for him, rejoices greatly at the groom's voice. So this joy of mine is complete. **He must increase, but I must decrease**" (John 3:27-30, HCSB).

After John had been placed in prison by Herod, John heard of the things Jesus was doing. Oddly, he sent his disciples to inquire whether Jesus was the Messiah, or if they should expect another. Jesus replied:

> "Go and report to John what you hear and see: the blind see, the lame walk, those with skin diseases are healed, the deaf hear, the dead are raised, and the poor are told the good news. And if anyone is not offended because of Me, he is blessed" (Matt. 11:4-6, HCSB).

Though John had been called to be a prophet, and even filled with the Holy Spirit from the womb of his mother, he also needed to exercise faith in Jesus. When John's disciples departed, Jesus spoke to the crowds:

> "What did you go out into the wilderness to see? A reed shaken by the wind? But what did you go out to see? A man clothed in soft

> garments? Indeed, those who wear soft *clothing* are in kings' houses. But what did you go out to see? A prophet? Yes, I say to you, and more than a prophet. For this is *he* of whom it is written: 'Behold, I send My messenger before Your face, Who will prepare Your way before You.' "**Assuredly, I say to you, among those born of women there has not risen one greater than John the Baptist**; but he who is least in the kingdom of heaven is greater than he. And from the days of John the Baptist until now the kingdom of heaven suffers violence, and the violent take it by force. For all the prophets and the law prophesied until John. And if you are willing to receive *it,* he is Elijah who is to come. He who has ears to hear, let him hear!" (Matt. 11:7-15, NKJV).

The people unquestionably regarded John to be a prophet of God (the chief priests and elders would not publicly give their opinion of John's baptism because they feared the people: Matt. 21:23-27). But Jesus explained to the crowd that as a prophet, John was more consequential and far reaching than the people had supposed. He was the fulfilment of the prophecies regarding the *messenger* who would be sent to prepare the way of the Lord and the *Elijah* who would restore relations between fathers and sons (Mal. 3:1; 4:5-6). Unlike other prophets who had been sent to the people, the people came to John in the wilderness. He preached to them a baptism of repentance, he heralded the coming of the Messiah, the baptism with the Holy Spirit and fire, and the coming wrath of God. Without controversy, John the Baptist was the greatest prophet of restoration and transition.

A New Paradigm, Transition, Reformation, and Restoration

Moses' prophetic anointing was without question, unique and unequaled. However, it would not remain so forever. Even Moses knew this, for he said, "The Lord your God will raise up for you a prophet like me from among your own brothers. You must listen to him" (Deut. 18:15, HCSB). Moses spoke prophetically of another prophet that would be just like him: a prophet who would transition God's people toward a new paradigm[15] of worship; who would reform the old order of priesthood, even revolutionizing it through a new covenant (Heb. 9:10); and who would restore all things at his second advent, including the kingdom to Israel (Acts 1:6; 3:21). In short, the

[15] By *paradigm*, we mean a new *model*, *example*, or *form* of worship that is either introduced, or initiated through the prophetic anointing.

prophet would initiate a new *transition*, *paradigm*, *reformation*, and *restoration*—all in one. The New Testament recognizes and acclaims Jesus Christ as the very prophet of which Moses spoke. Jesus' disciples acknowledged he was the prophet: "Philip found Nathanael and told him, 'We have found the One Moses wrote about in the Law (and so did the prophets): Jesus the son of Joseph, from Nazareth!'" (John 1:45, HCSB). Acts of the Apostles records that both Peter and Stephen, openly proclaimed Jesus to be the prophet spoken of by Moses (Acts 3:22-23; 7:37). Even some of the Jewish people recognized Jesus as the coming prophet (John 6:14, 7:40).

Jesus the Prophet

> So he came to a town of Samaria called Sychar, near the field that Jacob had given to his son Joseph. Jacob's well was there; so Jesus, wearied as he was from his journey, was sitting beside the well. It was about the sixth hour. A woman from Samaria came to draw water. Jesus said to her, "Give me a drink" (John 4:5-7, ESV).

One of the more renowned encounters in the gospel narratives took place in Samaria, at Jacob's well, between Jesus and a Samaritan woman. The story paints a beautiful picture of Jesus' willingness to cross social and religious boundaries to reach out and touch the life of this single Samaritan woman. Even the woman was surprised Jesus would break with social conventions (John 4:9). But Jesus saw beyond her gender, ethnicity, and religious background; he saw the spiritual need of her soul. Jesus spoke to the woman, addressing her longing for a meaningful life. He even raised the personal issue of her marital status, which somewhat reflected the unhappiness and lack of fulfillment she felt in her life. It did not take long for the woman to recognize the man before her was more than just a rabbi or teacher of the Law:

> The woman said to him, "**Sir, I perceive that you are a prophet.** Our fathers worshiped on this mountain, but you say that in Jerusalem is the place where people ought to worship." Jesus said to her, "Woman, believe me, the hour is coming when neither on this mountain nor in Jerusalem will you worship the Father. You worship what you do not know; we worship what we know, for salvation is from the Jews. **But the hour is coming, and is now here**, when the true worshipers will worship the Father in spirit and truth, for the Father is seeking such people to worship him. God is spirit, and those who worship him must worship in spirit and truth." The

> woman said to him, "I know that Messiah is coming (he who is called Christ). When he comes, he will tell us all things." Jesus said to her, "I who speak to you am he" (John 4:19-26, ESV).

Realizing Jesus was a prophet, the woman naturally questioned him about the subject of worship and the ongoing rivalry between the Jews and the Samaritans. The Samaritans had long worshipped on Mount Gerizim, while the Jews taught that Jerusalem was the place to worship God. Jesus responded to the woman's query by first pointing out a fundamental difference in Jewish and Samaritan worship: "You worship what you do not know; we worship what we know, for salvation is from the Jews." In other words, Jewish worship was founded upon prophetic revelation. As a prophet, Jesus spoke to the woman of a dramatic transition in worship that was coming very soon, and that was already present. The letter to the Hebrews refers to this transition as "the time of reformation" (Heb. 9:10, ESV). Where formerly, locations, rituals, and symbolic rites were an integral part of worship, the Messianic reformation would introduce a new paradigm in worship. One of the first changes concerned the very nature of worship. Jesus prophesied: "But the hour is coming, and is now here, when the true worshipers will worship the Father **in spirit and truth**, for the Father is seeking such people to worship him." The Law of Moses regulated external details of worship, such as the tabernacle, the priesthood, sacrifices, various rituals, sabbaths, and so forth; but the law could not change the internal state of man, that is, where spirit and truth reside (Ps. 51:6, 10-12). Indeed, the sinful desires of man, according to Apostle Paul, "weakened" the law of God (Rom. 8:3, ESV). The pattern and regulations of worship in the old covenant were only *temporary* and *symbolic*, waiting for the day and hour when the true pattern and reality of things would come.

> They serve a **copy and shadow** of the heavenly things. For when Moses was about to erect the tent, he was instructed by God, saying, "See that you make everything according to the pattern that was shown you on the mountain (Heb. 8:5, ESV. See also Heb. 9:9; 10:1).

According to the old covenant, the people of Israel were required to bring their sacrifices and offerings before the tabernacle, and later in history, before the temple in Jerusalem. They also had to rely on the earthly priests to offer up their sacrifices and enter the holy place on their behalf. But as we already discussed in our first chapter, the sacrifice of Christ changed everything. Because of Jesus' blood, the inner life of man—his heart and conscience—may be transformed. Moreover, he may also approach God in a direct way that previously had not been possible. The blood of Christ is the foundation of a new covenant and a new paradigm of worship.

> Therefore, brothers, since we have confidence **to enter the holy places by the blood of Jesus**, by the new and living way that he opened for us through the curtain, that is, through his flesh, and since we have a great priest over the house of God, let us draw near with a true heart in full assurance of faith, with our hearts sprinkled clean from an evil conscience and our bodies washed with pure water (Heb. 10:19-22, ESV).

There is another reason why worshippers no longer need to go to a specific location or temple to worship God; they have become themselves the new temple of God.

> Now, therefore, you are no longer strangers and foreigners, but fellow citizens with the saints and members of the household of God, having been built on the foundation of the apostles and prophets, Jesus Christ Himself being the chief corner*stone,* in whom the whole building, **being fitted together, grows into a holy temple in the Lord, in whom you also are being built together for a dwelling place of God in the Spirit** (Eph. 2:19-22, NKJV).

In the larger context of the above passage, Apostle Paul explains in more detail the redemptive work of Christ (Eph. 2:11-22): Through his blood and the preaching of the gospel of peace, the Gentiles have become participants of the same promises, hope, and privileges enjoyed by Jewish believers. Through Jesus, they even have access to the Father by the same Spirit. Through the cross, Christ abolished the hostility created by the law, and tore down the wall that separated the two people, creating in himself a new man that is neither Jewish nor Gentile, but a new creation (2 Cor. 5:17; Eph. 4:24; Col. 3:10). Moreover, the Lord uses both Jewish and Gentile believers as construction material to build a spiritual temple and dwelling place for God. This is certainly a paradigm without precedent.

The Offspring and the Promised Spirit

Jesus Christ is the offspring of both David and Abraham (Matt. 1:1). He is also the descendant of Shem and Seth (Luke 3:36, 38). He is the offspring of the woman who crushes the serpent's head through his life, death, and resurrection.[16] At his second coming, when he comes to restore all things, he will thoroughly defeat *all* his enemies.[17] According to Scripture, Jesus Christ has been given "the sure mercies of David" (Isa. 55:3, KJV), and "the blessing of Abraham" (Gal 3:14, NKJV). Regarding the latter, the Apostle Paul explains in more detail the meaning of the Abrahamic blessing and its relevance to Gentile believers:

> Christ redeemed us from the curse of the law by becoming a curse for us—for it is written, "Cursed is everyone who is hanged on a tree"—so that in Christ Jesus the blessing of Abraham might come to the Gentiles, so that we might receive **the promised Spirit through faith**. To give a human example, brothers: even with a man-made covenant, no one annuls it or adds to it once it has been ratified. **Now the promises were made to Abraham and to his offspring**. It does not say, "And to offsprings," referring to many, but referring to one, "And to your offspring," who is Christ (Gal. 3:13-16, ESV).

Paul unequivocally claims Jesus Christ to be the promised *offspring* of Abraham. He further explains, through *faith* we receive the blessing of Abraham— "the promised Spirit." Moreover, through faith in Christ, we also become Abraham's *offspring* and *heirs* (Gal. 3:29). The promised Spirit is a new paradigm of worship and of the prophetic anointing. In fact, it is through the baptism of the Holy Spirit the prophetic anointing continues to operate in the New Testament age. The Scriptures highlight at least four specific areas of this anointing:

Prophetic Praise and Worship

One of the primary purposes of the baptism of the Holy Spirit was so Jesus' disciples could receive power to be his witnesses (Luke 24:49; Acts 1:8). With the baptism also comes the *fire* of praise and worship (even this is an integral part of being his witnesses). On the day of Pentecost, when the

---

[16] Gen. 3:15; Gal. 4:4; Heb. 2:14; 1 John 3:8
[17] 1 Cor. 15:25-26

disciples were baptized and filled with the Holy Spirit, they began to praise God in different tongues. Some of the people mocked them and said they were drunk. But Peter and the apostles rose among the crowd and explained what was happening:

> "For these are not drunk, as you suppose, since it is *only* the third hour of the day. But this is what was spoken by the prophet Joel: 'And it shall come to pass in the last days, says God, That I will pour out of My Spirit on all flesh; **Your sons and your daughters shall prophesy**, Your young men shall see visions, Your old men shall dream dreams. And on My menservants and on My maidservants I will pour out My Spirit in those days; **And they shall prophesy**. I will show wonders in heaven above And signs in the earth beneath: Blood and fire and vapor of smoke. The sun shall be turned into darkness, And the moon into blood, Before the coming of the great and awesome day of the Lord. And it shall come to pass *That* whoever calls on the name of the Lord Shall be saved'" (Acts 2:15-21, NKJV).

According to the prophet Joel, the outpouring of the Spirit would be widespread and related to *prophesying*: "I will pour out of My Spirit on all flesh; Your sons and your daughters shall prophesy..." Under the Old Testament dispensation, only a limited number of people were anointed with the Spirit of God. But on the day of Pentecost, the anointing of the Holy Spirit was made available to all believers. When the disciples were baptized in the Holy Spirit, they spoke of "the magnificent acts of God" (Acts 2:11, HCSB). They were in effect, prophesying, that is, speaking forth the virtues of God. When Peter preached the gospel to the Gentiles and the Holy Spirit came upon them, they also spoke in tongues and *magnified* the Lord (Acts 10:46). In his journey to Ephesus, Paul encountered several disciples who only knew the baptism of John. Paul spoke to them of the Messiah and baptized them in the name of the Lord Jesus. When he laid his hands on them, the Holy Spirit came upon them and they spoke in tongues and *prophesied*. Even though we are not informed of what these disciples prophesied, the Biblical references (Acts 2:11; 10:46; 19:1-6) would strongly suggest they also spoke of the mighty works of God. Luke—the author of Acts—appears to corroborate a New Testament pattern: When believers receive the Holy Spirit, they will speak in other tongues and prophesy the praises of God.[18]

---

[18] There is a clear affinity between prophesying and worshipping in both the Old and New Testament. In the book of Chronicles, David and the officers of his

The Gift of Prophecy

According to Apostle Paul, the Holy Spirit empowers members of the body of Christ with different gifts for the benefit of all (1 Cor. 12:1-31). Among the various gifts and manifestations of the Spirit is that of *prophecy*. While all believers may prophecy the praises of God under the inspiration of the Holy Spirit, the gift of prophecy has a more specific purpose within the context of the church. Paul teaches the gift of prophecy serves to speak "edification and exhortation and comfort to men" (1 Cor. 14:3, NKJV). The apostle further writes that the gift serves as a source of *revelation*, *instruction*, and *encouragement*:

> Let two or three prophets speak, and let the others weigh what is said. If a **revelation** is made to another sitting there, let the first be silent. For you can all prophesy one by one, **so that all may learn and all be encouraged**, and the spirits of prophets are subject to prophets. For God is not a God of confusion but of peace (1 Cor. 14:29-33, ESV).

The gift of prophecy, of course, should be weighed or judged, to make sure it does not become unhinged or incoherent nonsense, but that it stays within the boundaries of *edification*, *exhortation*, and *comfort*. But more relevant to the subject of worship, Paul also explains how the gift of prophecy may positively impact *worship*, especially among unbelievers:

> But if all prophesy, and an unbeliever or outsider enters, he is convicted by all, he is called to account by all, the secrets of his heart are disclosed, and so, falling on his face, **he will worship God** and declare that God is really among you (1 Cor. 14:24-25, ESV).

The Ministry of the Prophet

The Lord gives special *ministries* to the church for the purpose of training believers for ministry and for the general edification of the body of Christ. The prophet is among these ministries. Apostle Paul writes:

> And he gave the apostles, **the prophets**, the evangelists, the shepherds and teachers, to equip the saints for the work of ministry, for building up the body of Christ until we all attain to the unity of the faith and of

army specifically chose the sons of Asaph, Heman, and Jeduthun "to prophesy accompanied by lyres, harps, and cymbals" (1 Chron. 25:1, HCSB). One of the functions of prophesy is to speak forth the inspired praises of God.

> the knowledge of the Son of God, to mature manhood, to the measure of the stature of the fullness of Christ" (Eph. 4:11-13, ESV).

One of the areas in which the saints need to be equipped is in the area of *effective* worship and devotion. I personally believe this is one of the areas in which the ministry of the prophet best impacts the body of Christ. While visions, dreams, revelations, prophesies, words of knowledge, and so forth, may be indicative of the prophetic anointing, the trademark of a prophet is the ability to teach and perfect other believers or saints for ministry and lead the body of Christ towards greater maturity, especially in the area of worship and service. The prophetic ministry is particularly important in church growth and expansion. In Acts of the Apostles, Luke describes an encounter among the prophets and teachers of Antioch and what took place during their worship service:

> Now in the church at Antioch there were prophets and teachers: Barnabas, Simeon called Niger, Lucius of Cyrene, Manaen (who had been brought up with Herod the tetrarch) and Saul. While they were worshiping the Lord and fasting, the Holy Spirit said, "Set apart for me Barnabas and Saul for the work to which I have called them." So after they had fasted and prayed, they placed their hands on them and sent them off (Acts 13:1-3, NIV).

The prophets and teachers of Antioch were a major contributing factor in the growth of the local church. But they also impacted the work of God on a larger scale. According to the above account, "While they were worshipping the Lord and fasting, the Holy Spirit said, 'Set apart for me Barnabas and Saul for the work to which I have called them.'" Because of prophetic ministry, and a willingness to listen to the voice of the Holy Spirit, new apostles were ordained and sent out. These chosen men would cause the church to expand and grow throughout Asia and Europe. Their missionary endeavors would not only increase exponentially the number of disciples, but also the worship of God on earth.

Eschatological Prophecy

A fourth area in which prophetic anointing operates is *eschatological prophecy*. Eschatology is the study of the *last things*, such as the end of the age, the second coming of Christ, the resurrection of the dead, the Messianic kingdom, the final judgment, and so forth. All the prophets, as well as the Lord and the apostles, spoke of events that would take place in the last days. The purpose of eschatological prophecy is not merely to foretell or forewarn of future events, but to inspire *hope* and encourage *faithfulness* in God's people. Within New Testament context, it serves to incite *watchfulness* so that believers are ready for the Lord's second coming.[19] Eschatological prophecy especially relates to biblical worship. In fact, both Old and New Testament worship are deeply rooted in eschatology. Earlier in our study, we discussed Zechariah's prophecy regarding the Feast of Booths and how the feast celebrated the Lord's blessings during Israel's pilgrimage in the wilderness. Zechariah prophetically identifies the feast with the coming of the Lord and an international participation of worship in Jerusalem (Zech. 14:16-19). Zechariah's prophecy is both inspirational and descriptive of *eschatological worship*, that is, when all the nations shall come and worship before the Lord (Ps. 22:27; 86:9). The prophet Joel prophesied of the outpouring of the Holy Spirit that would take place in the last days (Joel 2:28-32). Apostle Peter certainly understood the baptism of the Holy Spirit to be an eschatological fulfilment of Joel's prophecy (Acts 2:16-21).

Other passages in the New Testament reveal the connection between eschatological prophecy and worship. For example, the *Lord's Prayer* not only represents elements of adoration, supplication, confession, and devotion, but it is also prophetic in nature: "Your kingdom come, your will be done, on earth as it is in heaven" (Matt. 6:10, ESV). We are not denying the words have a relevant application; nonetheless, they are primarily a petition for the eschatological fulfilment of the kingdom of God. The *Lord's Supper* is an integral part of New Testament worship. When the Lord instituted the memorial meal, he also included an eschatological expectation of the kingdom of God. After Jesus had offered the bread and wine to his disciples, he said to them: "But I say to you, I will not drink of this fruit of the vine from now on until that day when I drink it new with you in My Father's kingdom" (Matt. 26:29, NKJV). When the Apostle Paul testified before Felix, the Roman governor of Judea, he identified his own personal expression of worship with the Law and the Prophets and the eschatological *hope* of the resurrection of the dead. He also related how that hope personally affected his own actions and behavior:

> "But this I confess to you, that according to the Way which they call a sect, **so I worship the God of my fathers**, believing all things which are written in the Law and in the Prophets. I have hope in

---

[19] Matt. 24:42; 25:13; Mark. 13:33, 35, 37; Luke 21:36

> God, which they themselves also accept, that there will be a resurrection of the dead, both of the just and the unjust. **This being so, I myself always strive to have a conscience without offense toward God and men**" (Acts 24:14-16, NKJV).

Revelation colorfully paints a picture of both prophetic eschatology and eschatological worship in action. For example, in one of the most epic visions in apocalyptic literature, Apostle John sees two prophets who appear on the world stage and prophecy against a backdrop of flagrant idolatry, murder, sorcery, immorality, and thievery (Rev. 9:20-21). Like the prophets of old, these two prophets challenge the status quo of sin and idolatry on an international level. God gives his two witnesses, exceptional powers to back their testimony. These powers are reminiscent of those that worked through Moses and Elijah.[20]

> "And I will give power to my two witnesses, and they will prophesy one thousand two hundred and sixty days, clothed in sackcloth. These are the two olive trees and the two lampstands standing before the God of the earth. And if anyone wants to harm them, fire proceeds from their mouth and devours their enemies. And if anyone wants to harm them, he must be killed in this manner. These have power to shut heaven, so that no rain falls in the days of their prophecy; and they have power over waters to turn them to blood, and to strike the earth with all plagues, as often as they desire" (Rev. 11:3-6, NKJV).

The two prophets will prophesy in the last days under a powerful anointing, while at the same time, they themselves will also be the fulfilment of eschatological prophecy. In the last of his visions, John sees a new heaven and a new earth, and the new Jerusalem, descending out of heaven from God. He does not see a temple in the city, for the Lord God and the Lamb are the temple (Rev. 21:22). A river of life flows from the throne of God and through the midst of the city square; on either side of the river is the tree of life (Rev. 22:1-3). But the climax of John's prophetic and eschatological visions is that of the final destiny of God's servants:

> And there shall be no more curse, but the throne of God and of the Lamb shall be in it, **and His servants shall serve Him**.

[20] Exod. 7:17; 1Kgs. a17:1; 2 Kgs. 1:9-15

> They shall see His face, and His name shall be on their foreheads. There shall be no night there: They need no lamp nor light of the sun, for the Lord God gives them light. And they shall reign forever and ever (Rev. 22:3-5, NKJV).

Revelation is clearly prophetic and eschatological within its purview, yet it also deals with the subject of worship more than any other book in the Bible. In fact, the Greek word for *worship*, προσκυνέω, *proskuneó*, appears twenty-four times in Revelation alone. The books prophetic visions, prophecies, events, and exhortations reveal the close relationship between eschatological prophecy and worship:

> And I fell at his feet to worship him. But he said to me, "See *that you do* not *do that!* I am your fellow servant, and of your brethren who have the testimony of Jesus. **Worship God! For the testimony of Jesus is the spirit of prophecy**" (Rev. 19:10, NKJV).

To summarize the four points, the prophetic anointing is manifested through the baptism of the Holy Spirit and subsequent expressions of prophetic praise and worship; through the gift of prophesy, operating within the context of community worship; through the ministry of the prophet; and through eschatological prophecy. The ultimate purpose of the prophetic anointing, within New Testament context, is to lead us to Jesus and inspire holiness and the worship of God.

CHAPTER 4
The Pillar of Covenant
(The Concord of Biblical Worship)

"Behold, I establish my covenant with you and your offspring after you, and with every living creature that is with you, the birds, the livestock, and every beast of the earth with you, as many as came out of the ark; it is for every beast of the earth. I establish my covenant with you, that never again shall all flesh be cut off by the waters of the flood, and never again shall there be a flood to destroy the earth." And God said, "This is the sign of the covenant that I make between me and you and every living creature that is with you, for all future generations: I have set my bow in the cloud, and it shall be a sign of the covenant between me and the earth" (Gen. 9:9-13, ESV).

By faith Noah, being warned by God concerning events as yet unseen, in reverent fear constructed an ark for the saving of his household. By this he condemned the world and became an heir of the righteousness that comes by faith (Heb. 11:7, ESV).

Through the story of Noah, we encounter for the first time in Scripture, certain biblical words and concepts that are closely related to the subject of worship, such as the *altar*, the distinction between *clean* and *unclean animals*, *burnt offerings*, *pleasing aroma*, and *covenant*. Our present study will deal with the last of these—*covenant*. Noah and his family had been locked, for a year, in a massive ark full of animals. The ark had navigated uncharted waters for many months, before resting on a summit in the mountain range of Ararat. When the waters dried up from the face of the earth, God directed Noah, his family, and all the creatures aboard to leave the ark. Once the passengers had disembarked from the three-story, floating zoo, "Noah built an altar to the Lord and took some of every clean animal and some of every clean bird and offered burnt offerings on the altar" (Gen. 8:20, ESV). In occasion of his celebratory worship, the Lord established a covenant with Noah, his family, and all the animals that came out of the ark. He solemnly promised that he would never again destroy all flesh and the earth with a flood. The Lord also gave Noah and all future generations a sign of his covenant—the *rainbow*.[1]

A Survey of Biblical Covenants

Biblical covenants are divine promises and binding agreements that God establishes with man. Some covenants were conditional—they required certain moral obligations for their fulfillment; some covenants were unconditional—they made no explicit demand for their fulfilment; and some were a combination of both—they made both conditional and unconditional promises. Some covenants include signs of the agreement (i.e., rainbow, circumcision, salt[2]); some assimilated or incorporated promises made in previous covenants. In one particular case, a newer covenant even superseded a former covenant, rendering it obsolete. Biblical covenants are typically identified with sacrifice.[3] They also share other important characteristics: First of all, they are *relational*: They demonstrate God's willingness to interact and engage with man, even establishing a rapport, albeit according to his own terms. They are also *revelational*: They reveal the heart of God, his attributes, and, either implicitly or explicitly, his will and purpose. Covenants are *generational*: They demonstrate the faithfulness of God and of his promises to every generation. The new covenant also relates to every generation,[4] but its promises are eternal.[5] And lastly, they are *definitional*: While covenants may vary in design, scope, and range, they provide worship with a spiritual *foundation*, *structure*, and *definition*. A brief survey of biblical covenants will help us better understand how they relate to the subject of worship and the worshipper.

---

[1] Gen. 9:13
[2] Lev. 2:13; Ez. 43:24
[3] Ps. 50:5
[4] Eph. 3:21
[5] Heb. 13:20

The Noahic Covenant

> "The secret counsel of the Lord is for those who fear Him, and He reveals His covenant to them" (Ps. 25:14, HCSB).

According to the account in Genesis, when God saw the great wickedness of mankind, he was displeased that he had made man. There was, however, one man who stood out of the crowd: "But Noah found favor in the eyes of the Lord. These are the generations of Noah. Noah was a righteous man, blameless in his generation. Noah walked with God" (Gen. 6:8-9, ESV). Because Noah walked with God and because of his godly character, the Lord found in him a man with whom he could share his "secret counsel" and reveal "His covenant." In fact, the Lord revealed to Noah that he was going to bring a flood on the earth that would destroy man and all living creatures, but with Noah, he would establish his covenant. Noah and his wife, and his sons and their wives were to enter an ark that Noah would build according to the word of the Lord (Gen. 6:14-18). The story of Noah teaches us the importance of godly character in establishing a covenant. In fact, every covenant of divine origin was made with or through the mediation of someone who feared and worshipped the Lord. All biblical covenants either implicitly or explicitly define the quality of character the Lord seeks in a worshipper. It is important we see this last point lest we fail to consider one of the primary purposes of covenant. Furthermore, biblical covenants also define the expressions of worship and their boundaries, much in the same way that pillars delineate the height, width, and depth of a temple. The Lord instructed Noah to build an ark for himself and his family, and for a male and female of every living creature. Many people are only familiar with this part of the story, but there is more. The Lord further directed Noah to also bring into the ark seven pairs of every clean animal and bird:

> The Lord then said to Noah, "Go into the ark, you and your whole family, because I have found you righteous in this generation. Take with you seven pairs of every kind of clean animal, a male and its mate, and one pair of every kind of unclean animal, a male and its mate, and also seven pairs of every kind of bird, male and female, to keep their various kinds alive throughout the earth" (Gen. 7:1-3, NIV).

While the animals and birds that Noah was to take on the ark served to save their species, the distinction and the exceptional ratio between the clean and unclean can only be understood within the context of covenant and sacrifice (which is, as we discussed in our first chapter, an integral part of worship). Through his instructions, God was *implicitly* confirming the type of animal Noah, his family, and future generations could use in sacrificial offerings. In fact, when the flood waters abated and Noah and his family and all the animals exited from the ark, Noah built an altar and offered some of every clean animal and clean bird as burnt offerings. Though the Lord God had not given Noah any explicit instruction or commandment, regarding burnt offerings, his actions reflected his calling as a prophet and priest of God. The abundance of sacrifice Noah offered expressed the gratitude and devotion he felt towards the Lord, for having brought him, his family, and all the animals through the cataclysm. The narrative also suggests the burnt offerings deeply touched the heart of God:

> And when the Lord smelled the pleasing aroma, the Lord said in his heart, "I will never again curse the ground because of man, for the intention of man's heart is evil from his youth. Neither will I ever again strike down every living creature as I have done. While the earth remains, seedtime and harvest, cold and heat, summer and winter, day and night, shall not cease" (Gen. 8:21-22, ESV).

The pleasing aroma of Noah's sacrifice demonstrated indeed that man could rise above the evil intentions of his own heart and take his rightful place in creation as the image of God and worshipper of the Creator. In response to Noah's extravagant worship, the Lord established his covenant with his prophet.

The Abrahamic Covenant

> On the same day the Lord made a covenant with Abram, saying: "To your descendants I have given this land, from the river of Egypt to the great river, the River Euphrates—the Kenites, the Kenezzites, the Kadmonites, the Hittites, the Perizzites, the Rephaim, the Amorites, the Canaanites, the Girgashites, and the Jebusites" (Gen. 15:18-21, NKJV).

God called Abram and told him to leave everything and go to a country that he would show him; he would make of Abram, a great nation. Abram obeyed the call of God and journeyed towards the land of Canaan. Once he entered the land, God renewed his promise to give him an offspring who would inherit the land. Abram built an altar and worshipped God. Afterwards, Abram moved towards Bethel, where he built another altar and worshipped God. "Then Abram **journeyed by stages** to the Negev" (Gen 12:9, HCSB). When a famine hit the land, Abram took his wife, his nephew, and his servants and moved further south to Egypt. While sojourning in Egypt, Abram greatly increased his wealth and livestock (Lot, Abram's nephew, obviously prospered as well). After some time, Abram journeyed back to Negev and then on to Bethel, "to the place of the altar which he had made there at first. And there Abram called on the name of the Lord" (Gen. 13:4, NKJV). The land, however, could not support the numerous livestock that both he and his nephew had acquired in Egypt. The local inhabitants probably also used the land for grazing their own livestock. Conflict eventually arose between Abram and Lot's herdsmen. To keep peace between them, Abram asked Lot to go his own way. He gave his nephew the first choice of all the land before them. Shortly after their separation, the Lord spoke to Abram:

> "Lift your eyes now and look from the place where you are—northward, southward, eastward, and westward; for all the land which you see I give to you and your descendants forever. And I will make your descendants as the dust of the earth; so that if a man could number the dust of the earth, then your descendants also could be numbered. Arise, walk in the land through its length and its width, for I give it to you." Then Abram moved his tent, and went and dwelt by the terebinth trees of Mamre, which are in Hebron, and built an altar there to the Lord (Gen.13:14-18, NKJV).

In the above account, the Lord had Abram look towards the four points of the compass, and even walk the length and width of the land, that he might comprehend the goodness and extent of the promise. While encamped near the terebinth trees of Mamre, God visited Abram again. This time he led Abram outside his tent and had him look towards the starry sky:

> And he brought him outside and said, "Look toward heaven, and number the stars, if you are able to number them." Then he said to him, "So shall your offspring be." And he believed the Lord, and he counted it to him as righteousness (Gen. 15:5-6, ESV).

God's personal interactions with Abram served to foster faith in his promises. In fact, according to the narrative, Abram believed the promise of God, and because he believed, the Lord counted his faith as righteousness. Faith is a relational term, an essential element in worship. In the ensuing conversation, the Lord reiterated his promise of the land inheritance. But Abram responded, "O Lord God, how am I to know that I shall possess it?" (Gen. 15:8, ESV). Abram's inquiry was certainly not born out of either unbelief or doubt. In fact, moments earlier, he had just believed the promise of God. The patriarch's question arose from curiosity. Theologian and Bible commentator, Albert Barnes comments on Abram's inquiry:

> When God announces himself as Yahweh, who purposed to give him the land, Abram asks, Whereby "shall I know that I shall possess it?" He appears to expect some intimation as to the time and mode of entering upon possession.[6]

The Lord responded to Abram's question, first, by revealing *how* and *when* future events would unfold for his descendants, and then, by giving him the surety of his promise with a covenant (Gen. 15:18-21). Surely it is not incidental the covenant was established immediately after God had credited Abram's faith as righteousness. Nor is it incidental the covenant was made in the solemnity of animal sacrifices (Gen. 15:9-10).

One of the things we learn from this simple outline of Abram's life is that covenant was not only about *the promises of God*; it was also about Abram's spiritual *journey* with the Lord. Even in the case of Noah, the Lord promised to establish a covenant with him, but first Noah had to respond in faith and obedience; he had to build the ark and journey through the flood waters to the new world before God made a covenant with him. Abram, likewise, had to respond first to the calling of God; travel through the promise land; believe the promises of God against all odds; and afterwards, enter a covenant with the Lord. But Abram's journey was far from over. When Abram was 99 years old, the Lord visited him again and renewed his promise to establish a covenant with him and his descendants. In that occasion, the Lord changed the names of Abram and his wife, Sarai:

> "No longer shall your name be called Abram, but your name shall be **Abraham**, for I have made you the father of a multitude of nations."
>
> And God said to Abraham, "As for Sarai your wife, you shall not call her name Sarai, but **Sarah** shall be her name. I will bless her, and moreover, I will give you a son by her. I will bless her, and she shall become nations;

---

[6] Barnes, Albert, *Notes on the Bible*, [1834], at sacred-texts.com.

kings of peoples shall come from her" (Gen. 17:5, 15-16, ESV).

The Lord also gave Abraham a sign of the covenant—*circumcision*.[7]

In due season, the Lord fulfilled his promise and Sarah gave birth to a son. Abraham called him, *Isaac*. Some years after the birth of Isaac, the Lord God asked Abraham to take undertake another journey. He was to take his son to the land of Moriah and offer him up as a sacrifice in a place the Lord would show him. Abraham obeyed the voice of the Lord. He packed up the donkey and, with Isaac and two of his young men, headed towards the land of Moriah. When they arrived at the place, Abraham left the donkey and two young men, and climbed the mountain with his son, Isaac. When they reached the place, Abraham built an altar, bound his son. and placed him on the altar. He then raised his knife. But the Angel of Lord called out and stopped Abraham: "He said, 'Do not lay your hand on the boy or do anything to him, for now I know that you fear God, seeing you have not withheld your son, your only son, from me'" (Gen. 22:12, ESV). Abraham suddenly noticed a ram, caught by the horns nearby in the thickets. He took the ram and offered it up as a burnt offering, in the place of his son, Isaac. When Abraham finished worshipping God, the Angel of the Lord spoke again, confirming the promises of God with a solemn oath. Paraphrasing the Angel's words, the Lord would bless Abraham above and beyond his present experience, because he obeyed the Lord's voice and did not withhold his only son. His offspring would become so numerous that Abraham would not be able to count them. His offspring would also defeat its enemy and become the source of blessing for every nation (Gen. 22:16-18). The words of the Angel of Lord have far reaching implications which are spelled out in the New Testament (Acts 3:25; Rom. 4:13, 16, 18; 9:7-8; Gal. 3:16).

As we mentioned earlier, the covenant was not only about the promises; it was also about the *journey* Abraham had embarked upon when he first responded to the calling of God. Abraham's journeys were *revelatory*: Abraham acquired a vision of the promises of God, of both the vastness and richness of the land of Canaan and the numerous descendants the Lord would give him that would inherit the land. But more importantly, Abraham acquired a greater vision of the God he served and worshipped. Abraham's journeys were *transformational*. Abraham learned to trust and have faith in God, despite the circumstances. Before the birth of Isaac, the Lord

---

[7] Gen. 17:9-14

transformed Abram and Sarai and changed their names to *Abraham*, which means, *Father of a multitude*, and Sarai, *Sarah*, which means, *princess*. Though they were childless, and nomads who lived in tents in a foreign land; for Abraham and Sarah to call themselves by those names was certainly an act of transformational faith. Abraham's journeys were also *devotional*. Abraham's itinerary throughout the promise land was marked with altars and special locations where he worshipped God. And it all began with a divine call and the promise of a covenant.

The Mosaic Covenant

> But Moses said to God, "Who am I that I should go to Pharaoh, and that I should bring the children of Israel out of Egypt?" So He said, "I will certainly be with you. **And this shall be a sign to you that I have sent you**: When you have brought the people out of Egypt, you shall serve God on this mountain" (Exod. 3:11-12, NKJV).

Moses had been shepherding his father-in-law's sheep in the western part of the wilderness, towards Mount Sinai, when the Angel of the Lord appeared to him in a burning bush. The sight of a burning bush was probably not extremely unusual in the dry wilderness, but Moses had never seen a burning bush that was not also consumed by the fire. The unusual phenomenon captured his attention. He felt compelled to get a closer look. As he approached the fiery sight, God called out to Moses from the bush. When Moses responded, the Lord said, "Do not draw near this place. Take your sandals off your feet, for the place where you stand is holy ground" (Exod. 3:5, NKJV). When Moses heard the Lord's voice, he was afraid and quickly hid his face. On that sacred soil, Moses received the divine commission to return to Egypt, deliver the children of Israel from the oppression and slavery of Pharaoh, and bring them to "a land flowing with milk and honey" (Exod. 3:17, NKJV). God not only gave Moses a mandate, but a sign that he had indeed been sent by the Lord. Moses would bring the people back to that very mountain to worship the Lord. God faithfully kept his promise. Exactly three months after the children of Israel crossed the Red Sea, they were encamped in the wilderness before the mountain of God. At Mount Horeb (i.e., Sinai),[8] worship took on a more defined meaning. In fact, the mountain became

---

[8] Exod. 19:1-2

a spiritual landmark in Israel's history of Israel. It was the place where the Lord established an extraordinary covenant with his people:

> While Moses went up to God. The Lord called to him out of the mountain, saying, "Thus you shall say to the house of Jacob, and tell the people of Israel: 'You yourselves have seen what I did to the Egyptians, and how I bore you on eagles' wings and brought you to myself. **Now therefore, if you will indeed obey my voice and keep my covenant, you shall be my treasured possession among all peoples**, for all the earth is mine; and you shall be to me a kingdom of priests and a holy nation.' These are the words that you shall speak to the people of Israel" (Exod. 19:3-6, ESV).

By obeying the Lord's voice and observing his covenant, the Lord would esteem Israel above all other nations. They would be his own "special treasure" and "a kingdom of priests and a holy nation."

According to the account in Exodus, Moses had to go back and forth between the mountain top and the foot of the mountain to mediate the covenant between God and his people (That was a lot of mountain-climbing for an eighty-year-old man). Moses communicated to the people of Israel the covenantal promises and conditions. The people unanimously agreed to obey the words of the Lord.[9] Moses then brought the people's decision back to the Lord. Subsequently, the Lord descended on Mount Sinai in clouds of smoke and fire, and in plain view of all the people. The Lord gave Moses the covenant, expressed in moral laws; ordinances for the Sabbath and national festival observances; various sanctions and warnings; and special directives, regarding the promise land. The covenant also stipulated the proper way Israel was supposed to worship God. It also warned against making covenants with the inhabitants of Canaan and their gods. Instead of forming treaties and alliances, the people of Israel were to drive out the inhabitants from the land and destroy their sacred pillars.[10] When Moses related to the people all that the Lord had said, the people, once again, promised to obey the Lord's words. In preparations to ratify the covenant, Moses recorded all the words of the Lord. The next morning, he set up an altar and twelve pillars at the

---

[9] Exod. 19:8

[10] Exod. 23:20-33

foot of the mountain to represent the twelve tribes of Israel:

> Then he sent young men of the children of Israel, who offered burnt offerings and sacrificed peace offerings of oxen to the Lord. And Moses took half the blood and put it in basins, and half the blood he sprinkled on the altar. Then he took the Book of the Covenant and read in the hearing of the people. And they said, "All that the Lord has said we will do, and be obedient." And Moses took the blood, sprinkled it on the people, and said, "This is the blood of the covenant which the Lord has made with you according to all these words" (Exod. 24:5-8, NKJV).

Moses then ascended the mountain, taking with him Aaron and his two sons and seventy elders of Israel. According to the word of God, they were to worship the Lord "**at a distance**" (Exod. 24:1, HCSB). Afterwards, Moses was to ascend even higher up the mountain to meet with the Lord.

> Then the Lord said to Moses, "Come up to Me on the mountain and be there; and I will give you tablets of stone, and the law and commandments which I have written, that you may teach them." So Moses arose with his assistant Joshua, and Moses went up to the mountain of God (Exod. 24:12-13, NKJV).

The expressions of worship and all the priestly services were defined and bound by covenant; sealed and ratified with the blood of a sacrifice; and confirmed in engraved tablets of stone. The covenant would allow men and women to gain closer proximity to God. Even though the seventy elders and Aaron and his sons worshipped God from a relative distance, and later, outside the veil or curtain of the sanctuary, they and the people of Israel were allowed to draw closer to the presence of God than had been possible for most of their ancestors. Nonetheless, it would take yet another covenant to remove the remaining distance, clear the clouds of Sinai's smoke, and pull back the veil of the sanctuary.[11]

The Phinehasic Covenant

> The Lord spoke to Moses, "Phinehas son of Eleazar, son of Aaron the priest, has turned back My wrath from the Israelites because he was zealous among them with My zeal, so that I did not destroy the

---

[11] Matt. 27:51; Heb. 9:3, 8; 10:19-20

Israelites in My zeal. Therefore declare: **I grant him My covenant of peace. It will be a covenant of perpetual priesthood for him and his future descendants**, because he was zealous for his God and made atonement for the Israelites" (Nu. 25:10-13, HCSB).

Except for the account in Numbers and a brief mention in Psalms 106:28-31, the Phinehasic Covenant is not brought up anywhere else in the Scriptures. Nonetheless, the covenant is meaningful and important to our discussion. All covenants are revelations of God; they reveal his nature, character, and purpose. Biblical covenants have also impacted worship in different ways. In the case of Phineas, the Lord confirmed through the covenant the character he seeks and approves of in a worshipper. According to the account in Numbers, the people had violated the covenant by going with the women of Moab, sacrificing, eating, and bowing before their gods. Because the people had bonded themselves with Baal of Peor, the anger of God was so greatly provoked that a deadly plague broke out in camp. Moses and the community wept before the entrance of the tent of meeting when an Israelite man brought a Moabite woman to his own tent in plain view of everyone. Phinehas, son of Eleazar and grandson of Aaron, grabbed a spear and followed the couple in the tent. With a deadly blow, he dispatched the couple, and the plague was immediately stopped. Commending Phinehas' righteous deed, the Lord declared: "I grant him My covenant of peace. It will be **a covenant of perpetual priesthood** for him and his future descendants, because he was zealous for his God and made atonement for the Israelites."

From the beginning the priesthood had been fraught with moral problems and political conflicts. For example, when Moses delayed returning from the mountain, the people surrounded Aaron (who would become the first High Priest) and demanded he make a god that would go before them. Aaron faltered before the people and made a golden calf. He even built an altar. He also let the people "get out of control, resulting in weakness before the enemies" (Exod. 32:25, HCSB). The Lord would have destroyed the people in his anger, but Moses interceded for them. In a later incident, Nadab and Abihu, sons of Aaron, offered "unauthorized fire before the Lord, which had not been commanded them" (Lev. 10:1, ESV). The two priests quickly incurred a fiery judgment from the Lord.[12] And in another occasion, Korah,

[12] Lev. 10:1-3

one of the Levite priests, incited a rebellion, challenging Moses' authority, and Aaron's role as high priest. He and his followers also encountered the judgment of God.[13] We are not suggesting the Phinehasic Covenant resolved all moral issues within the priesthood; there would be other serious problems. However, the covenant affirmed and memorialized a *model of character* according to the Lord. The point of the story of Phineas is that righteous character is not merely an ideal, but a real and achievable objective. Righteousness is always one of the outstanding attributes of men and women in the Scriptures who worshipped God.

As the grandson of Aaron, the office of high priest *naturally* fell to Phineas (Nu. 17:1-11), but God *supernaturally* granted him and his descendants, "a permanent priesthood." Genealogical succession was extremely important in past ages, especially under the old covenant. Genealogy was particularly related to the offspring of the woman and that of Abraham; the office of the high priest and the Levitical priesthood; the Davidic throne; and even Israel's individual tribal inheritance of the promise land. Succession was God's way of demonstrating the faithfulness of his promises across a spectrum of multiple generations. Covenantal succession also safeguarded divine appointments against false pretenders. But in the new covenant, all genealogical successions arrive at the end of the line. In fact, the Messiah is the final destination of all divinely appointed successions: Jesus is the promised offspring of the woman and offspring of Abraham; heir to David's throne; and "heir of the world" (Rom. 4:13, ESV). But more relevant to our present study, Christ became high priest, not through genealogical succession, but through divine declaration and oath (Heb. 5:5, 10). Succession was practically necessary because of death; all heirs and successors eventually died (e.g., patriarchs, high priests, kings). Christ, instead, lives forever, therefore, his priesthood is permanent. Succession was necessary as long as the old covenant and laws were in effect, but with the coming of the Messiah, the priesthood, the covenant, and even the law changed (Heb. 7:12-19, 23-25). With the passing of the old order of priesthood and genealogical succession, one thing certainly did not change: The succession of righteous character required in those who worship and serve God.

---

[13] Nu. 16:8-11

> But you have come to Mount Zion and to the city of the living God, the heavenly Jerusalem, and to innumerable angels in festal gathering, and to the assembly of the firstborn who are enrolled in heaven, and to God, the judge of all, **and to the spirits of the righteous made perfect**, and to Jesus, the mediator of a new covenant, and to the sprinkled blood that speaks a better word than the blood of Abel (Heb. 12:22-24, ESV).

The Davidic Covenant

> "Ought you not to know that the Lord God of Israel gave the kingship over Israel forever to David and his sons by **a covenant of salt**?" (2 Chr. 13:5, ESV).

After the reign of David had been established and peace ensued from all his enemies, David began to desire to build a more permanent residence for the ark of the covenant. Up until that time, the ark had been kept in a tent in Jerusalem. As we discussed in chapter two of our study, the Lord spoke to David through the prophet Nathan, promising to build him an enduring house and kingdom. His offspring, instead, would build the Lord's house.[14] Hearing the wonderful promises of God, David entered the tent, sat before the Lord, and articulated one of the most beautiful and eloquent expressions of thanksgiving and worship in the Old Testament (2 Sam. 7:18-29). The promises made to David were essentially understood as a *covenant of salt.*

The Davidic Covenant is important to our discussion for different reasons. The covenant entailed much more than a few personal promises made to David; it would ultimately impact biblical history and the way future generations would worship God. First of all, the covenant expressed a *redemptive quality*. When God promised David an offspring who would sit on his throne and build the temple, he also included a caveat:

> "I will be to him a father, and he shall be to me a son. When he commits iniquity, I will discipline him with the rod of men, with the stripes of the sons of men, but my steadfast love will not depart from

---

[14] In a later occasion, David explains to the leaders of Israel why he could not build a house for the Lord: "But God said to me, 'You are not to build a house for My name because you are a man of war and have shed blood.'" (1 Chron. 28:3, HCSB).

> him, as I took it from Saul, whom I put away from before you. And your house and your kingdom shall be made sure forever before me. Your throne shall be established forever. (2 Sam. 7:14-16, ESV).

The covenant also expressed a *future prospect.* The Lord promised David that his house and his kingdom would endure *forever* before him. The covenant not only looked forward to future generations; it also looked forward to the distant future, to another offspring of David whose throne and kingdom would be established forever.[15]

> "He will be great, and will be called the Son of the Highest; and the Lord God will give Him the throne of His father David. And He will reign over the house of Jacob forever, and of His kingdom there will be no end" (Luke 1:32-33, NKJV).[16]

Solomon, David's offspring, built a house where God's people could gather from all over the promised land, to sacrifice, celebrate, and worship God. The temple also served as a witness to surrounding nations of the faithfulness of God. Moreover, the descendants of David, who reigned in his place, invariably set the spiritual tone for the kingdom. In fact, the books of Kings and Chronicles document the histories of the kings of Judah (and Israel) and how they influenced worship and devotion among their subjects, sometimes for good, but more often than not, for evil. Only in Jesus Christ would the kingdom of David and worship find their fullest meaning.

The covenant God made with David and his offspring[17] is also referred to as a *covenant of salt.* Salt was used to season all grain offerings and burnt offerings (Lev. 2:13; Ezek. 43:24). Salt symbolically represented the *perpetuity* of the covenant (Num. 18:19). Since biblical covenants are generally associated with sacrifices, the question that naturally follows is: *What sacrifices are associated with the Davidic Covenant?* While the Scriptures do not mention any immediate sacrifice being offered in connection with the covenant, they do refer to a much later occasion when David offered up burnt offerings and grain offerings. According to the Scriptures, David had ordered a census to be taken of the people, and this greatly displeased the Lord. The Lord sent Gad the seer to speak with David and have him to choose one of three possible judgments for his transgression:

---

[15] Rev. 22:16

[16] 2 Sam. 7:11-16; Isa. 9:7

[17] 2 Chr. 7:18

> So Gad came to David and said to him, "Thus says the Lord: 'Choose for yourself, either three years of famine, or three months to be defeated by your foes with the sword of your enemies overtaking you, or else for three days the sword of the Lord—the plague in the land, with the angel of the Lord destroying throughout all the territory of Israel.' Now consider what answer I should take back to Him who sent me" (1 Chr. 21:11-12, NKJV).[18]

All three choices would dramatically impact the people of Israel, but the second one—the sword of David's enemies—would have a more immediate and direct consequence on David and his family. He knew what it was like to be pursued by an adversary (i.e., Saul and Absalom). But as the instigator of the census, he could hardly consider a judgment that would not personally affect him. David threw himself on the Lord's mercy rather than fall into the cruel hands of man. The Lord sent a three-day plague, which decimated the population throughout the land. When the plague approached Jerusalem, the Lord changed his mind and stopped the angel. David looked up and saw the angel of the Lord with his sword stretched out over the city. He and the elders, clothed in sackcloth, fell before the Lord. David interceded for the people, asking the Lord to spare them and instead, punish him and his family, for he had committed the evil in ordering the census (1 Chron. 21:16-17). So, the angel of the Lord spoke to Gad and directed him to tell David to build an altar to the Lord on the threshing floor of Ornan. David went to Ornan and purchased from him the land, the oxen, the grain, and the wood of the threshing tools:

> "So David gave Ornan six hundred shekels of gold by weight for the place. And David built there an altar to the Lord, and offered burnt offerings and peace offerings, and called on the Lord; **and He answered him from heaven by fire on the altar of burnt offering**. So the Lord commanded the angel, and he returned his sword to its sheath" (1 Chr. 21:25-27, NKJV).

This account is meaningful and relevant to the Davidic Covenant on two accounts. First of all, when David saw the angel of the Lord, held at

---

[18] Divine judgment was not only because of the census that David had ordered, but also because Israel had provoked the anger of the Lord (2 Sam. 24:1). The three choices that were given to David by Gad are among the judgments typically associated with idolatry and the anger of the Lord (Deut. 28:20-25; 32:15-27, see also Lev. 26:14-20). This may possibly suggest why Israel had provoked the wrath of the Lord.

abeyance, yet still poised for attack, he knew he and his house were in grave danger of being destroyed (1 Chron. 21:30). David certainly did not consider himself exempt from the sword of the angel, even though the Lord had promised to build him an enduring house and not destroy it. According to the account, the angel of the Lord sent Gad to instruct David *where* he should build the altar. David obeyed and offered up burnt offerings and peace offerings. The Lord responded with fire from heaven. He also commanded the angel to sheath his sword. The plague immediately stopped, and Jerusalem and David's house were spared. Secondly, the location of the altar was of utmost importance. David certainly understood the significance: "Then David said, 'This is the house of the Lord God, and this is the altar of burnt offering for Israel'" (1 Chr. 22:1, NKJV). Staying the plague and finding the location for the house of the Lord served as a sign and confirmation of the covenant God had made with David. Only God could choose the place where he would place is name (Deut. 14:23). Without such a revelation, the offspring of David could not build a house for the Lord. Moreover, without the sacrifice and staying of judgment, David would have had no offspring left to build the house. But the Lord showed mercy to David from the very beginning, proving himself faithful to the covenant of salt he established with him.

The New Covenant

No book in the New Testament better articulates the radical reforms that took place under the new covenant than the book of Hebrews. As discussed in the previous chapter, the reformation that Jesus ushered in made significant changes in both the *priesthood* and the *law* (Heb. 7:12; 9:10). Because Jesus was from the tribe of Judah, and not from Levi, he could not be a priest according to the old covenant. Instead, God made Jesus a priest according to another order of priesthood:

> So Christ did not take upon himself the glory of becoming a high priest. But God said to him, "You are my Son; today I have become your Father." And he says in another place, "**You are a priest forever, in the order of Melchizedek**" (Heb. 5:5-6, NIV).

Who was this Melchizedek?[19] *Why is his priestly order so much better than that of the*

[19] Gen. 14:1-24, for a full account of the circumstances surrounding Abram's encounter with Melchizedek.

Levitical priesthood? According to the Scriptures, Melchizedek was the king of *Salem*, which means, *peace.*[20] His name means *righteousness*. Melchizedek was a priest of God. When Abram returned from rescuing his nephew, Lot, and the people who were with him, who had been taken captive during a battle, Melchizedek went out to meet him. Bringing with him bread and wine, he blessed Abram. Abram gave Melchizedek a tithe of everything. But just as Melchizedek appears all of a sudden on the scene, he disappears from biblical history. Because of the mystery that shrouds this enigmatic biblical character, both he and his priesthood assume a divine quality of *permanency*: "Without father or mother, without genealogy, without beginning of days or end of life, like the Son of God he remains a priest forever. (Heb. 7:3, NIV). Melchizedek is, indeed, a *Christophany*, that is, a type of manifestation or appearance of Christ in the Old Testament. Christ's own priesthood is clearly patterned after the order of Melchizedek and not that of the Levitical order. The letter to the Hebrews succinctly explains:

> For it is clear that our Lord descended from Judah, and in regard to that tribe Moses said nothing about priests. And what we have said is even more clear if another priest like Melchizedek appears, one who has become a priest not on the basis of a regulation as to his ancestry but on the basis of the power of **an indestructible life**. For it is declared: "**You are a priest forever, in the order of Melchizedek**. The former regulation is set aside because it was weak and useless (for the law made nothing perfect), **and a better hope is introduced, by which we draw near to God**. And it was not without an oath! Others became priests without any oath, but he became a priest with an oath when God said to him: "The Lord has sworn and will not change his mind: 'You are a priest forever.'" Because of this oath, Jesus has become **the guarantor of a better covenant** (Heb. 7:14-22, NIV).
>
> "But in fact the ministry Jesus has received is as **superior** to theirs as the covenant of which he is mediator is superior to the old one, since the new covenant is established on **better promises**" (Heb. 8:6, NIV).

Christ received a *permanent priesthood* through an *indestructible life* and through a *divine oath*. And because his ministry is far *superior* to that of the high priest

[20] Heb. 7:1-3

under the old covenant, he has become both *guarantor* and *mediator* of a new and better covenant—one that is superior in every way.

One of the most significant reforms and benefits of the new covenant is that we may draw closer to God than ever before. Earlier in our study, we discussed the formidable *distance* between God and worshippers under the old covenant. This was principally due to the immense holiness of God and man's conscience of sin. While the tabernacle and priesthood somewhat helped to reduce the distance between God and man, it did not completely remove the obstacles. However, through faith in the blood of Jesus, God has become both accessible and approachable in worship:

> Therefore, brothers and sisters, since we have confidence to enter the Most Holy Place by the blood of Jesus, by a new and living way opened for us through the curtain, that is, his body, and since we have a great priest over the house of God, **let us draw near** to God with a sincere heart and with the full assurance that faith brings, having our hearts sprinkled to cleanse us from a guilty conscience and having our bodies washed with pure water (Heb. 10:19-22, NIV).

The old covenant regulated exterior practices of worship, but it was incapable of regulating the interior life of the worshipper. Though the worshipper offered sacrifices according to the law, the conscience remained unchanged in regard to sin and guilt. The fact that the high priest had to continually enter every year into the most holy place to offer sacrificial blood for his own sin and the sin of the people, demonstrated the ineffectiveness of animal blood:

> The Holy Spirit was showing by this that the way into the Most Holy Place had not yet been disclosed as long as the first tabernacle was still functioning. This is an illustration for the present time, indicating that the gifts and sacrifices being offered were not able to clear the conscience of the worshiper. They are only a matter of food and drink and various ceremonial washings—external regulations applying until the time of the new order (Heb. 9:8-10, NIV).

Through the new covenant, the heart and mind of man are radically changed: "This is the covenant I will make with them after that time, says the Lord. I will put my laws in their hearts, and I will write them on their minds" (Heb. 10:16, NIV). Because of the spiritual and dynamic transformation that takes place within the heart and mind, men and women may freely enter the presence of God to worship and serve him. They no longer have to stand at a distance as onlookers while someone else approaches God on their behalf. We no longer need priests and mediators who must deal their own weaknesses and mortality; nor do we need animal sacrifices and the symbolic ceremonies and rituals associated with the old covenant and order of priesthood. Jesus is the sum of all we will ever need; he is the *merciful*, *faithful*, and *great* high priest[21], the *one* sacrifice for sin, *once*, and *forever*[22]; and the mediator of a *new*, *better*, and *eternal* covenant.[23]

---

[21] Heb. 2:17; 4:14
[22] Heb.7:27; 10:10, 12, 14
[23] Heb. 8:6; 9:15; 12:24; 13:20

CHAPTER 5

The Pillar of Revelation

(The Inspiration of Biblical Worship)

Now the Lord said to Abram, "Go from your country and your kindred and your father's house to the land that I will show you. And I will make of you a great nation, and I will bless you and make your name great, so that you will be a blessing. I will bless those who bless you, and him who dishonors you I will curse, and in you all the families of the earth shall be blessed." So Abram went, as the Lord had told him, and Lot went with him. Abram was seventy-five years old when he departed from Haran. And Abram took Sarai his wife, and Lot his brother's son, and all their possessions that they had gathered, and the people that they had acquired in Haran, and they set out to go to the land of Canaan. When they came to the land of Canaan, Abram passed through the land to the place at Shechem, to the oak of Moreh. At that time the Canaanites were in the land. Then the Lord appeared to Abram and said, "To your offspring I will give this land." **So he built there an altar to the Lord, who had appeared to him**. *From there he moved to the hill country on the east of Bethel and pitched his tent, with Bethel on the west and Ai on the east.* **And there he built an altar to the Lord and called upon the name of the Lord**. *And Abram journeyed on, still going toward the Negeb (Gen. 12:1-9, ESV).*

The Lord *spoke* to Abram and told him to leave everything and go to a place that he would show him. He further promised to make a great nation of him. Abram obeyed the voice and calling of God. When he arrived in Canaan, "Abram passed through the land to the place at Shechem, to the oak of Moreh." The Lord appeared again to Abram, promising to give to his offspring, the land where he was presently sojourning. According to the narrative, "and there he built an altar to the Lord who had appeared to him." The altar served as a location of worship and renewal of his allegiance to the God who had called him. It also stood as a memorial to *divine revelation*. Divine revelation prompted Abram to act in faith and leave his country, his kindred and his father's house, and go to an unknown land the Lord would show him. Divine revelation that prompted Abram to build an altar and worship God upon the very ground promised to his offspring.

Abram, or Abraham as he was later called by the Lord, received many revelations throughout his lifetime. They came to him through different means: an audible voice, a vision, divine and angelic visitation.[1] In one particular instance, the patriarch even learned something about God in a less dramatic and more ordinary event. In Genesis, the narrative recounts that Abimelech the king of Gerar, and Phicol, the commander of his army, traveled south to Beersheba to meet with Abraham. The two men greeted Abraham with a powerful and suggestive salutation, followed by an unusual request, that is, coming for a king and an army commander:

> "God is with you in all that you do. Now therefore swear to me here by God that you will not deal falsely with me or with my descendants or with my posterity, but as I have dealt kindly with you, so you will deal with me and with the land where you have sojourned" (Gen. 21:22-23, ESV).

Abraham quickly responded to their request with an oath, but he also brought to Abimelech's attention a dispute that had arisen between their servants. The king's servants had confiscated a water well from Abraham's servants. But Abimelech assured Abraham he knew nothing of the matter, nor did he understand why Abraham had not spoken of it earlier.[2] Abimelech restored to Abraham the rights to the well. That day, the two men also established a treaty between themselves. Perhaps it was Abimelech and Phicol's unexpected greeting, or the way in which Abimelech responded to his remonstration, or perhaps even both; whatever the reason may have been, the encounter deeply affected Abraham. Suddenly, a thought entered Abraham's heart and mind—an *inspired thought*, recorded for all posterity: It is written: "Abraham planted a tamarisk tree in Beersheba and called there on the name of the Lord, **the Everlasting God**" (Gen. 21:33, ESV).

---

[1] Gen 12:1; 13:14; 15:1; 17:1; 18:1-33: 19:1; 22:1, 11,15

[2] Gen. 21:25-26

Abraham understood something of the eternal nature of God through his own life experience and expressed it in his worship. Personal experience has always played an important role in divine revelation. The prophets and psalmists of old also drew spiritual insight from their own personal experiences and observations. As strange as it may sound, the Lord often reveals himself in the ordinary and commonness of life.

The above examples from the life of Abraham reveal a distinct pattern and correlation between divine revelation and biblical worship. We are not suggesting every biblical revelation necessarily prompted an immediate response in worship, or that it *always* relates directly to the subject. What we are saying is that divine revelation is one of the major contributing factors in both the expression and the unfolding development of worship throughout biblical history. Divine revelations are *impartations* of knowledge and insight; *portals* of the unseen world of angels and demons; *visions* of divine promises, victories, and of future events and destinies. But most importantly, divine revelations have something to say about God. Through revelation, the Lord pulls back the veil of nature and allows his people a glimpse of himself, of his nature, character, and of his purpose and will. Nothing will impact worship more than *revelatory knowledge* of God. In ancient times, men often built altars and worshipped God in response to such revelations. In several instances, they even commemorated the revelation by changing the name of a particular location:

> And Abraham lifted up his eyes and looked, and behold, behind him was a ram, caught in a thicket by his horns. And Abraham went and took the ram and offered it up as a burnt offering instead of his son. So Abraham called the name of that place, **"The Lord will provide"**; as it is said to this day, "On the mount of the Lord it shall be provided" (Gen. 22:13-14, ESV).

> "There he [Jacob] erected an altar and called it **El-Elohe-Israel**" (Gen. 33:20, ESV).

> "And there he [Jacob] built an altar and called the place **El-bethel**, because there God had revealed himself to him when he fled from his brother" (Gen. 35:7, ESV).

> "And Moses built an altar and called the name of it, **The Lord Is My Banner**" (Exod. 17:15, ESV).

> "Then Gideon built an altar there to the Lord and called it, **The Lord Is Peace**. To this day it still stands at Ophrah, which belongs to the Abiezrites" (Judg. 6:24, ESV).

Revelations of God

The Lord God revealed himself in the past, and continues to do so in the present, in various ways. First and foremost, he reveals himself through the creative works of his hands. In one of his psalms, David proclaims creation to be a *universal revelation* of God: "The heavens declare the glory of God; the skies proclaim the work of his hands. Day after day they pour forth speech; night after night they reveal knowledge" (Ps. 19:1-2, NIV). In his letter to the Romans, Apostle Paul explains both the meaning and the implications of this universal revelation:

> The wrath of God is being revealed from heaven against all the godlessness and wickedness of people, who suppress the truth by their wickedness, since what may be known about God is plain to them, because God has made it plain to them. For since the creation of the world God's invisible qualities—his eternal power and divine nature—have been clearly seen, being understood from what has been made, so that people are without excuse. For although they knew God, they neither glorified him as God nor gave thanks to him, but their thinking became futile and their foolish hearts were darkened. Although they claimed to be wise, they became fools and exchanged the glory of the immortal God for images made to look like a mortal human being and birds and animals and reptiles. Therefore God gave them over in the sinful desires of their hearts to sexual impurity for the degrading of their bodies with one another. They exchanged the truth about God for a lie, and worshiped and served created things rather than the Creator—who is forever praised. Amen (Rom. 1:18-25, NIV).

According to the apostle's reasoning, God discloses certain truths about himself through creation for the purpose that men and women would indeed worship him. But when people refuse to give him the glory and allow their hearts and minds to become darkened by lust, they will no longer be interested in retaining the truth, especially if it is *inconvenient.* Instead, they open themselves up to false concepts of deity and false practices of worship.

This is what Paul means when he writes: "They exchanged the truth about God for a lie, and worshiped and served created things rather than the Creator—who is forever praised. Amen." Paul further points out that God holds men *accountable* for all that may be known of him in creation.

The metaphorical fingerprints of God are not only present in the things he has made, but also through his dealings with mankind. Luke records Paul's discourse to the Athenians, in which he eloquently speaks of God who interacts in the stream of history, operates within the boundaries of geopolitics, and even finds his way across the open ranges of art and philosophy:

> "From one man He has made every nationality to live over the whole earth and has determined their appointed times and the boundaries of where they live. He did this so they might seek God, and perhaps they might reach out and find Him, though He is not far from each one of us. For in Him we live and move and exist, as even some of your own poets have said, 'For we are also His offspring'" (Acts 17:26-28, HCSB).

It would be helpful in our discussion if we make a simple distinction between, what we may define as, *natural* and *supernatural* revelation.[3] Natural revelations are those fundamental truths of God, existing within the boundaries of nature and the visible cosmos (Rom. 1:19-20). Such truths are understood through man's natural endowments, that is, his ability to observe, understand, interpret, and draw conclusions. On the other hand, the Lord God occasionally reaches beyond the veil of nature and supernaturally reveals himself, his word, and the invisible world that surrounds us. Moses, Job, and the prophet Daniel unequivocally declare God to be the revealer of such things that are hidden from the natural mind and the senses of man:

> "The secret things belong to the Lord our God, but the things that are revealed belong to us and to our children forever, that we may do all the words of this law" (Deut. 29:29, ESV).

---

[3] *Natural revelation* is merely a categorical term for the purpose of our study. The term is somewhat of a semantic conundrum (at least for this author). Considering the divine origin and authorship of nature and the cosmos, natural revelation, in certain respects, is also supernatural. From a biblical perspective, even man's natural endowments are the supernatural work of the Creator.

> "He reveals the deep things of darkness and brings utter darkness into the light" (Job 12:22, ESV).
>
> "He reveals deep and hidden things; he knows what lies in darkness, and light dwells with him" (Dan. 2:22, ESV).

Supernatural (or divine) revelations come in different ways: the audible voice of God; divine and angelic visitations; dreams and visions; prophetic words and actions; miracles, signs, and wonders; spiritual discernment and, as we discussed earlier, through common life experiences. Both the Old and New Testament chronicle many extraordinary examples of divine revelation. Our study, however, will limit itself to those accounts that specifically illustrate the connection between divine revelation and biblical worship.

Old Testament Revelations

The Revelation of Jacob

As we stated earlier, nothing will inspire praise and worship more than a revelation from God. The man or woman who truly sees the things of God or catches a glimpse of heaven will never quite be the same. Jacob was such a man. In a dream, he saw the invisible world of God and angels. On his journey towards Haran in Paddan-aram, Jacob stopped for the night in an open field, not far from the city of Luz. Choosing a rock for his pillow, Jacob bedded down under the stars. That night he had a dream in which he saw a ladder, reaching from earth to heaven. Even stranger, he saw angels, descending and ascending the ladder. The Lord suddenly spoke and renewed to Jacob the promises he had made to Abraham and his father, Isaac. The Lord further promised to protect Jacob, to be with him and bring him back to the promise land.[4]

> Then Jacob awoke from his sleep and said, "Surely the Lord is in this place, and I did not know it." And he was afraid and said, "How awesome is this place! This is none other than the house of God, and this is the gate of heaven" (Gen. 28:16-17, ESV).

Jacob had more than a common dream; he had a revelation of God—one that would dramatically impact his life. Jacob took his stone pillow, set it up as a pillar, and poured oil on it. He called the place, *Bethel* (i.e., house of God). Jacob then made a solemn vow. Paraphrasing his words, if the Lord would

---

[4] Gen. 28:10-15

grant him divine protection, provision, and a safe passage to his father's house, then the Lord would be his God. Jacob further promised to return to the pillar that he set up and anointed and worship the Lord. He would even offer the Lord a tenth of all that he would receive from his hand (Gen. 28:20-22). Throughout Jacob's journeys and sojourns, the Lord showed himself faithful to the covenant he had made with Abraham, Isaac, and Jacob; he had blessed and watched over Jacob wherever he went. In later years, Jacob fulfilled his vow. He returned to Bethel with his family and the servants who were with him, to worship the Lord and only him. It is impossible to read in the Scriptures the life of Jacob and not see how dreams and revelations from God molded and transformed him into a worshipper of God (We will examine Jacob's vow in more detail in chapter eight).

The Revelation of Moses

Moses first encountered God on Mount Sinai in the burning bush. The bush burned with a supernatural fire that did not consume the leaves and branches. The Lord revealed to Moses his holiness. In fact, his holiness was so infectious, the very ground upon which Moses stood became holy. The Lord revealed to Moses that he wanted to rescue his people from slavery and the oppression of Egypt and bring them "to a good and spacious land, a land flowing with milk and honey…" (Exod. 3:8, HCSB).[5] In doing so, he also confirmed Moses' calling and mandate to be the Lord's emissary and the people's leader. God also gave Moses a sign that he had truly been called by the Lord: "I will certainly be with you, and this will be the sign to you that I have sent you: when you bring the people out of Egypt, you will all worship God at this mountain" (Exod. 3:12, HCSB). Moses obeyed the call of God and, together with his brother, Aaron, made his way to Egypt. The first thing on their agenda was to speak with the elders of Israel:

> Then Moses and Aaron went and gathered together all the elders of the people of Israel. Aaron spoke all the words that the Lord had spoken to Moses and did the signs in the sight of the people.

---

[5] We should consider some of the implications in this verse of Scripture. For milk and honey to flow, the land would have to be extremely fertile with grasslands so that cattle could produce an abundance of milk; and fertile with orchards, farmlands, cover crops, and even gardens so that bees could pollinate and produce an abundance of honey.

> And the people believed; and when they heard that the Lord had visited the people of Israel and that he had seen their affliction, **they bowed their heads and worshiped** (Exod. 4:29-31, ESV).

Seeing the supernatural signs Moses performed, and understanding the purpose and intent of God, and of his care for the plight of his people, the elders believed and "bowed their heads and worshiped" God. When Moses brought the people out of Egypt and to the foot of the mountain, the Lord established a covenant with them. He also supernaturally revealed to Moses the pattern or blueprints for a tabernacle—a sanctuary where God would dwell among his people, and where his people could worship him (Exod. 25:8-9, 40). The mountain of God,[6] as it was often called, proved to be a place of divine encounter and revelation, a place that served as a sign of Moses' calling, a place where the Lord began to dwell in the midst of his people, and ultimately, a place where his people would commit themselves through covenant to worship and service only him. The account and example of Moses reveals how divine revelations lead God's people towards a more meaningful expression of worship. Whether or not his people respond to divine revelation is another subject.

The Revelation of Joshua

Joshua succeeded Moses and led the children of Israel into the promise land. The Lord miraculously caused the waters of the Jordan to stop flowing so the people could pass through on dry ground. Having crossed the Jordan, the people encamped at Gilgal, where they circumcised every male who had been born during the forty years Israel had spent in the wilderness. They remained in Gilgal until all the men were healed. While in that location, they celebrated their first Passover, partaking of the food that came from the promise land. The time was quickly approaching when they would begin the conquest of Canaan. Joshua stood near Jericho, perhaps examining the city's formidable walls, and wondering how their armies would possibly conquer their first city. Suddenly, Joshua was not alone:

> When Joshua was by Jericho, he lifted up his eyes and looked, and behold, a man was standing before him with his drawn sword in his hand. And Joshua went to him and said to him, "Are you for us, or for our adversaries?" And he said, "No; but I am the

[6] Exod. 3:1; 4:27; 18:5; 24:13; 1 Re 19:8

> commander of the army of the Lord. Now I have come." **And Joshua fell on his face to the earth and worshiped and said to him, "What does my lord say to his servant?"** And the commander of the Lord's army said to Joshua, "Take off your sandals from your feet, for the place where you are standing is holy." And Joshua did so (Josh. 5:13-15, ESV).

The man who stood before Joshua, with sword unsheathed, revealed that he was the commander of the Lord's army, ready to fight for the Lord's cause. Joshua immediately fell to the ground and worshipped. Some might argue that Joshua merely prostrated himself in homage or reverence to a superior.[7] This, however, does not account for the fact that the man with the sword directed Joshua to remove his sandals, for the very ground where he stood was holy. The circumstances are quite reminiscent of the story of Moses, the difference being, Joshua was standing on holy ground before the commander of the Lord's army not before a burning bush. It is impossible not to correlate Joshua's experience with that of Moses. Furthermore, such a revelation would produce unfettered and expressed with facedown worship. Indeed, it is divine revelation that makes the difference between rendering homage and offering authentic worship. People knelt, bowed or prostrated themselves before Jesus in reverence, because they knew him to be a rabbi, a man of God, and a healer.[8] But then there were others who did so out of genuine adoration, because they knew his true identity.[9] Again, it is revelation that makes the difference between homage and worship.

Israel's first battle and victory in the land of Canaan began with a supernatural encounter with the commander of the Lord's army, with worship, and with a revelation the battle was not their own, but that it belonged to the Lord. Though we are not precisely informed, we may speculate that it was during this encounter the Lord *revealed* to Joshua how to take the city of Jericho.

The Revelation of Gideon

The conquest of Jericho is not the only battle the Scriptures identify with revelation and worship. After Israel had settled into their tribal territories, and Joshua and the elders of Israel eventually died, the next generation began

---

[7] The Hebrew verb, שָׁחָה, *shachach*, *to bow down*, is also translated, *to worship* (Gen. 22:5).

[8] Matt. 9:18, 15:25; Mark 10:17

[9] Matt. 14:33; 17:6; 28:9

to succumb to the idolatrous practices of the indigenous people who remained in the land of Canaan. Consequently, the Lord allowed Israel's enemies to oppress and dominate the people. Because of their grievous afflictions, the Lord raised up judges who would rescue Israel from their oppressors. The book of Judges especially relates how this became a regrettable and vicious cycle in Israel's early history.[10] In one of those many instances, the Lord called a man named, Gideon, to spearhead an attack against enemy occupation of the Midianites:

> And the angel of the Lord appeared to him and said to him, "The Lord is with you, O mighty man of valor." And Gideon said to him, "Please, my lord, if the Lord is with us, why then has all this happened to us? And where are all his wonderful deeds that our fathers recounted to us, saying, 'Did not the Lord bring us up from Egypt?' But now the Lord has forsaken us and given us into the hand of Midian." And the Lord turned to him and said, "Go in this might of yours and save Israel from the hand of Midian; do not I send you?" And he said to him, "Please, Lord, how can I save Israel? Behold, my clan is the weakest in Manasseh, and I am the least in my father's house." And the Lord said to him, "But I will be with you, and you shall strike the Midianites as one man" (Judg. 6:12-16, ESV).

Gideon asked the angel permission to go home that he might prepare an offering and return with it. The angel replied that he would remain there until he returned. Gideon prepared a big meal of goat, broth, and cakes and brought it back. The angel instructed Gideon to place the meat and cakes on a rock and pour the broth over the meal. When the angel touched the rock with his staff, fire came forth from the rock and consumed the gift. The angel suddenly disappeared. In that moment, Gideon realized he had been speaking with the angel of the Lord.[11] Fear filled his heart as he thought he would surely die: "But the Lord said to him, 'Peace be to you. Do not fear; you shall not die.' Then Gideon built an altar there to the Lord and called it, The Lord Is Peace. To this day it still stands at Ophrah, which belongs to the Abiezrites" (Judg. 6:23-24, ESV). The revelation of the Lord's peace became an occasion for Gideon to build an altar and worship God. Later that night, the Lord instructed Gideon to demolish the altar of Baal and cut down

[10] Judg. 2:16-23
[11] Judg. 6:22

the wooden Asherah—the *spiritual stronghold*[12] that prevented Israel from defeating its enemies—and build in their place an altar of stone to the Lord. Afterwards, Gideon was to offer one of his father's bulls on the altar as a burnt offering, using the Asherah for firewood. But fearing reprisal from his family and the local people, Gideon took ten of his servants, and by stealth of night, executed the Lord's instructions (Judg. 6:25-27). Gideon was led by supernatural revelation to restore the worship of Yahweh among his people and on the very soil that was part of the promise land. Worship is always the precursor of victory.

The book of Judges again recounts how divine revelation would play an important role in Gideon's leadership and victory over the enemy. According to the account, the Lord had reduced Gideon's army to three hundred men and instructed him to go against the enemy encamped in the valley. Gideon was overwhelmed by the disproportionate numbers between his army and that of the enemy. "And the Midianites and the Amalekites and all the people of the East lay along the valley like locusts in abundance, and their camels were without number, as the sand that is on the seashore in abundance" (Judg. 7:12, ESV). Though the Lord assured Gideon of victory, he also wanted to help him overcome his own fear. The Lord instructed Gideon to go down to the enemy camp with his servant and listen to their conversation.

> When Gideon came, behold, a man was telling a dream to his comrade. And he said, "Behold, I dreamed a dream, and behold, a cake of barley bread tumbled into the camp of Midian and came to the tent and struck it so that it fell and turned it upside down, so that the tent lay flat." And his comrade answered, "This is no other than the sword of Gideon the son of Joash, a man of Israel; God has given into his hand Midian and all the camp." **As soon as Gideon heard the telling of the dream and its interpretation, he worshiped.**[13] And he returned to the camp of Israel and said, "Arise, for the Lord has given the host of Midian into your hand" (Judg. 7:13-15, ESV).

---

[12] We will have much more to say about Gideon and the meaning of spiritual strongholds in the chapter, *The Pillar of Warfare.*

[13] Note "he worshipped" in Judg. 7:15 is the same Hebrew verb used in Joshua 5:14, "And Joshua fell on his face to the earth **and worshiped**..." (ESV).

Divine revelation from an unlikely source—a dream and its interpretation, and both from the mouth of the enemy—gave Gideon confidence to fight the battle and motivation to worship God.

The Revelation of David

In previous studies, we discussed the story of David and how it relates to the *Pillar of the Prophet* and that of the *Covenant.* However, it also relates to the *Pillar of Revelation.* The promises God made to David came by *prophetic revelation* though the prophet Nathan.[14] David shared with Nathan his intentions to build a house for the ark of the covenant. Nathan encouraged him to do all that was in his heart. But that same night, the Lord spoke to Nathan and gave him a specific word for the David. Nathan returned David that same evening and relayed to him the word of the Lord. David was profoundly touched and humbled. He entered the tent, sat in the Lord's presence and worshipped him, saying: "Therefore you are great, O Lord God. For there is none like you, and there is no God besides you, according to all that we have heard with our ears" (2 Sam. 7:22, ESV). Prophetic revelation even gave David the confidence and boldness to pray and request that the Lord would accomplish all that had been revealed to him:

> "For you, O Lord of hosts, the God of Israel, have made this **revelation** to your servant, saying, 'I will build you a house.' Therefore your servant has found courage to pray this prayer to you. And now, O Lord God, you are God, and your words are true, and you have promised this good thing to your servant. Now therefore may it please you to bless the house of your servant, so that it may continue forever before you. **For you, O Lord God, have spoken**, and with your blessing shall the house of your servant be blessed forever" (2 Sam. 7:27-29, ESV).

The revelation that David received through Nathan the prophet assured him that God would build him an enduring house and that his offspring would build the Lord's house. The establishing of the Davidic kingdom and the building of the Lord's house were certainly meant to promote the worship of Yahweh among his people. Even more so, the Messianic and eschatological fulfilment of David's revelation would cause biblical worship to reach far beyond Israel's borders and to every nation.[15]

---

[14] 2 Sam. 7:4-17

[15] Isa. 2:2-3; Luke 1:69; Acts 15:16-17; Heb. 3:5-6

The Revelation of Heavenly Fire and Divine Glory

David's son, Solomon, built the house of God, just as the Lord had revealed. Solomon gathered all of Israel's elders and heads of the tribes, to bring the ark of the covenant into the temple and to celebrate the dedication of the house.[16] Indeed, a great congregation assembled in Jerusalem for the event. Innumerable sacrifices were offered as the Levites brought up the ark from the city of David and placed in the inner sanctuary of the house. The construction of the temple had certainly been a massive undertaking; and when completed, it became one of the wonders of the ancient world. But Solomon was not fooled by its unparalleled beauty and grandeur. In his long and eloquent prayer of dedication, Solomon placed the house in proper perspective: "But will God indeed dwell with man on the earth? Behold, heaven and the highest heaven cannot contain you, how much less this house that I have built!" (2 Chr. 6:18, ESV).[17] Solomon understood the primary function of the temple was to serve as a house of prayer and worship (In his prayer of dedication, Solomon uses the Hebrew words for *to pray*, *to beseech* or *plead*, *prayer*, *cry*, and *supplication(s)* or *plea(s)*, altogether, no less than twenty-three times). When Solomon finished praying, the Lord tangibly revealed his glory:

> As soon as Solomon finished his prayer, fire came down from heaven and consumed the burnt offering and the sacrifices, and the glory of the Lord filled the temple. And the priests could not enter the house of the Lord, because the glory of the Lord filled the Lord's house. **When all the people of Israel saw the fire come down and the glory of the Lord on the temple, they bowed down with their faces to the ground on the pavement and worshiped and gave thanks to the Lord**, saying, "For he is good, for his steadfast love endures forever" (2 Chr. 7:1-3, ESV).

The sudden and overwhelming revelation of heavenly fire and divine glory prompted God's people to bow down, worship, and give thanks to the Lord. The supernatural manifestation revealed the God's acceptance of Solomon's request. Indeed, that very night the Lord spoke to Solomon:

> Then the Lord appeared to Solomon in the night and said to him:

---

16 2 Chron. 5:2-7

17 2 Chron. 6: 18-41, for the full text of Solomon's prayer

> "I have heard your prayer and have chosen this place for myself as a house of sacrifice. When I shut up the heavens so that there is no rain, or command the locust to devour the land, or send pestilence among my people, if my people who are called by my name humble themselves, and pray and seek my face and turn from their wicked ways, then I will hear from heaven and will forgive their sin and heal their land. Now my eyes will be open and my ears attentive to the prayer that is made in this place. For now I have chosen and consecrated this house that my name may be there forever. My eyes and my heart will be there for all time. And as for you, if you will walk before me as David your father walked, doing according to all that I have commanded you and keeping my statutes and my rules, then I will establish your royal throne, as I covenanted with David your father, saying, 'You shall not lack a man to rule Israel'" (2 Chr. 7:12-18, ESV).

The Lord further disclosed to Solomon that if the people turned to other gods and began to worship and serve them, he would remove them from the land and literally trash the house (2 Chron. 7:19-22). The temple stood erect and secure only as long as the land was inhabited by the people of the covenant, and as long as the edifice served its purpose—a house of prayer and worship.

New Testament Revelations

The Revelation of the Twelve

> But immediately Jesus spoke to them, saying, "Take heart; it is I. Do not be afraid." And Peter answered him, "Lord, if it is you, command me to come to you on the water." He said, "Come." So Peter got out of the boat and walked on the water and came to Jesus (Matt. 14:27-29, ESV).

Immediately after feeding more than five thousand people, Jesus made his disciples get in the boat and proceed to the other side of the lake. Jesus dismissed the crowds and went up into the mountain to pray. Meanwhile, the disciples were rowing against the wind and waves, late into the evening. During the early morning hours, the disciples espied a form, walking on the water. Supposing it to be a ghost, they were terrified and cried out in fear. "But immediately Jesus spoke to them, saying, 'Take heart; it is I. Do not be afraid.'" Perhaps still unsure, Peter replied, "Lord, if it is you, command me to come to you on the water." Jesus simply replied, "Come!" Peter immediately stepped out of the boat and walked on the water. But seeing the boisterous wind, he began to sink in his fear and in the water. Peter cried out to the Lord.

> Jesus immediately reached out his hand and took hold of him, saying to him, "O you of little faith, why did you doubt?" And when they got into the boat, the wind ceased. **And those in the boat worshiped him, saying, 'Truly you are the Son of God**'" (Matt 14:31-33, ESV).

The disciples had heard some of the demon-possessed, calling Jesus, 'Son of God,'[18] but when they actually saw a demonstration of the Lord's power over the physical elements, they were more than convinced he was the Son of God, and they worshipped him. The revelation of Jesus as the Son of God is a powerful motive and stimulus of worship. As aforementioned, one may render homage to a person of repute, such as a king, prophet, or rabbi; but Jesus is to be worshipped, because he is the Son of God. Sonship of Jesus Christ is tantamount to deity. When Jesus called God his Father, the Jews clearly understood the implications. Apostle John writes: "This was why the Jews were seeking all the more to kill him, because not only was he breaking the Sabbath, but he was even calling God his own Father, **making himself equal with God**" (John 5:18, ESV). The sonship and deity of Jesus Christ is a revelation of God, and nothing will more deeply impact the way a person worships God than personally knowing who Jesus is. While in the region of Caesarea Philippi, Jesus asked his disciples a question that highlights the importance of revelation:

> "Who do people say that the Son of Man is?" And they said, "Some say John the Baptist; others, Elijah; still others, Jeremiah or one of the prophets." "But you," He asked them, "who do you say that I am?" Simon Peter answered, "**You are the Messiah, the Son of the living God!**" And Jesus responded, "**Simon son of Jonah, you are blessed because flesh and blood did not reveal this to you, but My Father in heaven**" (Matt 16:13-17, HCSB).

Without a revelation from the heavenly Father,[19] people will only speculate as to who Jesus is, but they will not worship him.

---

[18] Matt. 8:29; Mk. 3:11

[19] Matt. 11:25-27

The Revelation of the Samaritan Woman

Nowhere in the Scriptures is the correlation between revelation and worship better articulated than in the account of Jesus' conversation with the Samaritan woman at the well of Jacob in the gospel of John. In the ensuing dialogue, the woman made an important observation, regarding one of the more noted contentions between the Jews and the Samaritans: "Our fathers worshiped on this mountain, but you say that in Jerusalem is the place where people ought to worship" (John 4:20, ESV). What Jesus says then to the woman discloses the importance of divine revelation: "You worship what you do not know; we worship what we know, for salvation is from the Jews" (John 4:22, ESV).

The Samaritans, at the best, imitated elements of Jewish teaching and tradition. Historically, the Samaritans descended from a mixture of foreign peoples the king of Assyria had forced to migrate to Samaria, to repopulate its cities after he had removed the people of Israel.[20] Because the Samaritans were not of pure Jewish extraction, the Jews did not allow them to help rebuild the temple[21] that had been destroyed during the Babylonian conquest of Judah. Subsequently, the Samaritans built their own temple on Mount Gerizim. The location, of course, was not a random choice; the mountain had a spiritual importance in Israel's history. Before the conquest of the promise land, Moses had instructed the people: "When the Lord your God brings you into the land you are entering to possess, you are to proclaim the blessing at Mount Gerizim and the curse at Mount Ebal" (Deut. 11:29, HCSB). The Samaritans apparently identified themselves with the patriarch, Jacob. The woman had asked Jesus if he were "greater than our father Jacob? He gave us the well and drank from it himself, as did his sons and his livestock" (John 4:12, ESV). The Samaritans had clearly embraced elements of Jewish identity, beliefs, hopes, and practices, but despite their religious background, Jesus affirms that revelation had been given to the Jews: "You worship what you do not know; we worship what we know, for salvation is from the Jews." The Apostle Paul further expands on this revelation:

> They are Israelites, and to them belong the adoption, the glory, the covenants, the giving of the law, the worship, and the promises. To them belong the patriarchs, and from their race,

---

[20] 2 Kgs. 17:24-33
[21] Ezra 4:1-3

> according to the flesh, is the Christ, who is God over all, blessed forever. Amen (Rom. 9:4-5, ESV).

In the ensuing conversation, Jesus revealed to the woman things were about to change for both Jew and non-Jew alike. The hour was coming when worship would no longer be contingent upon a location, but in spirit and truth. The woman answered Jesus that she knew the Messiah was coming and he would explain everything to the Samaritans. She apparently understood the connection between the things Jesus was saying about worship and the coming Messiah. But then the Lord revealed to her the greatest of all revelations: "Jesus said to her, 'I who speak to you am he'" (John 4:26, ESV). Jesus' prophetic revelation, concerning worship, was indeed a radical transition from past revelations, and certainly a break from centuries of tradition and religious culture. Moreover, the fact that Jesus disclosed such a revelation to a non-Jewish person, and that he openly revealed himself to be the Messiah to a woman, who was most likely marginalized by her own people, spoke volumes of the changes already in progress.

The Revelation of the Resurrection

The revelation of the resurrection of Jesus Christ has had more impact and influence in shaping worship than any other event in biblical history. In fact, the resurrection—like the deity of Christ—is one of the most monumental revelations of God. And it was first made to two of the women who followed Jesus.

> Now after the Sabbath, toward the dawn of the first day of the week, Mary Magdalene and the other Mary went to see the tomb. And behold, there was a great earthquake, for an angel of the Lord descended from heaven and came and rolled back the stone and sat on it. His appearance was like lightning, and his clothing white as snow. And for fear of him the guards trembled and became like dead men. But the angel said to the women, "Do not be afraid, for I know that you seek Jesus who was crucified. He is not here, for he has risen, as he said. Come, see the place where he lay. Then go quickly and tell his disciples that he has risen from the dead, and behold, he is going before you to Galilee; there you will see him. See, I have told you." So they departed quickly from the tomb with fear and great joy, and ran to tell his disciples. And behold, Jesus met them and said, "Greetings!" **And they came up and took hold of his feet and worshiped him** (Matt. 28:1-9, ESV).

Overwhelmed with fear and immense joy at the news that Jesus rose from the dead, the women ran to inform the disciples. Along the way, they encountered Jesus. They could only fall down and embrace his feet and worship him. Jesus instructed the women to tell his brothers to go to Galilee where they would meet him. The disciples followed the Lord's instructions and journeyed to the mountain Jesus had indicated: "**And when they saw him they worshiped him**, but some doubted" (Matt. 28:17, ESV). Jesus appeared to his disciples one last time in Bethany, before ascending into heaven. Again, the encounter led unto worship:

> And he led them out as far as Bethany, and lifting up his hands he blessed them. While he blessed them, he parted from them and was carried up into heaven. **And they worshiped him and returned to Jerusalem with great joy, and were continually in the temple blessing God** (Luke 24:50-53, ESV).

The above texts from the gospels of Matthew and Luke substantiate one of the most important doctrines in the New Testament—*the resurrection of Jesus Christ*. The verses also reveal the transition from Old to New Testament worship. The disciples worshipped *Jesus*, and they did so regardless of the location.

The Revelation of the Gentiles

When Jesus was just eight days old, his parents took him to the temple in Jerusalem to be circumcised according to the law of Moses. While the couple and their newborn were in the temple complex, they encountered an elderly man named, Simeon, who prophesied over the child:

> Simeon took him in his arms and praised God, saying: "Sovereign Lord, as you have promised, you may now dismiss your servant in peace. For my eyes have seen your salvation, which you have prepared in the sight of all nations: **a light for revelation to the Gentiles, and the glory of your people Israel**" (Luke 2:28-32, NIV).[22]

Some thirty years after this prophecy, Jesus called to himself, a band of disciples and trained them to preach the gospel. He also sought to impart in them a vision that reached far beyond their own borders and people. Jesus' itinerary even took the disciples beyond Judea and Galilee and into the

---

[22] Luke 2:28-35, for the full account of Simeon's prophecy.

regions of Samaria, Tyre, Sidon, and Decapolis.[23] The gospels even narrate occasions when Jesus' ministry directly touched the lives of Gentiles, such as the Roman Centurion; the woman from Syrian Phoenicia; the Samaritan leper; and of course, the Samaritan woman and people from her town.[24] Jesus was indeed "a light for revelation to the Gentiles."[25] Through personal example, the Lord clearly intimated that the future mission of the disciples would be without social, ethnic, political, and geographical boundaries. Moreover, just before he ascended into heaven, Jesus said to the disciples: "But you will receive power when the Holy Spirit comes on you; and you will be my witnesses in Jerusalem, and in all Judea and Samaria, **and to the ends of the earth**" (Acts 1:8, NIV).

A few years had gone by since the Lord's ascension. The church had had great success in reaching out to the Jewish populace, but nothing had been done to reach the Gentiles. Then one day, Peter had a *revelational vision*—one that would dramatically impact his life as well church history.

> The next day, as they were on their journey and approaching the city, Peter went up on the housetop about the sixth hour to pray. And he became hungry and wanted something to eat, but while they were preparing it, he fell into a trance and saw the heavens opened and something like a great sheet descending, being let down by its four corners upon the earth. In it were all kinds of animals and reptiles and birds of the air. And there came a voice to him: "Rise, Peter; kill and eat." But Peter said, "By no means, Lord; for I have never eaten anything that is common or unclean." And the voice came to him again a second time, "What God has made clean, do not call common." This happened three times, and the thing was taken up at once to heaven (Acts 10:9-16, ESV).

As Peter puzzled over the meaning of the vision, three men arrived at the house where he was staying and asked for him. The Holy Spirit instructed Peter to go with them "without hesitation," because they were sent by him (Acts 10:20, ESV). Peter introduced himself and asked them why they had come. The men explained that Cornelius, the Roman centurion, had sent them; he had seen in a vision an angel who told him to send for Peter.

---

[23] Mark 7:24, 31; John 4:4

[24] Matt. 8:5-13; Mk. 7:24-30; Luke 17:11-19; John 4:5-30; 39-42

[25] The word, *Gentile*, refers to people or nations who are not Jewish.

Peter received the three men in the house as his guests. The next day, he departed with them for Caesarea. Up until that time, the apostles and the church had only reached out to the Jews and Samaritans. But through a revelatory vision and the guidance of the Holy Spirit, Peter and those who were with him moved beyond their religious and cultural boundaries, entering the house of a Roman centurion. Prompted by Cornelius' account of how an angel had directed him to call for the apostle, Peter shared the gospel for the first time with a non-Jewish audience. Then something totally unexpected happened: The Holy Spirit fell on those who were gathered in the house, and they began to speak in tongues and magnify God, just as the first disciples had done when they were baptized in the Holy Spirit (Acts 10:44-48).[26] The new Gentile believers were then baptized in water.

The importance of Peter's revelatory vision should not be underestimated. It served as the catalyst to unlock the blessings of the gospel for the Gentiles. It was also instrumental in helping those of the circumcision, understand the purpose of God for the Gentiles and give him glory. Peter recounted to them his vision and all that had transpired in Cornelius's house: "When they heard these things they fell silent. And they glorified God, saying, 'Then to the Gentiles also God has granted repentance that leads to life'" (Acts 11:18, ESV). The inclusion of the Gentiles in the grace of God has ultimately caused the number of worshippers to increase exponentially on the earth and in heaven (Rev. 7:9-10).

The Revelation of Paul

> But I make known to you, brethren, that the gospel which was preached by me is not according to man. **For I neither received it from man, nor was I taught *it,* but *it came* through the revelation of Jesus Christ** (Gal. 1:11-12, NKJV).

Upon learning there were disciples of Jesus in the city of Damascus, a young and zealous man named, Saul, requested from the High Priest, letters to the synagogues of Damascus, stating his purpose. He then headed for the Syrian capital to arrest the disciples and bring them back to Jerusalem to stand trial. As he and some other men journeyed, a bright light suddenly shown around Saul, blinding him with its intensity:

---

[26] Acts 2:4-11; 10:44-48.

> Then he fell to the ground, and heard a voice saying to him, "Saul, Saul, why are you persecuting Me?" And he said, "Who are You, Lord?" Then the Lord said, "I am Jesus, whom you are persecuting. It *is* hard for you to kick against the goads." So he, trembling and astonished, said, "Lord, what do You want me to do?" Then the Lord *said* to him, "Arise and go into the city, and you will be told what you must do" (Acts 9:4-6, NKJV).[27]

In that very moment, on a dusty road to Damascus, Saul received a revelation of Jesus Christ that radically changed his life, his character, his theology, and his understanding of worship. The Name which he formerly persecuted and had forced believers to blaspheme, suddenly became the very Name he called, *Lord.* Saul, or *Paul,* as he was later called,[28] became an apostle and minister of Jesus Christ. He would also become one of the major contributors of New Testament writings.

Acts of the Apostles records that while Paul was preaching the gospel in the city of Corinth, some of the Jews dragged him before the proconsul and accused him: "This *fellow* persuades men to worship God contrary to the law" (Acts 18:13, NKJV). Paul was ready to give his defense, but before he could say a word, the proconsul Gallio rejected their complaint and expelled them from his judgment seat. This complaint brought before Gallio is important to our discussion because it reveals how the local Jews perceived and interpreted Paul's preaching. Paul testified to the Jews that Jesus was, indeed, the Messiah and the Son of God,[29] and that salvation and forgiveness of sin were through repentance and faith in Jesus' name.[30] Though Paul had the Scriptures and eye-witness accounts to substantiate his claims, non-believing Jews would perceive his message as an attack on the law of Moses and centuries of Jewish traditions, not to mention, prejudice. Besides the fact that Paul reached out the Gentiles, one of the things that definitely flew in the face of Jewish tradition was that he taught that men should call on the name of Jesus.[31] Even when he was arrested by the Romans in Jerusalem, Paul spoke and openly testified to as much before the crowd that had gathered around him:

---

[27] Acts 22:6-10; 26:14

[28] Acts 13:9

[29] Acts 17:3; 18:5; 2 Cor. 1:19-20

[30] Acts 16:31; 20:21

[31] Acts 22:16; Rom. 10:12-14; 1 Cor. 1:2; 2 Tim. 2:22

> Someone named Ananias, a devout man according to the law, having a good reputation with all the Jews residing there, came and stood by me and said, 'Brother Saul, regain your sight.' And in that very hour I looked up and saw him. Then he said, 'The God of our fathers has appointed you to know His will, to see the Righteous One, and to hear the sound of His voice. For you will be a witness for Him to all people of what you have seen and heard. And now, why delay? Get up and be baptized, and wash away your sins **by calling on His name**'" (Acts 22:12-16, HCSB).

Unbelieving Jews would inevitably interpret Paul's teaching as blasphemous, especially since the Hebrew Scriptures taught that "everyone who calls on the name of Yahweh will be saved…" (Joel 2:32, HCSB).[32]

The Revelation of the Mystery of Christ

Apostle Paul certainly received many revelations from God throughout his life. In fact, in one of his letters, he speaks of "the surpassing greatness *and* extraordinary nature of the revelations" which he had received of the Lord (2 Cor. 12:7, HCSB). While space does not allow us to examine every revelation of Paul, we will remark on one that particularly affects the dynamics of worship: The inclusion and integration of the Gentiles in the spiritual temple of God and in body of Christ:

> For this reason I, Paul, a prisoner of Christ Jesus on behalf of you Gentiles—assuming that you have heard of the stewardship of God's grace that was given to me for you, **how the mystery was made known to me by revelation, as I have written briefly**. When you read this, you can perceive my insight into the mystery of Christ, which was not made known to the sons of men in other generations as it has now been revealed to his holy apostles and prophets by the Spirit. This mystery is that the Gentiles are fellow heirs, members of the same body, and partakers of the promise in Christ Jesus through the gospel (Eph. 3:1-6, ESV).

Paul writes that the mystery of Christ was made known to him by revelation. *But what is this mystery and how does it impact worship?* In the previous chapter of his letter to the Ephesians, Paul *briefly* explains that through the redemptive

---

[32] 1 Kgs. 18:24; 1 Chron. 16:8; Ps. 99:6; 105:1; 116:4, 13, 17; Lam. 3:55; Jonah 1:14; Zeph. 3:9; Zech. 13:9

work of Christ, the Gentiles have become part of the family of God, integrated in the same spiritual temple (Eph. 2:11-22).[33] In the text cited above, Paul further elaborates that the Gentiles are now "fellow heirs, members of the same body, and partakers of the promise in Christ Jesus through the gospel." This revelation marked and defined Paul's ministry among Gentiles (Eph. 3:8-10). But it also marked and defined a new paradigm and dynamic in worship: The Gentiles may join God's people in praising and worshipping him. Moreover, their inclusion has caused praise and worship to proliferate among the Gentiles:

> For I say that the Messiah became a servant of the circumcised on behalf of God's truth, to confirm the promises to the fathers, **and so that Gentiles may glorify God for His mercy**. As it is written: Therefore I will praise You among the Gentiles, and I will sing psalms to Your name. Again it says: Rejoice, you Gentiles, with His people! And again: Praise the Lord, all you Gentiles; all the peoples should praise Him! And again, Isaiah says: The root of Jesse will appear, the One who rises to rule the Gentiles; the Gentiles will hope in Him (Rom. 15:8-12, HCSB).

The Revelation of John

According to the book of Revelation, John had been exiled to the isle of Patmos for his faith and testimony of Jesus Christ. While on the island, he received a revelation of the second coming of Jesus Christ. John committed that revelation to parchment and sent it to the seven churches in Asia. That parchment, known to us as the book of *Revelation*, has reached well beyond the borders of Asia and across centuries of church history, blessing, encouraging, and challenging generations of believers to worship God, even in the face of grievous and aggravated persecution. Although Revelation addresses specific issues and problems relating to the seven churches in Asia, a great deal of the book deals with events that will transpire shortly before the second coming of the Lord Jesus Christ. Chapter after chapter, a series of visions unfold, many of which are highly symbolic in nature. Some of the visions clearly and unambiguously reveal a connection between divine revelation and worship.

---

[33] In effect, what had been impossible during the post-exilic construction of the temple (i.e., a collaboration between the Jews and Samaritans), God accomplished through the redemptive work of Christ.

In one of his visions, John sees and hears a heavenly ensemble of those who won the victory over their adversary:

> Then I saw another sign in heaven, great and amazing, seven angels with seven plagues, which are the last, for with them the wrath of God is finished. I also saw something like a sea of glass mixed with fire, and those who had won the victory over the beast, his image, and the number of his name, were standing on the sea of glass with harps from God. They sang the song of God's servant Moses and the song of the Lamb: "Great and awe-inspiring are Your works, Lord God, the Almighty; righteous and true are Your ways, King of the Nations. Lord, who will not fear and glorify Your name? Because You alone are holy, **for all the nations will come and worship before You because Your righteous acts have been revealed**" (Rev. 15:1-4, HCSB).

John is greatly astonished at a sign he sees in heaven; seven angels with seven plagues that complete the wrath of God. He then hears the victors singing the song of Moses and the song of the Lamb, which exalt God, his works, his ways, and his name. They also sing prophetically that all nations will come and worship before the Lord, inspired and moved by a clear manifestation of his righteousness. Since the garden of Eden, the devil has casted doubt and suspicion on the integrity of God; but when the fulness of his wrath is ultimately revealed and poured out on an incorrigible and unrepentant world, his holy and righteous character will clearly be vindicated. Moreover, that all nations will come and worship before God is an eschatological event, contingent upon the revelation of his judgments: "Arise, O God, judge the earth; For You shall inherit all nations" (Ps. 82:8, NKJV).[34]

Towards the end of all the visions, John experiences a first-hand revelation. Perhaps overwhelmed by the magnitude of the prophecies and revelations he had just witnessed, when the angel speaks again to him, his response is rather unexpected and even perplexing:

> Then he said to me, "Write: 'Blessed *are* those who are called to the marriage supper of the Lamb!'" And he said to me, "These are the true sayings of God." And I fell at his feet to worship him. But he said to

[34] Zech. 14:3, 16-19

> me, "See *that you do* not *do that!* I am your fellow servant, and of your brethren who have the testimony of Jesus. **Worship God!** For the testimony of Jesus is the spirit of prophecy" (Rev. 19:9-10, NKJV).

And shortly after:

> Then he said to me, "These words *are* faithful and true." And the Lord God of the holy prophets sent His angel to show His servants the things which must shortly take place. "Behold, I am coming quickly! Blessed *is* he who keeps the words of the prophecy of this book." Now I, John, saw and heard these things. And when I heard and saw, I fell down to worship before the feet of the angel who showed me these things. Then he said to me, "See *that you do* not *do that.* For I am your fellow servant, and of your brethren the prophets, and of those who keep the words of this book. **Worship God**" (Rev. 22:6-9, NKJV).

Some Bible commentaries think John was simply overcome by all he had seen and heard; consequently, he fell down to worship the angel. Others, instead, suggest the apostle may have simply confused the angel for God, the Lord Jesus, or the Angel of the Lord. Whatever may have been the reasons, the angel immediately corrected John's misguided actions, informing him that he was simply a fellow servant, a brother among the prophets, and of those who keep the words of the very revelation that John was supposed to write down. On both of these occasions, the angel redirected John to worship God. Worshipping God is the natural and, more importantly, the *correct* response to divine revelation.

The Revelation of the Believer

Divine revelation is an integral part of the New Testament church and worship. The Lord continues, as in the Old Testament, to impart spiritual revelation through supernatural means, such as dreams, visions, prophecy, divine and angelic encounters, etc. Such events, however, are infrequent and uncommon occurrences, at least for most believers. Nonetheless, the Lord has provided the church and every believer with a readily available resources of revelation, namely, the word of God and the Holy Spirit.

The Scriptures are replete with truths, directives, promises, and, of course, divine revelations. Through the Scriptures the Lord reveals his nature, character, and will. He also reveals his redemptive and eschatological plan and purpose for mankind and the earth. Moreover, the Lord reveals through his word the character he wants to form in each believer. But merely reading the Scriptures is not enough. If biblical revelations remain abstract, objective, and impersonal, they do little to inspire and motivate believers to worship and serve God. That is why we also need the Holy Spirit. He makes the Scriptures become concrete, relevant, and personal, as though the Lord were speaking directly to us.

The gospel of Luke recounts that after his resurrection, Jesus appeared to two of the company of disciples, as they walked towards the town of Emmaus. They conversed with him as though he were a stranger, for they were prevented from recognizing him. Because it was late in the evening, the disciples invited this unknown traveler to their home. When Jesus blessed and broke bread, their eyes were suddenly opened and they recognized the Lord, moments before he disappeared from their table: "And they said to one another, 'Did not our heart burn within us while He talked with us on the road, and while He opened the Scriptures to us?'" (Luke 24:32, NKJV). The two disciples had heard Scriptures read in the synagogue and temple; they had probably also heard them recited in their homes as children. But when Jesus expounded the Scriptures and gave their meaning, he caused the hearts of the two disciples to burn. It is the anointing and power of the Holy Spirit that makes the difference (Luke 4:18; Acts 1:2). According to the Apostle Paul, the Holy Spirit reveals to us the things of God:

> But as it is written: What eye did not see and ear did not hear, and what never entered the human mind—God prepared this for those who love Him. **Now God has revealed these things to us by the Spirit**, for the Spirit searches everything, even the depths of God (1 Cor. 2:9-10, HCSB).

The Lord also discloses revelation through the gifts of the Spirit and the body of Christ. In his letter to the Corinthians, Paul speaks of revelation as an integral part of their worship service.

> "How is it then, brethren? Whenever you come together, each of you has a psalm, has a teaching, has a tongue, has **a revelation**, has an interpretation. Let all things be done for edification" (1 Cor. 14:26, NKJV).[35]

The revelation to which Paul refers is special knowledge the Holy Spirit imparts to believers for the benefit and edification of the body of Christ. Of

---

[35] 1 Cor. 14:6, 26, 30

course, all such revelation is subject and subordinate to the Scriptures (The Holy Spirit will never give a revelation that contradicts the word of God).

The word of God and the Holy Spirit are essential resources of divine revelation for every believer. Divine revelation, however, must be received and assimilated by faith (Heb. 4:2). Passive acceptance is not the same as having faith. From a biblical perspective, faith involves trusting, obeying, and even acting upon that which God reveals. Without faith, revelation will not produce positive, spiritual results, especially when it comes to worship. The gospel of Matthew brings to light a particular truth, regarding the relationship between revelation and faith: "Now the eleven disciples went to Galilee, to the mountain to which Jesus had directed them. And when they saw him they worshiped him, but some doubted" (Matt. 28:16-17, ESV). Jesus revealed himself to the disciples at an undisclosed location on a mountain in Galilee. But not all of the disciples worshipped him; some doubted. Worship will not flow from the heart full of doubt, unbelief, and fear. These are actually antithetical and even toxic to worship. Revelation requires faith just as much as worship requires revelation.

CHAPTER 6
The Pillar of Warfare
(The Conflict of Biblical Worship)
Part One

And Abimelech said to Isaac, "Go away from us, for you are much mightier than we." So Isaac departed from there and encamped in the Valley of Gerar and settled there. And Isaac dug again the wells of water that had been dug in the days of Abraham his father, which the Philistines had stopped after the death of Abraham. And he gave them the names that his father had given them. But when Isaac's servants dug in the valley and found there a well of spring water, the herdsmen of Gerar quarreled with Isaac's herdsmen, saying, "The water is ours." So he called the name of the well Esek, because they contended with him. Then they dug another well, and they quarreled over that also, so he called its name Sitnah. And he moved from there and dug another well, and they did not quarrel over it. So he called its name Rehoboth, saying, "For now the Lord has made room for us, and we shall be fruitful in the land." From there he went up to Beersheba. And the Lord appeared to him the same night and said, "I am the God of Abraham your father. Fear not, for I am with you and will bless you and multiply your offspring for my servant Abraham's sake." So he built an altar there and called upon the name of the Lord and pitched his tent there. And there Isaac's servants dug a well (Gen. 26:16-25, ESV).

Isaac was the very offspring the Lord God had promised his parents, Abraham and Sarah. He was the son of laughter and heir of all the promises the Lord had made to his father. Like his father, Isaac was also a prophet. He met with the Lord and heard his voice; but more importantly, he knew how to worship God. The blessing of the Lord was clearly on Isaac; nonetheless, he faced numerous conflicts and struggles during his lifetime. When Isaac was in his late thirties, his mother, Sarah died. Isaac took her death rather hard. Abraham was advancing in age when he decided to send his most trusted servant to find a wife for his son. Abraham made his servant swear he would not choose one of the daughters of the Canaanites, but that he would seek a wife among Abraham's kindred in Aram-naharaim, a town in the Mesopotamia region.[1] The servant departed with ten camels, loaded with all types of gifts. When the servant arrived at his destination, he prayed the Lord would guide him to the right woman. The Lord answered his prayer and caused him to encounter Rebekah straightaway. Rebekah was unmarried and a descendent of Abraham's brother. Equally important, she was willing to leave her family, and make the long trek to the land of Canaan.

> And Rebekah lifted up her eyes, and when she saw Isaac, she dismounted from the camel and said to the servant, "Who is that man, walking in the field to meet us?" The servant said, "It is my master." So she took her veil and covered herself. And the servant told Isaac all the things that he had done. Then Isaac brought her into the tent of Sarah his mother and took Rebekah, and she became his wife, and he loved her. So Isaac was comforted after his mother's death (Gen. 24:64-67, ESV).

The fact that Isaac was comforted by the love he felt for Rebekah may be indicative of an inner struggle caused by the death of his mother. We do not know the extent or depth of that struggle, but the account suggests her death left him disconsolate and perhaps even depressed. The loss of a family member or close friend often causes sorrow and grief. Subsequently, it may also produce depression, a sense of loneliness, and even bitterness and anger. Such sentiments certainly make it difficult to find and express feelings of love and devotion towards God. But worship is not only about feelings; it is also about faith and trust, especially in the face of a conflicting emotions and states of mind.

Some twenty years had gone by, but Rebekah still remained without child. This was a rather odd predicament, since God had promised Isaac's father, "I will surely bless you, and I will surely multiply your offspring as the stars of heaven and as the sand that is on the seashore…" (Gen. 22:17, ESV).

---

[1] Gen. 24:1-4, 10

Isaac prayed on behalf of his wife. The Lord answered and Rebekah conceived and became pregnant. But then another problem arose; the children struggled with each other in Rebekah's womb. Concerned, Rebekah sought the Lord: "And the Lord said to her, 'Two nations are in your womb, and two peoples from within you shall be divided; the one shall be stronger than the other, the older shall serve the younger'" (Gen. 25:23, ESV). When the children were born, the younger of the two, Jacob, came out, holding the heel of his brother, Esau. This was certainly an ominous portent of future struggles.

Some years later, when a famine broke out in the land, Isaac moved his family to the Philistine town of Gerar. Once again, he was faced with inner conflict. Because Rebekah was exceptionally beautiful, Isaac was afraid the local men would kill him and take his wife. Like his father, Abraham, Isaac lied about his wife, saying she was his sister. When Abimelech, the king of Gerar, discovered the truth, he reproved Isaac and warned the people they would be put to die if they touched Rebekah. Isaac prospered and increased greatly during his stay in Gerar, but his prosperity eventually caused him serious problems. The Philistines envied Isaac because he had become wealthy and powerful. There were also other signs of hostility. The Philistines had clogged up with dirt all the wells Isaac's father had dug. This was a rather unfriendly response on their part, considering the fact that Abraham and Abimelech, king of Gerar, had established a covenant or treaty of peace. But then again, a treaty may also imply the presence of hostility and potential for conflict. Because of the growing fear and resentment among the people, Abimelech asked Isaac to depart from their land.

Isaac resettled his family in the nearby valley of Gerar. He reopened the wells his father had dug. However, when he dug new wells in the valley, the herdsmen of Gerar fought with him over water rights:

> But when Isaac's servants dug in the valley and found there a well of spring water, the herdsmen of Gerar quarreled with Isaac's herdsmen, saying, "The water is ours." So he called the name of the well **Esek**, because they contended with him. Then they dug another well, and they quarreled over that also, so he called its name **Sitnah**. And he moved from there and dug another well, and they did not quarrel over it. So he called its name **Rehoboth**, saying, "For now the Lord has made room for us, and we shall be fruitful in the land" (Gen. 26:19-22, ESV).

Isaac called the wells, "Esek" and "Sitnah," which mean *contention* and *hostility*.

Isaac moved from the area and dug another well, calling it, "Rehoboth," which means, *broad spaces*. Eventually, Isaac moved his family further south to Beersheba. Here, the Lord appeared again to Isaac, encouraging him not to fear, for the Lord was with him. The Lord further promised that he would multiply Isaac's offspring, according to the promise he made with his father, Abraham. Isaac responded in worship: "So he built an altar there and called upon the name of the Lord and pitched his tent there. And there Isaac's servants dug a well" (Gen. 26:25, ESV).

While in Beersheba, Abimelech, king of Gerar, along with his friend, Ahuzzath, and Phicol, commander of the army, came to meet with Isaac. The patriarch was not happy to see them since Abimelech had treated him unjustly by sending him away from Gerar. Abimelech, however, assured Isaac of the friendly nature of their visit. The king said, "We see plainly that the Lord has been with you" (Gen. 26:28, ESV).[2] The king explained they wanted to make a treaty with Isaac that he would treat them well and do them no harm, just as they believed they had done when they sent him away peacefully.

> So he made them a feast, and they ate and drank. In the morning they rose early and exchanged oaths. And Isaac sent them on their way, and they departed from him in peace. That same day Isaac's servants came and told him about the well that they had dug and said to him, "We have found water." He called it Shibah; therefore the name of the city is Beersheba to this day (Gen. 26:30-33, ESV).

Isaac faced various conflicts and struggles during his lifetime, yet the blessing of God was upon him, evidenced in several ways: Abraham's servant found him the perfect wife; he received answers to his prayer, regarding

---

[2] Gen. 21:22. Abimelech's greeting to Abraham and Isaac are somewhat similar. It is interesting to note that on both occasions, Abimelech visited the patriarchs with Phicol, the commander of the army. Perhaps they possibly perceived Abraham and Isaac as a potential military threat (or a possible alliance). Such a notion is not without merit, considering the account given in Genesis, chapter fourteen: "When Abram heard that his relative had been taken prisoner, he assembled his **318 trained men**, born in his household, and they went in pursuit as far as Dan. **And he and his servants deployed against them by night**, attacked them, and pursued them as far as Hobah to the north of Damascus. He brought back all the goods and his relative Lot and his goods, as well as the women and the other people" (Gen. 14:14-16, HCSB). According to the account, Abram defeated Chedorlaomer, king of Elam, and the other three kings who fought by his side (Gen. 14:17). This was certainly no small feat.

Rebecca's barrenness; he prospered in all his endeavors; he received a divine visitation and renewal of the promises that God had made to his father; he formed a treaty of peace with the Philistines; and even his servants continually succeeded in digging wells and finding water. The life of Isaac teaches us a solemn truth: genuine worship is often born in the crucible of conflict and struggle. In fact, the very enmity manifested towards the promised offspring constitutes one of the fundamental principles of worship and the theme of our current study.

The Spiritual Nature of Enmity

> "**And I will put enmity between you and the woman**, and between your offspring and hers; he will crush your head, and you will strike his heel" (Gen. 3:15, NIV).

The enmity and contention Isaac encountered from the Philistines were symptomatic of an ancient hostility, whose roots go back to the Garden of Eden. Genesis recounts that when God judged the serpent for its role in the transgression of the woman, God himself placed perpetual "enmity" between the serpent and woman and their respective offspring. Enmity conveys a much deeper meaning than the natural abhorrence people often may feel towards snakes and vipers. Indeed, we would fail to understand the meaning of God's judgment on the serpent and how it correlates to redemption, unless we grasp the spiritual nature of enmity. First of all, the book of Revelation unveils the true identity of the serpent: "So the great dragon was thrown out—**the ancient serpent, who is called the Devil and Satan**, the one who deceives the whole world. He was thrown to earth, and his angels with him" (Rev. 12:9, HCSB).[3] Secondly, *offspring* does not merely refer to those who are naturally or physically born to either the serpent or the woman, but rather to their spiritual progeny. Cain and Abel were both offspring of the same woman, yet Cain rose up against his brother and murdered him. The first letter of John explains why he did so: "We should not be like Cain, who was of **the evil one** and murdered his brother. And why did he murder him? Because his own deeds were evil and his brother's righteous" (1 John 3:12, ESV). The *evil one* is a New Testament term for the devil.[4] By opening the door to sin, Cain allowed the evil one to take advantage of his anger and sway him to murder his own brother. Cain effectively showed himself to be the

---

[3] Rev. 20:2

[4] Matt. 13:19, 38-39; Luke 8:12. Jesus refers to the devil as the *wicked* or *evil one*.

spiritual offspring of the serpent. Thirdly, God is the one who places enmity between the serpent and the woman and their offspring. And the principal cause of enmity is the very favor and approval of the Lord. Let us consider, again, the story of Cain and Abel:

> In the course of time Cain brought to the Lord an offering of the fruit of the ground, and Abel also brought of the firstborn of his flock and of their fat portions. And the Lord had regard for Abel and his offering, but for Cain and his offering he had no regard. So Cain was very angry, and his face fell. The Lord said to Cain, "Why are you angry, and why has your face fallen? If you do well, will you not be accepted? And if you do not do well, sin is crouching at the door. Its desire is contrary to you, but you must rule over it" (Gen. 4:3-7, ESV).

We should not overlook the circumstances that prompted Cain to murder his brother. In fact, the spiritual nature of enmity becomes crystal clear in the context of worship. According to the account, the Lord regarded Abel's sacrifice, but not that of Cain. The Lord not only had regard for the choice of his sacrifice, but he also approved of his spiritual character. Abel's offering was not only an expression of worship, but a demonstration of his faith and righteousness.[5] Divine favor appointed Abel as the promised offspring.[6] Cain, on the other hand, offered the fruit of the ground, which suggests the works of his own hands. The Lord God did not regard Cain or his offering. Cain took it personal and became angry and dejected. But the Lord exhorted Cain: "If you do well, will you not be accepted? And if you do not do well, sin is crouching at the door. Its desire is contrary to you, but you must rule over it." Cain ignored God's counsel and instead followed his baser passions. Inviting his brother into the field, Cain raised his hand against Abel and murdered his brother (Gen. 4:8). The first homicide was committed because God had regard for a man and his expression of worship. Because of the murderous nature of the ancient serpent, and because the offspring of the woman is destined to crush his head, enmity will continue to fester and spread, until it eventually escalates in open war. Enmity is not only the spiritual divide between the serpent and the woman and their respective offspring, but also the battle line drawn between the hosts of heaven and the hordes of hell. Worship and the souls of men are the spoils of that war.

---

[5] Heb. 11:4

[6] Gen. 4:25. Note Eve's response when Seth is born.

When speaking of enmity and war, it should not be inferred that the offspring of the woman is merely on the defensive. Abel indeed struck the first blow to the serpent when he worshipped God and established a prophetic paradigm. Though the evil one used Cain to do his will and kill the promised offspring, but he could not stop the purpose of God. The prophet Isaiah writes: "The Lord advances like a warrior; He stirs up His zeal like a soldier. He shouts, He roars aloud, He prevails over His enemies" (Isa. 42:13, HCSB).[7] It was the Lord who mobilized the patriarchs and the people of Israel in the conquest of the promise land. Today, he is mobilizing his church in the conquest and recovery of the world through the preaching of the gospel. The Lord's purpose, expressed in the Abrahamic Covenant, is to bless all families and nations through his offspring (the Messiah).[8] This blessing is realized in the gospel, but it will not come to *complete* fruition until the promised offspring entirely crushes the head of the enemy and all families and nations are brought under his dominion.[9] Biblical history is indeed a history of worship, warfare, and conquest—a history that embraces both heaven and earth. In fact, an overwhelming amount of biblical data corroborates the premise that spiritual warfare is one of the supporting pillars of biblical worship.

Spiritual Incursions into the Promise Land

> Abram traveled through the land as far as the site of the great tree of Moreh at Shechem. At that time the Canaanites were in the land. The Lord appeared to Abram and said, "To your offspring I will give this land." So he built an altar there to the Lord, who had appeared to him (Gen. 12:6-7, NIV).

According to the account in Genesis, Abraham obeyed the voice of God and left his country for a land that the Lord would show him. One of Abraham's first recorded stops in the promise land was near "the great tree of Moreh at Shechem." The Lord appeared to Abraham and renewed his promise to give the land to his offspring. Abraham built an altar to the Lord in that place. As he ventured deeper into the land,

---

[7] Moses declares in his song: "The Lord is a man of war; The Lord is His name" (Exod. 15:3, NKJV).

[8] Gen. 12:3; 18:18; 22:18

[9] 1 Cor. 15:24-28

Abraham set up other altars where he would worship and call upon the name of the Lord. These altars represented a sort of spiritual *beachhead* within Canaan. The word, *beachhead*, typically refers to a military position, set up along any waterfront within enemy territory. Abraham's itinerary in the promise land was not an *excursion*, but a spiritual *incursion* into a demonically and politically hostile territory—a territory that his offspring would one day possess.

According to the above passage of Scripture, "at that time the Canaanites were in the land." The Canaanites did not worship the God of Abraham; instead, they served a pantheon of divinities.[10] The Scriptures identify all other the gods with demons.[11] Because the Canaanites worshipped these god-masquerading demons, the gates of hell were open and the evil one could freely operate throughout Canaan. Since the land was promised to Abraham and his offspring, Abraham set up several altars in various locations where he worshipped and called on the name of the Lord. Besides *Shechem*, he set up an altar near *Bethel*, one in *Hebron*; and one in the mountainous region of *Moriah*.[12] Isaac built an altar in the southern region, in a place called *Beersheba*.[13] Jacob built altars also in *Shechem* and in *Bethel*.[14] Altogether, the patriarchs built seven altars along the mountainous range of Canaan to the southern desert of the Negeb. As we have mentioned, these altars were important places of worship and devotion. Genesis recounts that four of the locations were places of divine revelation. Each altar was a significant memorial and served as a spiritual beachhead in a territory that had been polluted by every type of wickedness and demonic activity. The day would eventually come when the Lord would judge the Canaanite nations for their iniquity and give the land to the offspring of Abraham. But the conquest of the land began the moment Abraham responded to the calling of God.

---

[10] It would be a mistake to assert that only Abraham worshipped the Lord in the promise land, or that the territory was completely devoid of any virtue. We have the testimony of Melchizedek, king of Salem (i.e., Jerusalem), who was also "the priest of God Most High" (Gen. 14:18, NKJV); and also, that of Abimelech, king of Gerar (Gen. 20:3-6). Even Abraham discovered to his surprise, there were those who feared God among the Philistines (Gen. 20:11).

[11] Lev. 17:7; Deut. 32:17; Ps. 106:34-37; 1 Cor. 10:20

[12] Gen. 12:6-8; 13:18; 22:2

[13] Gen. 26:23-25

[14] Gen. 33:18-20; 35:1, 14-15

Mount Sinai and the Wilderness Journeys

> "For ask now of the days that are past, which were before you, since the day that God created man on the earth, and ask from one end of heaven to the other, whether such a great thing as this has ever happened or was ever heard of. Did any people ever hear the voice of a god speaking out of the midst of the fire, as you have heard, and still live? Or has any god ever attempted to go and take a nation for himself from the midst of another nation, **by trials, by signs, by wonders, and by war**, by a mighty hand and an outstretched arm, and by great deeds of terror, all of which the Lord your God did for you in Egypt before your eyes?" (Deut. 4:32-34, ESV).

The Lord sent Moses to deliver the people of Israel out of the hands of the Egyptians and bring them back to the very mountain where he had spoken to him from the burning bush, to serve and worship him. Once the covenant was confirmed between the Lord and his people, Moses would then lead the people to the promise land. But before Moses could complete his mission, he would encounter along the way, considerable conflicts, struggles, and even war. When Moses and his brother Aaron returned to Egypt, their mission immediately unleashed a sequence of conflicts: Moses met with defiance and resistance from Pharaoh; the magicians of Egypt also opposed him, even simulating some of his miraculous signs; and the people of Israel encountered a battle *en route* to Mount Sinai and other campaigns during their journey in the wilderness. But perhaps more surprising were the conflicts and struggles Moses encountered among his own people. The people continuously relapsed into unbelief, rebellion, idolatry, and other heathen practices. One of the worst incidents occurred at Mount Sinai, the very place where Israel was supposed to worship and serve God. In the third month of their journey, Moses brought Israel to the foot of the mountain of God. The Lord then called Moses to the mountain, where he spent over month, receiving from God, the stone tablets with the covenant laws engraved on them, and other ordinances and directives. Though the people initially promised to observe the covenant, which had been ratified with the sprinkling of sacrificial blood,[15] attitudes and behavior dramatically changed during Moses' absence.

---

[15] Exod. 24:7-8

> When the people saw that Moses delayed to come down from the mountain, the people gathered themselves together to Aaron and said to him, "Up, make us gods who shall go before us. As for this Moses, the man who brought us up out of the land of Egypt, we do not know what has become of him." So Aaron said to them, "Take off the rings of gold that are in the ears of your wives, your sons, and your daughters, and bring them to me." So all the people took off the rings of gold that were in their ears and brought them to Aaron. And he received the gold from their hand and fashioned it with a graving tool and made a golden calf. And they said, "These are your gods, O Israel, who brought you up out of the land of Egypt!" When Aaron saw this, he built an altar before it. And Aaron made a proclamation and said, "Tomorrow shall be a feast to the Lord" (Exod. 32:1-5, ESV).

Apparently, the task of getting the people of Israel out of Egypt had been far easier than getting Egypt out of the people. Because of Moses' extended absence, the people began acting just like the Egyptians and the surrounding nations. They wanted an image of the One who shrouded himself in thick clouds of smoke and fire on the summit of the mountain. Aaron made for them, a molten image of a calf; he even built an altar for the image. The following morning, the people began to debase themselves:

> "And they rose up early the next day and offered burnt offerings and brought peace offerings. And the people sat down to eat and drink and rose up to play" (Exod. 32:6, ESV).

Their idolatrous actions were not only a direct violation of the covenant and a deplorable act against a holy God, the people had also debased themselves before their enemies: "Moses saw that the people were running wild and that Aaron had let them get out of control and so become a laughingstock to their enemies" (Exod. 32:25, NIV). The Lord had clearly commanded the people not to make an image of anything that is in heaven or on the earth—including their own God—to bow down and worship it. He wanted his people to trust and believe in him, the invisible God who hides himself in columns of thick smoke. But the people wanted, instead, something more tangible and even recognizable. The Egyptians had idols of their deities; thanks to Aaron, Israel now had a golden calf. The people of Israel had been called to be God's chosen people, but many of them still thought and acted like their former lords and masters in Egypt. Moses prayed and interceded on behalf of the people, but the Lord responded:

> "Whoever has sinned against me, I will blot out of my book. But now go, lead the people to the place about which I have spoken to you; behold, my angel shall go before you. Nevertheless, in the day when I visit, I will visit their sin upon them." Then the Lord sent a plague on the people, because they made the calf, the one that Aaron made (Exod. 32:33-35, ESV).

The Lord promised to send his angel, but he would not go himself, lest he consume the people in his wrath. But Moses pleaded that God would not let them depart without his presence. The Lord granted Moses' request and promised that his presence would accompany them.[16] After revealing his glory to Moses, the Lord instructed him to carve new tablets of stone (Moses had broken the former ones in his anger over the calf). The Lord then renewed the covenant and wrote the Ten Commandments on the new tablets. Soon after, the construction project of the tabernacle commenced. Moses took from the people a voluntary offering of all the material necessary for the sanctuary. Bezalel and Aholiab, whom the Lord had called by name, and their fellow artisans began to build the tabernacle, manufacture all its furnishings, and weave and make the special garments for the priesthood. When the tabernacle was set up as the Lord had commanded, a cloud covered the tent of meeting, and the resplendent presence of the Lord filled the tabernacle (Exod. 40:34). Whenever the cloud lifted from the tabernacle, Moses and the people of Israel would set out again on their journey.

As Moses led the people towards the promise land, he ran into many more conflicts and struggles. One of these conflicts had devastating consequences on Israel and their destiny. When the people approached the promise land, the Lord ordered Moses to send twelve men to explore or spy out the land of Canaan (Nu. 13:2). When the men returned, they spoke well of the land, even showing Moses, Aaron, and the people some of the fruit they had gathered. However, ten of the men discouraged the people with bad reports of large and fortified cities, and of the giants in the land.[17] Caleb, instead, encouraged the people to go in at once and take the land. But the people responded to the bad accounts; they wept and complained that their

---

[16] Exod. 33:12-17
[17] Num. 13:28-33

children would perish by the sword of their enemies. Joshua, son of Nun, and Caleb, whom both were among the twelve, tore their clothes and sought to encourage the people to take the land and to not fear, because the Lord was with them. But the people were ready to stone the two men. Suddenly, the Lord's glory appeared at the tent of meeting. The Lord was extremely angry and spoke to Moses that he was ready to strike and destroy the people with a pestilence and make a new nation of Moses. But Moses, being a prophet and a man of God, interceded once again for the people. And though the Lord pardoned the people, he also made a solemn and severe promise:

> "Not one of you will enter the land I swore with uplifted hand to make your home, except Caleb son of Jephunneh and Joshua son of Nun. As for your children that you said would be taken as plunder, I will bring them in to enjoy the land you have rejected. But as for you, your bodies will fall in this wilderness. Your children will be shepherds here for forty years, suffering for your unfaithfulness, until the last of your bodies lies in the wilderness. For forty years—one year for each of the forty days you explored the land—you will suffer for your sins and know what it is like to have me against you.' I, the Lord, have spoken, and I will surely do these things to this whole wicked community, which has banded together against me. They will meet their end in this wilderness; here they will die" (Nu. 14:30-35, NIV).

When forty years had passed, the Lord raised up Joshua son of Nun to lead the people into the promise land. Canaan, however, would not be a cakewalk, but a conquest. Israel would have to face a series of battles. The land needed to be purged of its wicked inhabitants; of all its idols and foreign gods; and of its promiscuous practices. When the Lord had renewed the covenant for a second time, after the golden calf incident, he gave more explicit instructions to Israel, regarding Canaan:

> "Observe what I command you this day. Behold, I am driving out from before you the Amorite and the Canaanite and the Hittite and the Perizzite and the Hivite and the Jebusite. Take heed to yourself, lest you make a covenant with the inhabitants of the land where you are going, lest it be a snare in your midst. But you shall destroy their altars, break their sacred pillars, and cut down their wooden images (for you shall worship no other god, for the Lord, whose name is

> Jealous, is a jealous God), lest you make a covenant with the inhabitants of the land, and they play the harlot with their gods and make sacrifice to their gods, and one of them invites you and you eat of his sacrifice, and you take of his daughters for your sons, and his daughters play the harlot with their gods and make your sons play the harlot with their gods" (Exod. 34:11-16, NKJV).

The people of Israel were to utterly destroy all artifacts of veneration and worship, and institute the worship of Yahweh throughout the land. There could be no treaty or compromise with the people. The Lord God was sending his people into the promise land to wage a war against the Canaanites and their idolatry and promiscuity. In essence, Israel was sent to crush the serpent's head.

Invasion and Conquest of the Land

One of the first battles Israel engaged in was against the city of Jericho. Joshua was near Jericho, perhaps contemplating how they might take the city. The city presented itself as a formidable stronghold with impregnable walls. Joshua had previously sent two men to spy out the land and the ominous city before they had even crossed the Jordan. The spies had come back with a good report: "The Lord has surely given the whole land into our hands; all the people are melting in fear because of us" (Josh. 2:24, NIV). Even so, the city walls appeared to be an insurmountable barrier to their success. Suddenly, a man with an unsheathed sword appeared before Joshua.

> When Joshua was by Jericho, he lifted up his eyes and looked, and behold, a man was standing before him with his drawn sword in his hand. And Joshua went to him and said to him, "Are you for us, or for our adversaries?" And he said, "No; but I am the commander of the army of the Lord. Now I have come." And Joshua fell on his face to the earth and worshiped and said to him, "What does my lord say to his servant?" And the commander of the Lord's army said to Joshua, "Take off your sandals from your feet, for the place where you are standing is holy." And Joshua did so (Josh. 5:13-15, ESV).

Upon learning the man was commander of the Lord's army, Joshua fell on his face in worship, and removed his sandals. The Lord gave Joshua instructions how to take the city (Josh. 6:2-5). But it was worship that first set the stage for victory. The very presence of the commander of the

Lord's army with drawn sword underscores the spiritual nature of the conquest of the land and the battle Israel was about to undertake. The passage also intimates another particularly important principle, regarding the conquest. The commander of the Lord's army was not there to take sides with Israel or their adversaries, but to command the Lord's army and do his will. In short, it was the Lord who was directing the conquest, and whoever was on his side was the victor. When David fought against Goliath, he restated in unambiguous terms, this important principle:

> David said to the Philistine: "You come against me with a dagger, spear, and sword, but I come against you in the name of Yahweh of Hosts, the God of Israel's armies—you have defied Him. Today, the Lord will hand you over to me. Today, I'll strike you down, cut your head off, and give the corpse of the Philistine camp to the birds of the sky and the creatures of the earth. Then all the world will know that Israel has a God, and this whole assembly will know that it is not by sword or by spear that the Lord saves, **for the battle is the Lord's**. He will hand you over to us" (1 Sam. 17:45-47, HCSB).

The second book of Chronicles recounts the time an immense army of Moabites, Ammonites, and some Meunites mobilized against Judah and King Jehoshaphat. As this massive army approached their territory, the king proclaimed a fast for Judah. All the people came from the cities and gathered at the temple to seek the Lord. The Spirit of the Lord came upon Jahaziel (a descendant of Asaph), and he prophesied:

> And he said, "Listen carefully, all Judah and you inhabitants of Jerusalem, and King Jehoshaphat. This is what the Lord says: 'Do not be discouraged because of this vast number, **for the battle is not yours, but God's**. Tomorrow, go down against them. You will see them coming up the Ascent of Ziz, and you will find them at the end of the valley facing the Wilderness of Jeruel. **You do not have to fight this battle**. Position yourselves, stand still, and see the salvation of the Lord. He is with you, Judah and Jerusalem. Do not be afraid or discouraged. Tomorrow, go out to face them, for Yahweh is with you'" (2 Chron. 20:15-17, HCSB).

Jehoshaphat and the people Judah believed the word of the Lord, they even appointed singers to go before the army with songs of praise. "The moment they began their shouts and praises, the Lord set an ambush against the

Ammonites, Moabites, and the inhabitants of Mount Seir who came to fight against Judah, and they were defeated" (2 Chron. 20:22, HCSB). Again, we see the battle is the Lord's, and the victors are those who are on his side.

Returning to our account, the book of Joshua records Israel's systematic conquest of much of the promised territory.[18] Even though much of the land had been taken, the Lord pointed out to an elderly Joshua that there was still more land that needed to be conquered. The Lord affirmed to Joshua, "I will drive them out before the Israelites, only distribute the land as an inheritance for Israel, as I have commanded you" (Josh. 13:6, HCSB). Reuben, Gad, and half the tribe of Manasseh had already received as their inheritance, the land east of the Jordan.[19] Therefore, Joshua divided by lots the land of Canaan among the remaining nine tribes[20] and the other half of the tribe of Manasseh. Each tribe was to enter into its own inheritance and complete the conquest by driving out the remaining inhabitants. Ironically, Israel had managed to conquer the most fortified city in the land of Canaan, but they were unable to drive out the remaining inhabitants from some of the strongholds within territories of their inheritance. The book of Judges explains why:

> The Angel of the Lord went up from Gilgal to Bochim and said, "I brought you out of Egypt and led you into the land I had promised your fathers. I also said: I will never break My covenant with you. You are not to make a covenant with the people who are living in this land, and you are to tear down their altars. **But you have not obeyed Me**. What is this you have done? Therefore, I now say: I will not drive out these people before you. They will be a thorn in your sides, and their gods will be a trap for you." When the Angel of the Lord had spoken these words to all the Israelites, the people wept loudly. So they named that place Bochim and offered sacrifices there to the Lord (Judg. 2:1-5, HCSB).

The angel of the Lord declared that he had brought the people out of Egypt and led them to the promise land. He promised that he would never break his covenant with his people. He instructed them not to make treaties with the inhabitants of the land, but to utterly destroy all

---

[18] Josh. 8:1-9:2; 10:1-11:23

[19] Josh. 13:8

[20] The tribe of Joseph was counted for two tribes, Manasseh and Ephraim.

their places of worship and devotion.[21] The angel of the Lord asks the people, "What is this you have done?" The question is rhetorical because the answer is obviously self-evident: The people had failed to obey the word of the Lord. The Lord could not fully honor a covenant while it was being violated by his own people. To do so would be to condone their treaties with the enemies of God and their idolatrous behavior. The angel of the Lord further declared that he would not drive out the remaining nations; instead, they would be "a thorn in your sides, and their gods will be a trap for you."

There is yet another reason why the Lord did not give Israel immediate victory over all the enemy-nations dwelling in Canaan. The book of Judges further explains:

> **These are the nations the Lord left in order to test Israel, since the Israelites had fought none of these in any of the wars with Canaan. This was to teach the future generations of Israelites how to fight in battle, especially those who had not fought before**. These nations included the five rulers of the Philistines and all of the Canaanites, the Sidonians, and the Hivites who lived in the Lebanese mountains from Mount Baal-hermon as far as the entrance to Hamath. **The Lord left them to test Israel, to determine if they would keep the Lord's commands, He had given their fathers through Moses**. But they settled among the Canaanites, Hittites, Amorites, Perizzites, Hivites, and Jebusites. The Israelites took their daughters as wives for themselves, gave their own daughters to their sons, and worshipped their god. (Judg. 3:1-6, HCSB).

According to the passage, the Lord left some of the nations in Canaan to teach future generations how to fight and do warfare. He also wanted to test and see if his people would indeed obey his commandments given to them through Moses. Unfortunately, rather than fight for their inheritance and obey the word of God, the people *compromised*, *conformed*, and even *integrated* with the inhabitants and their culture of idolatry. In the process, many in Israel lost their own spiritual, ethical, and cultural identity.

---

[21] Deut. 7:5; 12:3

Spiritual Strongholds in the Promise Land

The Scriptures recount the continual conflict and struggle between light and darkness, truth and falsehood, the altar of the Lord and that of Baal, and between the hosts of heaven and the hordes of hell. The book of Judges especially reveals how God's people and the promise land were caught in the middle of this ongoing spiritual war. Worship has been, is, and will always be the deciding factor in who wins or loses each battle. Indeed, the outcome of spiritual warfare is always decided at the altar of God. The book of Judges narrates the early history of Israel as the people settled into the promise land. It also recounts the vicious cycle of *decline*, *dominance*, and *deliverance*: The people would stray from the covenant, serve, and worship foreign gods, and end up being subjugated and oppressed by an enemy. But then God would be merciful and raise up a judge or deliverer who would set the people free from their oppressors. In one such occasion, Israel was severely oppressed by the Midianite people. God chose a man named, Gideon, to liberate his people. Even before Gideon was called to be a leader, he already showed that he knew how to resist the enemy: "Gideon threshed wheat by the winepress, to hide it from the Midianites" (Judg. 6:11, KJV). But more importantly, Gideon knew how to worship the Lord. In the former chapter, we discussed how Gideon prepared an offering of goat's meat, unleavened bread, and broth and brought it to the angel. Gideon followed the angel's instructions and placed the meat and unleavened bread on a rock and poured the broth over them. When the angel touched the rock with his staff, fire came from the rock and burned up the offering. When the angel suddenly disappeared, Gideon became fearful that he would die because had seen the Lord's face. But then the Lord spoke and reassured him that he would not die. "Then Gideon built an altar there to the Lord and called it, The Lord Is Peace. To this day it still stands at Ophrah, which belongs to the Abiezrites" (Judg. 6:24, ESV).

The Lord instructed Gideon to begin by destroying the spiritual strongholds of the enemy in their midst—the altar of Baal and the Asherah pole (i.e., a wooden pole or tree, dedicated to the goddess, Asherah).[22] Both the altar of Baal and the Asherah pole were in direct violation of the commandments of the Lord:

---

[22] Deut. 16:21

> Be careful not to make a treaty with the inhabitants of the land that you are going to enter; otherwise, they will become a snare among you. Instead, you must tear down their altars, smash their sacred pillars, and chop down their Asherah poles. You are never to bow down to another god because Yahweh, being jealous by nature, is a jealous God (Exod. 34:12-14, HCSB).

The Lord further instructed Gideon, "and build an altar to the Lord your God **on the top of the stronghold**[23] here, with stones laid in due order. Then take the second bull and offer it as a burnt offering with the wood of the Asherah that you shall cut down" (Judg. 6:26, ESV). Several Bible commentaries believe that the stronghold in this passage refers to the town of Ophrah as a stronghold or place of refuge. Strongholds were vital and strategic positions and places of security and defense in times of conflict and war. One thing is certain: the altar of Baal and the Asherah pole constituted a *demonic* stronghold in the land. Both needed to be destroyed and the worship of God restored before Israel could achieve victory. Concerning spiritual strongholds, Apostle Paul writes:

> For though we live in the world, we do not wage war as the world does. The weapons we fight with are not the weapons of the world. **On the contrary, they have divine power to demolish strongholds**. We demolish arguments and every pretension that sets itself up against the knowledge of God, and we take captive every thought to make it obedient to Christ (2 Cor. 10:3-5, NIV).

Gideon followed the Lord's instructions during the night, for fear of the people. He destroyed the altar and cut down the Asherah pole. He then erected an altar to the Lord—a divinely-ordained stronghold—and used the wood of the Asherah pole to offer up a burnt offering to the God of Israel. This, of course, was perceived as a hostile act and an open challenge to those who venerated Baal. Gideon's actions angered many of those who were caught in the spiritual web of the enemy. But it also stirred up the hearts of those who truly worshipped God and who wanted to throw off the yoke of Midianite oppression. Gideon went on to lead a small band of people who vanquished an enormous host of enemies with the help and strength of the Lord. Victory over the

---

[23] Heb. מָעוֹז, *maoz* or *mauz, a place or means of safety, protection* [e.g., 2 Sam. 22:33; Ps. 31:2; Prov. 10:29; Isa. 23:14; Jer. 16:19, etc.].

Midianites, however, began with a small meal offering, placed on a rock before to the angel of the Lord; an altar built to worship to the God of peace; the destruction of the enemy's stronghold; and the building of a new altar to the Lord, on the very spot where Baal and Asherah had previously been worshipped. Victory in any spiritual conflict or struggle always begins with worship.

CHAPTER 7

The Pillar of Warfare

(The Conflict of Biblical Worship)

Part Two

When the people of Ashdod got up early the next morning, there was Dagon, fallen with his face to the ground before the ark of the Lord. So they took Dagon and returned him to his place. But when they got up early the next morning, there was Dagon, fallen with his face to the ground before the ark of the Lord. This time, both Dagon's head and the palms of his hands were broken off and lying on the threshold. Only Dagon's torso remained. That is why, to this day, the priests of Dagon and everyone who enters the temple of Dagon in Ashdod do not step on Dagon's threshold. The Lord's hand was heavy on the people of Ashdod, terrorizing and afflicting the people of Ashdod and its territory with tumors (1 Sam. 5:3-6, HCSB).

During the life of the prophet Samuel, the era of judges transitioned to a time when kings began to reign over the people of Israel. Notwithstanding the change, the old battle between the demon-gods of Canaan and the worship of the one true God continued into this new age. In fact, worship has always been the deciding factor in the outcome of Israel's political and geographic conflicts. According to the first book of Samuel, shortly before Israel chose her first king, Israel did not enjoy a healthy, spiritual panorama. Idolatry flourished among the people. The sons of Israel's High Priest, Eli, were wicked. Moreover, the Philistines oppressed the people and eventually moved to make war against them. In their first battle, Israel lost almost 4,000 men. The elders decided to bring in their midst the ark of the covenant, presuming that God would give them the victory. Instead of victory, Israel suffered devastating losses: They lost the battle; they lost 30,000 foot-soldiers; and they lost the ark to their enemy.

The Philistines brought the ark back to Ashdod, one of their principal cities, and placed it in the temple of Dagon, their god. Even though the Lord had not helped Israel in the battle, he still sent the Philistines a clear message who was indeed God. When the people of Ashdod rose early in the morning, they found that the statue of Dagon, fallen and lying face down before the ark of the Lord. They put the statue back in its place, but the next morning, they found it, once again, lying face down before the ark, only this time its head and hands were cut off and left lying on the threshold of the temple. But the Lord not only subjugated and destroyed the idol of Dagon, he also grievously afflicted the people of Ashdod and their territories with tumors. The Philistines attempted to resolve the problem by moving the ark to the city of Gath, but even there, the people were afflicted with tumors. According to the account, the Philistines attempted to move the ark to the city of Ekron, but the people cried out for fear of death. Subsequently, the Philistine leaders sought advice from their priests and diviners, who instructed them to make five gold tumors and five gold mice—to represent the five rulers of the Philistines, the tumors that afflicted the people, and the mice that devastated the land—and place them in a box as a restitution offering.[1] Then they were to send the ark and the box of gold tumors and mice back to Israel on a new cart, drawn by two cows. The incident with the ark teaches us about the spiritual nature of the war between Israel and the Philistines; beyond the number of soldiers, weaponry, and war strategies is the all-important question of covenant and worship. In fact, the ark represented both the covenant and presence of God. Israel had lost the ark in battle because they continually violated the covenant through idolatry. The Philistines could not keep the ark because they worshipped Dagon and because they had not entered into any covenant with God. The presence of God only dwells among those who observe his covenant and worship only him.

The compiled histories of the books of Kings and Chronicles continue to recount the ongoing and unremitting war between the God of Israel and the gods of Canaan. King David, unlike Saul, his predecessor, was wholly devoted to the Lord.[2] The kingdom was consolidated under his rule and leadership. Israel's enemies were put down as its territories greatly increased.

---

[1] 1 Sam. 6:2-6
[2] 1 Sam. 13:14

David also brought the ark of the covenant to Jerusalem and placed it in a tent he had especially erected for it. He also organized worship services in both the tent in Jerusalem and the tabernacle of the Lord, set up in the high place of Gibeon (1 Chr. 16:37-39). David even drafted a plan and set aside material for the construction of a future temple in Jerusalem. After the reign of David, Solomon, his son, sat on the throne. The Lord greatly blessed him with wisdom and riches. It was Solomon who built a house for the Lord. Under his leadership, the kingdom of Israel entered a *golden age* of expansion and prosperity. Unfortunately, Solomon disobeyed the commandment of the Lord and intermarried with many foreign women. They caused him to stray from the ardent devotion he had for the Lord God in his youth. Solomon not only condoned the altars of foreign gods in Jerusalem, but he also helped built them.

> At that time, Solomon built a high place for Chemosh, the detestable idol of Moab, and for Milcom, the detestable idol of the Ammonites, on the hill across from Jerusalem. He did the same for all his foreign wives, who were burning incense and offering sacrifices to their gods (1 Kgs. 11:7-8, HCSB).

Solomon's actions greatly angered the Lord. The Lord spoke to Solomon that ten of the tribes of the kingdom would be torn from the hands of his son. The Lord also raised up enemies who opposed him. When Solomon died, his son, Rehoboam, sat on the throne and reigned over Israel. But discontent soon arose among the people and the kingdom divided. Ten tribes went with Jeroboam, but two tribes remained loyal to Rehoboam. The schism almost caused a civil war, until the prophet, Shemaiah rose up and declared the word of the Lord to Rehoboam and the people that they were not to fight against their brothers, but return to their homes, for the schism was according to the Lord's design (1 Kgs.12:24).

The Kingdom of Israel

The ten tribes of Israel followed their new king, Jeroboam, and created a new and separate kingdom. But Jeroboam feared the people would go to Jerusalem to worship, reconcile with king Rehoboam and the tribes of Judah and Benjamin, and then kill him. Instead of trusting the Lord and the prophetic word that had been given through Shemaiah, Jeroboam initiated his own religion. He did not merely give the people one of the gods of the Canaanites; instead, he manipulated the people's faith and heritage and offered them a corrupt and perverted version of the one true God:

> So the king sought advice. Then he made two golden calves, and he said to the people, "Going to Jerusalem is too difficult for you. Israel, here is your God who brought you out of the land of Egypt." He set up one in Bethel, and put the other in Dan. This led to sin; the people walked in procession before one of the calves all the way to Dan (1 King 12:28-30, HCSB).

Because of its syncretistic and deceptive character, the unworthy image of God was worse than the false gods of the Canaanites and surrounding nations. It possessed some element of truth, even offering familiar points of reference (e.g., Bethel and Dan[3]); nonetheless, it was a pure falsehood that three open the floodgates to moral license and to the enemy. Jeroboam disregarded the word of the Lord and lowered the spiritual standards of the people under his rule. He made his own priesthood, built shrines, and offered sacrifices and burned incense. He even created special holidays that were to be celebrated on different calendar days than the feasts celebrated by Judah.[4] In short, Jeroboam offered his kingdom a complete package deal, one that disconnected the people from their true heritage and identity. Jeroboam's sin, however, would not go unchallenged. A prophet from Judah traveled all the way to Bethel and confronted the king in his madness:

> The man of God cried out against the altar by a revelation from the Lord: "Altar, altar, this is what the Lord says, 'A son will be born to the house of David, named Josiah, and he will sacrifice on you the priests of the high places who are burning incense on you. Human bones will be burned on you.'" He gave a sign that day. He said, "This is the sign that the Lord has spoken: 'The altar will now be ripped apart, and the ashes that are on it will be poured out'" (1 Kgs. 13:2-3, HCSB).

The king stretched forth his arm and commanded his men to arrest the prophet; but the Lord struck Jeroboam's hand with a form of paralysis. The altar suddenly broke apart, and the ashes poured out. The king asked the prophet to pray to the Lord that his hand might be restored. When the

---

[3] Gen. 28:19; Jdgs. 18:30

[4] 1 Kgs. 12:31-33

prophet prayed, Jeroboam's hand was immediately healed. Regrettably, he did not repent of his sin. Jeroboam's family and descendants would be wiped out, according to the word of the Lord, but his name would live on in ignominy for generations to come. In fact, he would become the moral standard—an extremely low one, indeed—against which the other kings of Israel would be measured and identified.[5]

Ironically, the Lord who had instructed his people to drive out the Canaanites from the land and to destroy all their altars and objects of devotion, eventually fought against his own people, removing them from the promise land. They had continuously violated the covenant, defying every sacred principle of worship. The second book of Kings reports:

> So they left all the commandments of the Lord their God, made for themselves a molded image *and* two calves, made a wooden image and worshiped all the host of heaven, and served Baal. And they caused their sons and daughters to pass through the fire, practiced witchcraft and soothsaying, and sold themselves to do evil in the sight of the Lord, to provoke Him to anger. Therefore the Lord was very angry with Israel, and removed them from His sight; there was none left but the tribe of Judah alone (2 Kgs. 17:16-18, NKJV).

The Assyrians invaded the land and besieged Samaria. After three years, they captured the city and deported the Israelites to distant lands (circa 722-721 B.C.).[6]

The Kingdom of Judah

Despite the division and loss of ten tribes, the kingdom of Judah initially prospered under the rule of Rehoboam. The second book of Chronicles explains:

> Those from every tribe of Israel who set their hearts on seeking the Lord, the God of Israel, followed the Levites to Jerusalem to offer sacrifices to the Lord, the God of their ancestors. They strengthened the kingdom of Judah and supported Rehoboam son of Solomon three years, following the ways of David and Solomon during this time (2 Chron. 11:16-17, NIV).

Rehoboam was the legitimate heir to the throne of David, but the strength and support of his kingdom came from the other tribes of Israel that followed

---

[5] 1 Kgs. 15:33-34; 16:1-2, 18-19, 25-26, 30-31; 22:51-52; 2 Kgs. 3:1-3; 10:29, 31; 13:1-2, 6, 10-11; 14:23-24; 15:8-9, 17-18, 23-24, 27-28; 17:22

[6] 2 Kgs. 17:1-6

the Levites to Jerusalem to worship the Lord. Regrettably, this pattern of worship and celebration was short lived—three years to be exact. It is written: "After Rehoboam's position as king was established and he had become strong, he and all Israel with him abandoned the law of the Lord" (2 Chron. 12:1, NIV). Rehoboam was not the only one guilty of departing from the law of the Lord. Many in Judah followed the idolatrous and promiscuous practices of the former inhabitants of the land:

> Judah did what was evil in the Lord's eyes. They provoked Him to jealous anger more than all that their ancestors had done with the sins they committed. They also built for themselves high places, sacred pillars, and Asherah poles on every high hill and under every green tree; there were even male cult prostitutes in the land. They imitated all the detestable practices of the nations the Lord had dispossessed before the Israelites (1 Kgs. 14:22-24, HCSB).

In the fifth year of Rehoboam, Shishak king of Egypt attacked Jerusalem. He also captured the fortified cities of Judah. The prophet Shemaiah declared to Rehoboam and the leaders of Judah the Lord had forsaken them because they had forsaken the Lord. The leaders and the king responded to the prophetic word and humbled themselves, acknowledging that the Lord was just (2 Chron. 12:6). Seeing they had humbled themselves, the Lord spoke again, through the mouth of Shemaiah, that he would not destroy Jerusalem by Shishak's hand. Shishak did leave Jerusalem, but only after he plundered the treasures of the temple and of the king's palace. Rehoboam once again, secured his throne. Yet, despite all the Lord had done, his heart was not right before the Lord. He continued to do evil because he never committed himself to seek the Lord (2 Chron. 12:14).

Idolatry quickly tarnished the golden age of the kingdom (the kingdom of Judah literally began using bronze instead of gold[7]). When the kingdom divided, war and conflict plagued both kingdoms. They often made war with each other, destroying life and wasting time, energy, and resources, instead of going against their common enemy—the Canaanites and their false gods. The Lord sent his prophets to speak to the people and to their leaders. The prophets challenged them for their gross negligence of the covenant and violation of the law of the Lord, but for the most, their

---

[7] 1 Kgs. 14:25-28; 2 Chron. 12:9-10. Rehoboam had bronze shields made to replace the gold shields that Shishak had carried away.

warnings went unheeded. The people continued to provoke the Lord to anger, until judgment befell both kingdoms. As we discussed earlier, Samaria and the kingdom of Israel fell to the Assyrians; the people were deported to foreign lands (circa 722-721 B.C.). Circa a hundred and thirty-six years later, the Babylonians besieged and conquered Jerusalem and the kingdom of Judah, deporting the people to their own country (the process of deportation lasted between 597-581 B.C.). The deportation of Judah was by no means the end of the story for the Jewish people and the promise land (or even that of spiritual warfare). After seventy years, the Lord caused a remnant of his people to return to Judah from exile. The people rebuilt both the house of God and the city of Jerusalem. There would be, of course, centuries of continued conflict and struggle. Foreign powers would dominate the land and the people. Some would even attempt to take control of temple worship (e.g., Antiochus IV Epiphanes; Caius Caesar). But in the midst of a Roman occupation, the Messiah would suddenly appear and challenge the devil's control over the world.

The Invisible War

We have briefly discussed some of the conflicts and struggles of the patriarchs and the people of Israel, chronicled in the Scriptures. Behind most these, rages an invisible war. The book of Daniel provides a revelatory glimpse into this spiritual and ongoing battle. According to the account, Daniel had been mourning and praying twenty-one days for his people. During those days, he had only eaten a very meager diet that reflected his broken heart, when suddenly, a man dressed in white linen and wearing a belt of pure gold appeared before Daniel. The prophet colorfully describes the likeness of this man:

> "His body was like beryl, his face like the appearance of lightning, his eyes like torches of fire, his arms and feet like burnished bronze in color, and the sound of his words like the voice of a multitude" (Dan. 10:6, NKJV).

Trembling and losing all physical strength, Daniel fell in a deep sleep. The man robed in white linen set the prophet on his hands and knees and spoke words of comfort:

> "O Daniel, man greatly beloved, understand the words that I speak to you, and stand upright, for I have now been sent to you." While he was speaking this word to me, I stood trembling. Then

> he said to me, "Do not fear, Daniel, for from the first day that you set your heart to understand, and to humble yourself before your God, your words were heard; and I have come because of your words. **But the prince of the kingdom of Persia withstood me twenty-one days; and behold, Michael, one of the chief princes, came to help me, for I had been left alone there with the kings of Persia**. Now I have come to make you understand what will happen to your people in the latter days, for the vision *refers* to *many* days yet *to come*."
>
> Then he said, "Do you know why I have come to you? **And now I must return to fight with the prince of Persia; and when I have gone forth, indeed the prince of Greece will come**. But I will tell you what is noted in the Scripture of Truth. (No one upholds me against these, except Michael your prince" (Dan. 10:11-14, 20-21, NKJV).

This messenger with human likeness, and yet so dissimilar, had been sent to Daniel with the task of revealing to him what would happen to his people in the latter days. The messenger, however, had encountered resistance from the "prince of the kingdom of Persia for twenty-one days, but "Michael, one of the chief princes" had come to help him. The messenger further informed Daniel that he was going to "return to fight against the prince of Persia." Since the messenger is clearly an angelic being, and Michael is also referred to as an archangel,[8] it is not difficult to understand the spiritual and prophetic nature of the revelation: the man in linen not only gives Daniel (and those who read his writings) prophetic insight of events, regarding his own people, he also offers a glimpse of an unseen war that rages in the spiritual realm, the outcome of which impacts and sway the major political powers of this world.

The Apostle Paul sheds even more light on the nature of this invisible war. In his letter to the Ephesians, he writes that believers are to put on the full armor of God so that they may resist and fight against the tactics of an invisible enemy: "For we do not wrestle against flesh and blood, but against the rulers, against the authorities, against the cosmic powers over this present darkness, against the spiritual forces of evil in the heavenly places" (Eph. 6:12, ESV).[9] Paul affirms that Christ has taken captive, the invisible powers, "When **He had disarmed the rulers and authorities**

---

[8] Jude 1:9; Rev. 12:7

[9] Eph. 3:10; Col. 2:15

[those supernatural forces of evil operating against us], He made a public example of them [exhibiting them as captives in His triumphal procession], having triumphed over them through the cross" (Col. 2:15, AMP). Even though these invisible rulers and authorities of darkness have been disarmed, this does not mean they will not attempt to deceive and make us believe they are still armed and powerful. This is why we must arm ourselves with the weapons of God and take authority over the enemy (we will discuss our spiritual weapons towards the end of the study).

The Revelation of War and Worship

Revelation, like no other book in the Bible, pulls back the curtains and allows the reader to understand the spiritual war that rages in heaven and earth. The principal theme of Revelation is the coming of the Lord and the in-breaking of the kingdom of God on earth (Rev. 11:15). Within context of this theme, worship and war interact and permeate the pages of Revelation. All types of imagery, symbolism, and specific key words are employed which relate to these two parallel subjects. While there are far too many examples to mention, suffice it to point out a few key examples for the sake of our study. First of all, Revelation reveals that worship is the general atmosphere of heaven. Beginning in chapter four, John has a vision of the throne room, in which he sees the awesome beauty of the one who is seated on the throne. Four creatures are standing like sentinels at the four corners of the throne, continually declaring the holiness of God. In his vision, John also sees twenty-four elders who appear to be heavenly worship-leaders. Each time the four creatures sound off their praise, the elders prostrate in worship before God, casting down their crowns and extolling the attributes of God.

John suddenly sees the one who is seated on the throne, holding in his right hand, a scroll with seven seals. In a loud voice and in the hearing of every sentient creature, a mighty angel proclaims: "Who is worthy to open the scroll and break its seals?" (Rev. 5:2, ESV). But no one answers the call. John, who had been caught up to heaven to *see* the things that were to come, understands the impasse and begins to weep. But one of the elders comforts and assures him that there is one who is worthy to open the book. John then sees a Lamb who had been slain, standing between the throne and the four creatures and elders. The Lamb approaches and takes the book from the one who is seated on the throne. Suddenly, an innumerable host of angels join the four creatures and elders in praising the Lamb and the one who sits on the throne. The throng of all creation then joins in the chorus of worship.

Again, the elders prostrate in worship before the throne. This concert of heavenly worship continues to grow in number and increase in volume throughout the unfolding revelations of the book. Yet, despite the prevailing and pervading atmosphere of worship, not to mention, all the wonderments of heaven itself, Revelation also describes in prophetic imagery, a horrific war breaking out in heaven, immediately following the revelation of the Messiah:

> She gave birth to a son, a male child, who "will rule all the nations with an iron scepter." And her child was snatched up to God and to his throne. The woman fled into the wilderness to a place prepared for her by God, where she might be taken care of for 1,260 days. Then war broke out in heaven. Michael and his angels fought against the dragon, and the dragon and his angels fought back. But he was not strong enough, and they lost their place in heaven. The great dragon was hurled down—that ancient serpent called the devil, or Satan, who leads the whole world astray. He was hurled to the earth, and his angels with him (Rev. 12:5-9, NIV).

Ironically, angels, who were created and ordained to worship and serve God, must fight against other angelic beings—Satan and his angels.[10] But God's faithful angel-warriors overcome Satan and his followers and hurl them to the earth. Expelled from heaven, Satan turns his attention to the *offspring* of the woman: "Then the dragon was enraged at the woman and went off **to wage war against the rest of her offspring**—those who keep God's commands and hold fast their testimony about Jesus" (Rev. 12:17, NIV). Within context of the chapter, the foci of the dragon's wrath are the man-child, the woman, and her spiritual offspring. Since the man-child is caught up to the throne of God (12:5), and the woman is protected in the wilderness from the serpent (12:14-16), the dragon directs his rage towards the offspring of the woman. In fact, the following chapters provides more details of this satanic aggression against the offspring.

The dragon will seek to control all of mankind, both politically and spiritually. According to Revelation, a beast will rise out of the sea, possessing

---

[10] "His tail [the dragon] swept a third of the stars out of the sky and flung them to the earth" (Rev. 12:4, NIV). According to one interpretation, Satan convinced a good part of the angels of God to take sides with his cause. In the Scriptures, *stars* are typically symbolic of angels (Job 38:7; Rev. 1:20). While there are other interpretations of the word, *stars*, the text clearly affirms that Satan's angels were cast down to earth with him (Rev. 12:9; cf. Matt. 25:41).

immense political control over the inhabitants of the earth. They will marvel at the beast, follow and worship it, just as they worshipped the dragon:

> **And they worshipped the dragon**, for he had given his authority to the beast, **and they worshipped the beast**, saying, "Who is like the beast, and who can fight against it? And the beast was given a mouth uttering haughty and blasphemous words, and it was allowed to exercise authority for forty-two months. It opened its mouth to utter blasphemies against God, blaspheming his name and his dwelling, that is, those who dwell in heaven. **Also it was allowed to make war on the saints and to conquer them.** And authority was given it over every tribe and people and language and nation, **and all who dwell on earth will worship it**, everyone whose name has not been written before the foundation of the world in the book of life of the Lamb who was slain" (Rev. 13:4-8, ESV).

This beast is empowered by the dragon; it is also similar to the dragon in character: *belligerent*, *arrogant*, and *blasphemous*. The beast will exercise authority over those who dwell on earth. Furthermore, it will wage war against those who worship God. Indeed, worship will become the litmus test of allegiance to the dragon and beast.

Subsequently, John sees another beast, rising from the earth:

> Then I saw another beast rising out of the earth. It had two horns like a lamb and it spoke like a dragon. It exercises all the authority of the first beast in its presence, **and makes the earth and its inhabitants worship the first beast**, whose mortal wound was healed. It performs great signs, even making fire come down from heaven to earth in front of people, and by the signs that it is allowed to work in the presence of the beast it deceives those who dwell on earth, telling them to make an image for the beast that was wounded by the sword and yet lived. And it was allowed to give breath to the image of the beast, so that the image of the beast might even speak and might cause those who would not worship the image of the beast to be slain. Also it causes all, both small and great, both rich and poor, both free and slave, to be marked on the right hand or the forehead, so that no one can buy or sell unless he has the mark, that is, the name of the beast or the number of its name (Rev. 13:11-17, ESV).

This second beast is *spiritually* deceptive, and savage and ruthless in nature. Its words are powerful and persuasive, for it speaks like the dragon. In fact, it is also referred to as "the false prophet" (Rev. 16:13, ESV). The second beast performs signs and wonders; it will even make an image of the first beast come alive and speak. Worship of the first beast will become monolithic and totalitarian, even upon pain of death, but the type of worship the second beast imposes is not born of love and devotion, but of deception, superstition, fear of death, and subjugation. In fact, people will not even be able to buy or sell unless they receive the mark of the beast.

John's account of this beast is highly reminiscent of the dilemma the Jews faced in Babylon, in the book of Daniel:

> Then Nebuchadnezzar, in rage and fury, gave the command to bring Shadrach, Meshach, and Abed-Nego. So they brought these men before the king. Nebuchadnezzar spoke, saying to them, "*Is it* true, Shadrach, Meshach, and Abed-Nego, *that* you do not serve my gods or worship the gold image which I have set up? Now if you are ready at the time you hear the sound of the horn, flute, harp, lyre, *and* psaltery, in symphony with all kinds of music, and you fall down and worship the image which I have made, *good!* But if you do not worship, you shall be cast immediately into the midst of a burning fiery furnace. And who *is* the god who will deliver you from my hands?" (Dan. 3:13-15, NKJV).

The king gave Shadrach, Meshach, and Abed-Nego another opportunity to prostrate themselves and worship his image, but the three men were clear and unambiguous in their response to the king. They declared that their God was more than capable of delivering them from the fiery furnace and from the king, but even if he chose not to, they would neither serve the king's gods nor worship his image of gold (Dan. 3:16-18). Furious, Nebuchadnezzar commanded that the furnace should be heated seven times hotter than normal, and then gave orders that Shadrach, Meshach, and Abed-Nego should be bound and thrown into the furnace. But the Lord sent his angel and rescued the three Hebrew men:

> Then King Nebuchadnezzar was astonished; and he rose in haste *and* spoke, saying to his counselors, "Did we not cast three men bound in the midst of the fire?" They answered and said to the king, "True, O king." "Look!" he answered, "I see four men loose, walking in the midst of the fire; and they are not hurt, and the form of the fourth is like the Son of God" (Dan. 3:24-25, NKJV).

Nebuchadnezzar approached the mouth of the furnace and called the three men out of the furnace. Upon inspection, he and all his satraps, administrators, governors, and counselors found that the three men were completely unscathed by the fire and even by the smoke. Nebuchadnezzar made a decree that no one should speak against the God of Shadrach, Meshach, and Abed-Nego, upon the pain of a horrible death and utter destruction of one's home. The king even gave promotions to the three men in his kingdom. But alas, unlike Nebuchadnezzar, the dragon and the two beasts of Revelation will never change their behavior. They will always be relentless in their rage and hate against the Lord and the saints of God, until the day Christ returns and stops Satan's murderous onslaught.

Returning to Revelation: During this trying period of political and religious dominance under the beast, the Lord will continue to reach out to all the inhabitants of the earth with the gospel, inviting them to cross the battleline and become worshippers of the Creator instead of demons.[11]

> Then I saw another angel flying in the midst of heaven, having the everlasting gospel to preach to those who dwell on the earth—to every nation, tribe, tongue, and people—saying with a loud voice, "**Fear God and give glory to Him, for the hour of His judgment has come; and worship Him who made heaven and earth, the sea and springs of water**" (Rev. 14:6-7, NKJV).

The spiritual conflict will escalate until the beast makes a concerted political move to wage an all-out-war against the Lamb and the saints of God:

> And I saw, coming out of the mouth of the dragon and out of the mouth of the beast and out of the mouth of the false prophet, three unclean spirits like frogs. For they are demonic spirits, performing signs, who go abroad to the kings of the whole world, **to assemble them for battle on the great day of God the Almighty**. (Rev. 16:13-14, ESV)

> And the ten horns that you saw are ten kings who have not yet received royal power, but they are to receive authority as kings for one hour, together with the beast. These are of one mind, and they hand over their power and authority to the beast. **They will make war on**

[11] Rev. 9:20

> **the Lamb**, and the Lamb will conquer them, for he is Lord of lords and King of kings, and those with him are called and chosen and faithful" (Rev. 17:12-14, ESV).

The enemies of God, however, will not prevail. The Lord Jesus Christ will return in majesty and power, sitting on a white horse. He will judge and make war against his adversaries:

> Then I saw heaven opened, **and behold, a white horse!** The one sitting on it is called Faithful and True, and in righteousness **he judges and makes war**. His eyes are like a flame of fire, and on his head are many diadems, and he has a name written that no one knows but himself. He is clothed in a robe dipped in blood, and the name by which he is called is The Word of God (Rev. 19:11-13, ESV).

The rider of the white horse will destroy the beast, the false prophet, and all the kings and their armies who go to war against him and his army. The beast and false prophet will then be cast alive into the lake of fire, while the kings and their armies will be slain with the sword that proceeds from the mouth of the one who rides the white horse, and the birds will feed on their bodies (Rev. 19:19-21). Satan, instead, will be bound for a thousand years (Rev. 20:1-3). At the end of a thousand years, Satan will be released and, once again, he will deceive the nations and gather them to war against the saints and against Jerusalem. But he will not prevail; instead, he will duly meet the same fate as the beast and false prophet:

> And when the thousand years are ended, Satan will be released from his prison and will come out to deceive the nations that are at the four corners of the earth, Gog and Magog, **to gather them for battle**; their number is like the sand of the sea. And they marched up over the broad plain of the earth and surrounded the camp of the saints and the beloved city, but fire came down from heaven and consumed them, and the devil who had deceived them was thrown into the lake of fire and sulfur where the beast and the false prophet were, and they will be tormented day and night forever and ever (Rev. 20:7-10, ESV).

Various interpretations have been put forward regarding this mysterious period called the *millennium*.[12] Regardless of the differing views and

[12] I personally believe in a pre-millennial view of the Lord's second coming.

opinions, the themes of worship and war are clearly woven throughout all the eschatological visions of Revelation. War is in the heart of the dragon, that ancient serpent. Satan opposes God and all that he represents, particularly the offspring in Rev. 12:17. Personally, I believe the *offspring* in this verse refers to those who belong to Christ. Writing to the churches in Galatia, Apostle Paul affirms: "And if you are Christ's, then **you are Abraham's offspring**, heirs according to the promise" (Gal. 3:29, ESV). And because we are the offspring, we are the objects of the devil's wrath. But the offspring of Abraham is also destined to possess the gate of his enemies (Gen. 22:17). In fact, Revelation informs us the day will come when Satan will be cast in the lake of fire, and the mouth of the tempter, the accuser of the brethren, the dragon, and ancient serpent will forever be silenced. This, however, will only the beginning of the universal purging. The last judgment will be pronounced from the great white throne, and Death and Hades will also be cast in the lake of fire, together with those whose names are not found in the book of life. God will then make all things new: a new heaven and new earth where there will be no more room for death, sorrow, pain, sin, and, above all, war. The tabernacle of God will dwell among his people, he will comfort them of all their afflictions (Rev. 21:1-8). And they will serve and worship God for all eternity (Rev. 22:3).

The Sword and the Harp: *Spiritual Warfare and Worship*

> "May the Lord, my rock, be praised, who trains my hands for battle and my fingers for warfare."
>
> "God, I will sing a new song to You; I will play on a ten-stringed harp for You— the One who gives victory to kings, who frees His servant David from the deadly sword" (Ps. 144:1, 9-10, HCSB).

In Psalm 144, David praised the Lord, his rock, who trained his hands for battle and fingers for warfare—the same hands and fingers that held a harp and plucked its chords to praise and worship God. Worship and warfare are, indeed, inseparable. To worship God invariably means we must also contend with his adversaries: the devil, the world, and even our own flesh. That is why, like David, the Lord trains our hands for battle and our fingers for warfare through his word and through the Holy Spirit.

First of all, as we have already noted, the devil is a powerful and formidable foe—an adversary in every sense of the word. The Scriptures characterize him as a *liar* (John 8:44); a *tempter* (1 Thess. 3:5); a *deceiver* (Rev. 12:9); and an *accuser*

(Rev. 12:10). He will do all he can to *hinder* and interfere with the work of God (1 Thess. 2:18). He will especially attempt to corrupt our minds and lead us astray from our devotion to Christ (2 Cor. 11:3). But God has given us weapons so that we may fight and resist him: He even gives us a tactical advantage through his word. Apostle Paul writes:

> "Put on the whole armor of God, that you may be able to stand against the schemes of the devil" (Eph. 6:11, ESV).[13]

Paul further describes in vivid detail the spiritual armor God has given us to combat the devil and evil:

> Therefore take up the whole armor of God, that you may be able to withstand in the evil day, and having done all, to stand firm. Stand therefore, having fastened on the belt of truth, and having put on the breastplate of righteousness, and, as shoes for your feet, having put on the readiness given by the gospel of peace. In all circumstances take up the shield of faith, with which you can extinguish all the flaming darts of the evil one; and take the helmet of salvation, and the sword of the Spirit, which is the word of God, (Eph. 6:13-17, ESV).

As discussed earlier, Revelation teaches that in the end times, Satan will, above all, wield political and religious power over the world, deceiving and forcing its inhabitant to worship the beast (Rev. 13:11-17). He will especially display his wrath against the saints of God. But the Lord has given his people a lethal weapon to defeat him: "And they have conquered him by the blood of the Lamb and by the word of their testimony, for they loved not their lives even unto death" (Rev. 12:11, ESV).

Secondly, the world is also an enemy with which we must contend. By the world, we mean a collective of men and women whose minds are governed by their own desires and passions. They are also deceived and easily influenced by the devil (1 John 5:19). The world lures men with all its desires (1 John 2:16-17). The world stands in direct opposition to God. James writes in his letter:

> "You adulterous people! Do you not know that friendship with the world is enmity with God? Therefore whoever wishes to be a friend of the world makes himself an enemy of God" (Jas. 4:4, ESV).

---

[13] It is amazing all the war terminology used extensively throughout the New Testament.

As shocking as it may sound, for the believer to be friends with the world constitutes spiritual adultery. We cannot truly worship God if we are embracing his enemy. Apostle Paul's answer for the world is, again, the cross of Christ: "But far be it from me to boast except in the cross of our Lord Jesus Christ, by which the world has been crucified to me, and I to the world" (Gal. 6:14, ESV). Besides the lusts of this world, we must also combat against deceptive arguments and false philosophies the world continually spews out like venom, especially against the knowledge of God:

> For though we live in the body, we do not wage war in an unspiritual way, since the weapons of our warfare are not worldly, but are powerful through God for the demolition of strongholds. We demolish arguments and every high-minded thing that is raised up against the knowledge of God, taking every thought captive to obey Christ (2 Cor. 10:3-5, HCSB).

We should not underestimate the power of persuasion and influence these arguments and philosophies have over people and, in some cases, even over some believers. But the Lord has placed in our hands, the necessary weapons to destroy strongholds and bring down the towers of human reasoning and philosophy that oppose the knowledge of God.

Lastly, another hostile adversary with which we must contend is the flesh. Worship, by nature, is spiritual. Jesus said, "God is spirit, and those who worship him must worship in spirit and truth" (John 4:24, ESV). But nothing will more quickly defile our worship and devotion than our own flesh. The term, *flesh*, has different usages in the New Testament, but mostly it is used to refer to those inner desires and passions that war against the law of God in our mind, and against our very soul (Rom. 7:23-24; 1 Peter 2:11). In his letter to the Romans, Apostle Paul writes that the mind that is subjected to the desires and passions of the flesh is hostile to God, and those who live according to the flesh cannot please him (Rom. 8:7-8). In his letter to the Galatians, he further attests that the flesh is also opposed to the Spirit of God within the believer, not to mention, a source of continual frustration:

> "But I say, walk by the Spirit, and you will not carry out the desire of the flesh. For the flesh sets its desire against the Spirit, and the Spirit against the flesh; **for these are in opposition to one another**, so that you may not do the things that you please" (Gal. 5:16-17, NASB).

According to James, the works of the flesh, particularly jealousy and ambition, stand in direct opposition to the wisdom and peace of God (Jas. 3:13-18). James also affirms that the fleshly passions are the source of infighting within the church: "What causes quarrels and what causes fights among you? Is it not this, that **your passions are at war within you**?" (Jas. 4:1, ESV). As strange as it sounds, we need to be armed against our own flesh. The Lord has provided us with the best weapons possible to resist carnality: the *cross* and the *Spirit of God.* Apostle Paul writes:

> Now those who belong to Christ Jesus have **crucified the flesh with its passions and desires**. If we live by the Spirit, let us also walk by the Spirit. Let us not become boastful, challenging one another, envying one another (Gal 5:24-26, NASB).

The message of the cross is indeed the power of God for those who are being saved (1 Cor. 1:18), but it is also God's answer for the flesh, the world, and the devil (Gal. 6:14, Rev. 12:11). Through faith, the cross of Christ becomes a fixed point of identity for the believer. Our flesh may fight, scream, and protest, but it no longer has free range to do as it pleases. Paul further exhorts believers to "walk by the Spirit." There is no better way of counteracting the works of the flesh than by being in tune to the prompting of the Spirit. The Spirit will never lead us down the path of the flesh. Instead, the Spirit will always produce good fruit in our lives. The Lord also gives us grace that we may overcome sinful desires of the flesh, but there are *conditions*:

> But he gives more grace. Therefore it says, "God opposes the proud but gives grace to the humble." Submit yourselves therefore to God. Resist the devil, and he will flee from you. Draw near to God, and he will draw near to you. Cleanse your hands, you sinners, and purify your hearts, you double-minded. Be wretched and mourn and weep. Let your laughter be turned to mourning and your joy to gloom. Humble yourselves before the Lord, and he will exalt you (Jas. 4:6-10, ESV).

Our flesh is the doorway to the world and a foothold in our lives for the devil. But God gives us grace to overcome the enticements of the flesh. However, we must appropriately respond to God ("Submit yourselves…to God…" "Draw near to God…"; "Humble yourselves before the Lord…"), to the devil ("Resist…and he will flee from you"), and to any compromise or double mindedness that leaves the door open to the flesh, the world and the enemy ("Cleanse your hands, you sinners, and purify your hearts…"). James describes true repentance and change of attitude ("Be wretched and mourn and weep"). The line or general direction in James' exhortation essentially relates to one of the other seven principles of worship: *devotion*, which is the theme of our next chapter.

CHAPTER 8

The Pillar of Devotion

(The Heart of Biblical Worship)

God said to Jacob, "Arise, go up to Bethel and dwell there. Make an altar there to the God who appeared to you when you fled from your brother Esau." So Jacob said to his household and to all who were with him, "Put away the foreign gods that are among you and purify yourselves and change your garments. Then let us arise and go up to Bethel, so that I may make there an altar to the God who answers me in the day of my distress and has been with me wherever I have gone." So they gave to Jacob all the foreign gods that they had, and the rings that were in their ears. Jacob hid them under the terebinth tree that was near Shechem (Gen. 35:1-4, ESV).

Jacob departed from Beersheba and made his way towards the town of Haran in the Mesopotamian region. Isaac and Rebekah had thought it best to send their son to Rebekah's relatives in Haran, but for different reasons. With the help of his mother, Jacob had deceived his father, making Isaac believe he was Esau, so that he could steal the blessing that should have gone to the first-born son. When Rebekah heard Esau harbored bitterness and intended to kill his brother after their father had died, she instructed Jacob to flee to Haran, to her brother Laban's house, until Esau's wrath had passed. Rebekah spoke to Isaac of the great displeasure it would cause her if Jacob were to take one of the local women for a wife—the very thing Esau had done.[1] So Isaac called Jacob and sent him to Rebekah's relatives, charging him not to take one a wife from one of the Canaanite women, but to marry one of Laban's daughters.

---

[1] Gen. 26:34-35

As Jacob journeyed northward through the land, he stopped near the city of Luz for the night. He took one of the stones for his head and lay down to sleep. That night, Jacob had a dream that would change his life and the lives of his future offspring. He dreamed of a ladder that from earth reached to heaven, and angels were ascending and descending upon it.

> And behold, the Lord stood above it and said, "I am the Lord, the God of Abraham your father and the God of Isaac. The land on which you lie I will give to you and to your offspring. Your offspring shall be like the dust of the earth, and you shall spread abroad to the west and to the east and to the north and to the south, and in you and your offspring shall all the families of the earth be blessed. Behold, I am with you and will keep you wherever you go, and will bring you back to this land. For I will not leave you until I have done what I have promised you" (Gen. 28:13-15, ESV).

Jacob woke up frightened. He understood the Lord was in that very place where he laid down and that it was none other than "the house of God" and "the gate of heaven" (Gen. 28:17, ESV). Jacob took the stone upon which he laid his head and set up a pillar and anointed it with oil. He then made a solemn vow before the Lord:

> "If God will be with me and will keep me in this way that I go, and will give me bread to eat and clothing to wear, so that I come again to my father's house in peace, then the Lord shall be my God, and this stone, which I have set up for a pillar, shall be God's house. And of all that you give me I will give a full tenth to you" (Gen. 28:20-22, ESV).

Jacob arrived at Laban's house and was received with open arms. Jacob dwelled with his uncle and worked for him. Eventually, he married Laban's two daughters, Leah and Rachel. Jacob's household grew in numbers, as well as did his own flocks and livestock. But Laban mistreated Jacob, cheating him ten times of his wages. Nonetheless, Jacob continued to prosper and acquire wealth. When Jacob realized he was no longer in good standing with Laban and his sons, he informed his wives of his intention to return to the land of Canaan. He explained how the angel of God had spoken to him in a dream and told him to return to his own land. Jacob's wives were in full agreement.

As Jacob journeyed with his household and livestock toward the land of Canaan, he had divine and angelic encounters along the way. These were evident signs of divine favor, protection, and encouragement from God. Jacob knew first-hand the awesome love and faithfulness of God. His personal experiences are well summarized in his prayer:

> And Jacob said, "O God of my father Abraham and God of my father Isaac, O Lord who said to me, 'Return to your country and to your kindred, that I may do you good,' **I am not worthy of the least of all the deeds of steadfast love and all the faithfulness that you have shown to your servant**, for with only my staff I crossed this Jordan, and now I have become two camps. Please deliver me from the hand of my brother, from the hand of Esau, for I fear him, that he may come and attack me, the mothers with the children. But you said, 'I will surely do you good, and make your offspring as the sand of the sea, which cannot be numbered for multitude'" (Gen. 32:9-12, ESV).

God answered his prayer. Jacob met peacefully with his brother, Esau. He received Jacob and even showed him favor. Esau returned to Seir, but Jacob moved on to Succoth (Gen. 33:17). After spending some time in that place, Jacob and his family continued their journey until they reached the city of Shechem. When they arrived, they encamped on a plot of land that Jacob purchased from the sons of Hamor. Long before Jacob ever returned to Bethel to fulfill his vow, he already expressed his devotion to God on that humble plot of land near Shechem: "There he erected an altar and called it El-Elohe-Israel" (Gen. 33:20, ESV). Jacob and his growing household remained in that region for some time, until troubles arose between his sons and the people of Shechem. Hamor's son had kidnapped and raped their sister, Dinah. Jacob's sons took revenge and killed all the men of Shechem and plundered their city and fields. They seized their wealth, their women and children, and all they found in their homes. Jacob, of course, feared repercussions from the surrounding inhabitants. But the Lord instructed Jacob to go to Bethel, where he had first appeared to him, and build an altar. In effect, the Lord was calling the patriarch back to the very place where he had made his solemn vow:

> So Jacob said to his household and to all who were with him, "Put away the foreign gods that are among you and purify yourselves and change your garments. Then let us arise and go up to Bethel, so that I may make there an altar to the God who answers me in the day of my distress and has been with me wherever I have gone" (Gen. 35:2-3, ESV).

Jacob's wives and their servants had come from Mesopotamia; most of them were probably devoted to the god of their ancestors and native region. Moreover, the company of people who were with Jacob most likely had their own deities and objects of devotion. But the time had come for Jacob's household and those under his authority to break with their past; they were going to Bethel, the house of God, to worship the Lord. Everybody gathered their gods and golden earrings and gave them to Jacob, who then took the objects and hid them under a terebinth tree. Afterwards, they set out for Bethel: "and there he built an altar and called the place El-bethel, because there God had revealed himself to him when he fled from his brother" (Gen. 35:7, ESV). Bethel, the house of God and the place of revelation, thus became the place of worship and devotion.

Jacob's Devotion

Devotion is a fundamental principle of biblical worship. Without devotion, worship would be a religious exercise without heart, a sacrifice without cost, and a cold altar without the fire of passion. The word, *devotion*, has its root in the Latin verb, *devovere*, which conveys the act of consecrating through a vow. In common parlance, it is typically used to express ideas of *affection*, *zeal*, *commitment*, and *dedication*. While both the etymological and modern usage of the word suggests *how* devotion is expressed, it practically says nothing about *why* devotion should thus be expressed. That is why the story of Jacob is important; his life-experiences vividly portray both the *expression* and *motivation* behind biblical devotion. According to the account, Jacob made a vow in the house of God (i.e., Bethel) that if God protected and provided for him, and brought him back peacefully to his father's house, the Lord would be his God. He would then return to Bethel, and the pillar he erected would be the house of God. In other words, Jacob would return to that location and build an altar to worship God with sacrifices. Moreover, he would give a tenth of all the Lord would give him (The tenth or tithe refers to the portion of flocks and livestock Jacob would offer in sacrifice on the altar).

Through Jacob's example, we learn several things concerning biblical devotion: First of all, *devotion is a response to divine revelation*. The future patriarch's devotion essentially began the moment he woke up and realized he was in the house of God. He responded to that revelation with a prayer for God's blessing and by making a solemn vow. During his journeys and sojourns, Jacob experienced revelations of the goodness and faithfulness of

God (Gen. 32:10).[2] Jacob even testified to his family and company of people that were with him of "the God who answers me in the day of my distress and has been with me wherever I have gone." *Devotion is a life-long commitment* and not a momentary gesture. While Jacob's devotion was initially expressed in a vow (the first time the word, *vow*, appears in the Scriptures), in reality, he proved his devotion to God under different circumstances, time and again, long before he ever fulfilled his vow at Bethel.[3] *Devotion embraces a person's family and all he possesses.* The injunction that Jacob gave his family and those with him: "Put away the foreign gods that are among you and purify yourselves and change your garments," served to *consecrate* and *secure* their undivided devotion, before departing for Bethel. For Jacob to ask anything less of them would have been a compromise.

Without dispute, the life and example of Jacob exerted a tremendous influence on the customs and traditions of the people of Israel. This is borne out by a short commentary found within the very story of Jacob: "Therefore to this day the people of Israel do not eat the sinew of the thigh that is on the hip socket, because he touched the socket of Jacob's hip on the sinew of the thigh" (Gen. 32:32, ESV). But more importantly, his *devotional* experience became a spiritual pattern among his descendants. In fact, the Old Testament presents a strong correlation between Jacob's devotion and the devotional practices prescribed and practiced under the old covenant.

Vows and Votive Offerings

Vows were an important expression of devotion in the Old Testament. They were solemn and binding pledges or promises made to God.[4] Vows were usually fulfilled by offering sacrifices,[5] or by consecrating oneself, persons, property, or various things to God.[6] The law required all the males to appear before the Lord three times a year, "at the Feast of Unleavened Bread, at the Feast of Weeks, and at the Feast of Booths" (Deut. 16:16, ESV). During the feasts, they were to bring offerings required by the law. But sometimes people felt the need or desire to go above and beyond the requirements of the law. Sometimes people

[2] Gen. 32:12; 24-32; 35:9

[3] Gen. 32:9-12; 24-32; 33:20; 35:14

[4] Deut. 23:21-23

[5] Num. 6:1-21 (Nazirite vow and sacrifice); 29:39; Deut. 12:5-6

[6] Lev. 7:16, 27:1-34

were in distress or despair,[7] such as Hannah,[8] who was childless and afflicted, or Jonah, trapped inside the belly of a fish.[9] In such cases, men and women often made vows to God, pledging to sacrifice and express their worship and devotion *at a future date*. Vows were a serious matter and not something to be trifled with (Ecc. 5:4-6; Prov. 20:25). Unfortunately, sometimes people would hastily make vows, only to regret them later; other times they would merely disregard the vow. The Lord spoke to Moses and gave the people clear guidelines for making vows and taking oaths.[10] Most Old Testament vows dealt with animal sacrifices and the consecration or setting apart of oneself, people, property, houses, and things for the Lord. Vow offerings and consecrated things were to be brought to the place of the Lord's choosing, (i.e., the tabernacle and later, the temple):

> But you shall seek the place that the Lord your God will choose out of all your tribes to put his name and make his habitation there. There you shall go, and there you shall bring your burnt offerings and your sacrifices, your tithes and the contribution that you present, your vow offerings, your freewill offerings, and the firstborn of your flock.
>
> But the holy things that are due from you, and your vow offerings, you shall take, and you shall go to the place that the Lord will choose, and offer your burnt offerings, the flesh and the blood, on the altar of the Lord your God. The blood of your sacrifices shall be poured out on the altar of the Lord your God, but you may eat the meat (Deut. 12:5-6, 26-27, ESV).

This also meant the fulfillment of vows or whatever might be consecrated to the Lord was contingent upon the services of the Levitical priesthood. The priests performed all votive offerings and sacrifices related to the Nazirite vow.[11] Moreover, if a person chose to redeem whatever he had consecrated to the Lord, it was the priest who would give him the pecuniary valuation.[12]

Vows were also practiced in the New Testament times by some

---

[7] Ps. 66:13-15
[8] 1 Sam. 1:9-11
[9] Jonah 2:9
[10] Lev. 27:1-29; Num. 30:1-16
[11] Num. 6:1-21
[12] Lev. 27:1-25

Jewish believers.[13] However, with the destruction of the Temple in the year 70 A.D., vow offerings and all other types of offerings were no longer possible. Besides, with the coming of the Messiah and the Messianic reformation, worship became defined by a new paradigm:

> "For when there is a change in the priesthood, there is necessarily a change in the law as well" (Heb. 7:12, ESV).
>
> "In speaking of a new covenant, he makes the first one obsolete. And what is becoming obsolete and growing old is ready to vanish away" (Heb. 8:13, ESV).

Vows and oaths relating to old covenant worship always pointed to a future date when the devotee would go to the divinely designated place and fulfill his or her pledge; but in Christ, all such vows and oaths have been replaced by the *immediacy of worship*. In Christ, the place and the hour or time of worship is here and now.[14]

Separation

Jacob gave his family and the company of people who were with him a specific, three-fold injunction: "Put away the foreign gods that are among you and purify yourselves and change your garments" (Gen. 35:2, ESV). His instructions represent a biblical pattern of devotion. The first of his injunctions: "Put away the foreign gods that are among you..." conveys the meaning of *separating* oneself from all other deities, including practices associated with them. The Scriptures are unequivocal that God demands the exclusive worship and total devotion of his people. The exclusiveness of worship is, in fact, an intrinsic part of the Ten Commandments:

> I am the Lord your God, who brought you out of the land of Egypt, out of the place of slavery. **Do not have other gods besides Me**. Do not make an idol for yourself, whether in the shape of anything in the heavens above or on the earth below or in the waters under the earth. You must not bow down to them or worship them; for I, the Lord your God, am a jealous God, punishing the children for the fathers' sin, to the third and fourth generations of those who hate Me, but showing faithful love to a thousand generations of those who love Me and keep My commands (Exod. 20:2-6, HCSB).

Biblical devotion allows no room for any other god or idol. Indeed, there are

---

13 Acts 18:18, 22; 21:23-24

14 John 4:21-23

no other gods but the Lord God:

> "I am the Lord; that is my name; my glory I give to no other, nor my praise to carved idols" (Is. 42:8, ESV).
>
> "I am the Lord, and there is no other, besides me there is no God" (Isa. 45:5, ESV).

According to the Scriptures, all other gods are nothing but *demons*. In his song, Moses laments those among his people who have fallen into the snare of these demons:

> They stirred him to jealousy with strange gods; with abominations they provoked him to anger. **They sacrificed to demons that were no gods**, to gods they had never known, to new gods that had come recently, whom your fathers had never dreaded (Deut. 32:16-17, ESV).[15]

New Testament teaching also equates idolatry with the worship of demons and of things made by the hands of man:

> What am I saying then? That an idol is anything, or what is offered to idols is anything? Rather, that the things which the Gentiles sacrifice **they sacrifice to demons and not to God**, and I do not want you to have fellowship with demons" (1 Cor. 10:19-20, NKJV).
>
> The rest of the people, who were not killed by these plagues, did not repent of the works of their hands to stop **worshiping demons and idols** of gold, silver, bronze, stone, and wood, which are not able to see, hear, or walk (Rev. 9:20, HCSB).

Similar to Jacob's injunction, Joshua, son of Nun, had also incited the children of Israel to put away their foreign gods:

> "Now therefore fear the Lord and serve him in sincerity and in faithfulness. **Put away the gods that your fathers served beyond the River and in Egypt, and serve the Lord**. And if it is evil in your eyes to serve the Lord, choose this day whom you will serve, whether the gods your fathers served in the region beyond the River, or the gods of the Amorites in whose land you dwell. But as for me and my house, we will serve the Lord" (Josh. 24:14-15, ESV).

---

[15] Ps. 106:36-38

In response to Joshua's exhortation, the people remonstrated their determination not to forsake the Lord by serving other gods. They further declared they would only serve the Lord God, for he had delivered them from Egypt and helped them drive out the Amorites from the promise land.[16] Despite the people's insistence, Joshua admonished them with one final and provocative challenge (and perhaps with a bit of reverse psychology):

> But Joshua said to the people, "**You are not able to serve the Lord, for he is a holy God**. **He is a jealous God**; he will not forgive your transgressions or your sins. If you forsake the Lord and serve foreign gods, then he will turn and do you harm and consume you, after having done you good." And the people said to Joshua, "No, but we will serve the Lord." Then Joshua said to the people, "You are witnesses against yourselves that you have chosen the Lord, to serve him." And they said, "We are witnesses." He said, "**Then put away the foreign gods that are among you, and incline your heart to the Lord**, the God of Israel" (Josh. 24:19-23, ESV).

The gods of Mesopotamia, of Egypt, and of the Amorites perhaps allowed worshippers to share their devotion with other gods, but not so, the God of Israel: "You are not able to serve the Lord, for he is a holy God. He is a jealous God." His holiness and jealousy demand *undivided devotion.*

The prophet Samuel, like Jacob and Joshua, also challenged the people of his day to put away their foreign gods and serve and worship only the Lord:

> And Samuel said to all the house of Israel, "If you are returning to the Lord with all your heart, **then put away the foreign gods and the Ashtaroth from among you and direct your heart to the Lord and serve him only**, and he will deliver you out of the hand of the Philistines" (1 Sam. 7:3, ESV).

Like an unbroken thread, the concept of putting away foreign gods continues in the New Testament. The first letter of John concludes with a brief but pointed exhortation: "Little children, guard yourselves from idols" (1 John 5:21, HCSB). Idolatry was prevalent in the first century and very much a problem in the church, particularly among Gentile believers. In his letter to the church in Corinth, the Apostle Paul deals with idolatry

---

[16] Josh. 24:16-18

and related concerns he had with some of the believers. His exhortation is equally relevant for today:

> **Do not be unequally yoked with unbelievers.** For what partnership has righteousness with lawlessness? Or what fellowship has light with darkness? What accord has Christ with Belial?[17] Or what portion does a believer share with an unbeliever? What agreement has the temple of God with idols? For we are the temple of the living God; as God said, "I will make my dwelling among them and walk among them, and I will be their God, and they shall be my people. Therefore go out from their midst, **and be separate from them**, says the Lord, and touch no unclean thing; then I will welcome you, and I will be a father to you, and you shall be sons and daughters to me, says the Lord Almighty" (2 Cor. 6:14-18, ESV).

Paul exhorts the Corinthian believers not to be "unequally yoked" with unbelievers. This, however, does not mean believers could or should not socialize or associate with unbelievers. In fact, the apostle writes elsewhere to the Corinthians:

> I wrote to you in my letter not to associate with sexually immoral people—not at all meaning the sexually immoral of this world, or the greedy and swindlers, or idolaters, since then you would need to go out of the world. But now I am writing to you not to associate with anyone who bears the name of brother if he is guilty of sexual immorality or greed, or is an idolater, reviler, drunkard, or swindler—not even to eat with such a one (1 Cor. 5:9-11, ESV).

Paul, instead, refers to being bound in a *spiritual* relation, such that sooner or later, the believer would be forced to compromise his or her faith, conscience, and holiness to maintain the union with the unbeliever. Paul's exhortation draws its analogy from the Old Testament: "You shall not plow with an ox and a donkey together" (Deut. 22:10, ESV). The ox and the donkey were considered, respectively, a clean and unclean animal.[18] The two animals are also an incompatible work team in strength, size, and

---

[17] Judg. 19:22. The verse literally speaks of the *sons of Belial*: (בְּנֵי־בְלִיַּעַל, *ḇə-nê-ḇə-lî-ya-'al*). The story in Judges, chapter nineteen, provides an excellent background for the meaning of *Belial.*

[18] Lev. 11:1-3; Deut. 14:3-8

behavior. Likewise, to be unequally yoked with an unbeliever forms a spiritually, unsuitable relationship. We may clearly infer the spiritual nature and incongruity of such a union from the five specific questions Paul asks the Corinthians:

1. "For what partnership has righteousness with lawlessness?"
2. "Or what fellowship has light with darkness?"
3. "What accord has Christ with Belial?"
4. "Or what portion does a believer share with an unbeliever?"
5. "What agreement has the temple of God with idols?"

In each question, Paul probes a specific area that needs to be safeguarded against compromise: *righteousness*, *light*, *devotion*, *spiritual inheritance*, and *God's dwelling place.* In each question, the apostle employs five specific words that convey the concept of being spiritually yoked: "partnership"; "fellowship"; "accord"; "portion"; and "agreement."[19] To be yoked together with someone that loves and worships God is actually beneficial; it serves, among other things, for reciprocal growth and edification.

Paraphrasing the Old Testament, Paul explains why spiritual separation is so vital for believers[20]:

> "I will make my dwelling among them and walk among them, and I will be their God, and they shall be my people. **Therefore go out from their midst, and be separate from them, says the Lord**, and touch no unclean thing; then I will welcome you, and I will be a father to you, and you shall be sons and daughters to me, says the Lord Almighty" (2 Cor. 6:16-18, ESV).

Separation, or holiness, is never an end in itself, and it is definitely not for the purpose of making a show of one's devotion.[21] The whole reason for separation is so that God may dwell among his people and that he may be a father to us, and we, his sons and daughters.

The divine call, "go out from their midst, and be separate from them" is similarly given in the book of Revelation:

---

[19] Many years ago, I heard missionary and mission-leader, Jamon Tipton preach on 2 Cor. 6:14-18. Though I do not recall the specific message, I distinctly remember brother Jamon, highlighting in the text, the five questions and nouns considered in this study. As then, I still think he made a brilliant observation.

[20] Exod. 29:45; Lev. 26:12; 2 Sam. 7:14; Isa. 52:11; Jer. 31:33; 32:38; Ezek. 20:34, 41; 37:27

[21] Is. 65:5

> And he cried mightily with a loud voice, saying, "Babylon the great is fallen, is fallen, and has become a dwelling place of demons, a prison for every foul spirit, and a cage for every unclean and hated bird! For all the nations have drunk of the wine of the wrath of her fornication, the kings of the earth have committed fornication with her, and the merchants of the earth have become rich through the abundance of her luxury." And I heard another voice from heaven saying, "**Come out of her, my people, lest you share in her sins, and lest you receive of her plagues**. For her sins have reached to heaven, and God has remembered her iniquities" (Rev. 18:2-5, NKJV).

The book of Revelation portrays Babylon as a bloodthirsty prostitute who is dressed extravagantly and who is drunk on the blood of the saints, those who testified of Jesus (Rev. 17:6). She represents a city that wields power over all the nations through her fornication, that is, through her idolatry.[22] From a premillennial perspective, she is symbolic of a monolithic, world power of the last days. The wine of her bloodthirsty fornication is so intoxicating that all separation between state, religion, and even economics, is totally lost. But judgment will come to Babylon for her iniquities. Therefore, the call is given that God's people should come out of her lest they also partake of her judgment.

In Western civilization, the spread of Christianity has contributed immensely to the defrocking of the pantheon of ancient gods. This, of course, does not mean that polytheism, occultism, and other ancient idolatrous practices have been eradicated from the Western hemisphere; they are merely not as ubiquitous as they are in some Eastern cultures. Though the church has made progress, and in some cases, even stopped paganism, the world continuously and inexorably moves towards Babylon. In fact, in recent years, there has been a popular resurgence of ancient deities, witchcraft, and black magic in literature, games, and Hollywood movies. It is no wonder, considering that the world is under the influence of the devil (1 John 5:19), and that "the mystery of lawlessness is already at work…" (2 Thess. 2:7, NKJV). The weeds of idolatry and occultism grow well in the fertile soil of wickedness, fear,

---

[22] Exod. 34:15-16; 2 Chron. 21:11; etc. The Hebrew word, זָנָה, *zanah*, which means, *to commit fornication, be a harlot*, is used to describe those who go after other gods to worship them.

darkness, and ignorance. The call to put away one's "foreign gods" applies today, just as much as it did in the days of the patriarchs, ancient Israel, and the early church.

Purification

Following his order to put away their foreign gods, Jacob enjoined upon his household and the company of people with him: "and purify yourselves…" (Gen. 35:2, ESV). This imperative certainly means more than merely taking a bath. In fact, it would have been rather senseless and awkward for the people to bathe and change clothes just before a long days' journey on a dusty road to Bethel. The injunction, instead, represented a type of washing that symbolized spiritual purification. The people were to literally purge themselves of any past devotions and cleanse themselves of having even touched their foreign gods. In short, purification was a sort of *baptism* of devotion.

The Scriptures describe purification as an intrinsic part of biblical worship and devotion. Aaron and his sons were to be washed *before* they dressed in holy attire and entered the tabernacle to serve God (Exod. 29:4-9; 40:12; Lev. 8:6). The Lord instructed Moses to also place a brazen basin of water between the altar and the tabernacle so that Aaron and his sons could also wash their hands and feet before entering the tabernacle: "When they go into the tent of meeting, or when they come near the altar to minister, to burn a food offering to the Lord, they shall wash with water, so that they may not die" (Exod. 30:20, ESV). The practice of washing was more than practical and hygienic; it also communicated the idea of purifying oneself from spiritual filth and defilement. In the opening chapter of the book of Isaiah, the Lord God holds in contempt the people's worship and devotion, because they were contaminated with iniquity, injustice, oppression, and even bloodshed. The Lord exhorts the people to wash and cleanse themselves from all such defilement:

> Hear the word of the Lord, ye rulers of Sodom; give ear unto the law of our God, ye people of Gomorrah. To what purpose is the multitude of your sacrifices unto me? saith the Lord: I am full of the burnt offerings of rams, and the fat of fed beasts; and I delight not in the blood of bullocks, or of lambs, or of he goats. When ye come to appear before me, who hath required this at your hand, to tread my courts? Bring no more vain oblations; incense is an abomination unto

> me; the new moons and sabbaths, the calling of assemblies, I cannot away with; it is iniquity, even the solemn meeting. Your new moons and your appointed feasts my soul hateth: they are a trouble unto me; I am weary to bear them. And when ye spread forth your hands, I will hide mine eyes from you: yea, when ye make many prayers, I will not hear: your hands are full of blood. **Wash you, make you clean; put away the evil of your doings from before mine eyes; cease to do evil**; Learn to do well; seek judgment, relieve the oppressed, judge the fatherless, plead for the widow (Isa. 1:10-17, KJV).

Similarly, the prophet Jeremiah declares: "O Jerusalem, **wash**[23] **your heart from evil**, that you may be saved. How long shall your wicked thoughts lodge within you?" (Jer. 4:14, ESV).

The theme of washing and spiritual purification continues into the New Testament. Testifying of his conversion experience to the crowd in Jerusalem—the same crowd that had only moments earlier attacked and beaten him, Apostle Paul declared:

> "Someone named Ananias, a devout man according to the law, having a good reputation with all the Jews residing there, came and stood by me and said, 'Brother Saul, regain your sight.' And in that very hour I looked up and saw him. Then he said, 'The God of our fathers has appointed you to know His will, to see the Righteous One, and to hear the sound of His voice. For you will be a witness for Him to all people of what you have seen and heard. And now, why delay? **Get up and be baptized, and wash away your sins by calling on His name**'" (Acts 22:12-16, HCSB).

The word, *baptism*, literally conveys the meaning of *washing* in the original language.[24] Baptism is identified with spiritual and ceremonial purification:

> Now a discussion arose between some of John's disciples and a Jew over **purification**. And they came to John and said to him, "Rabbi, he who was with you across the Jordan, to whom you bore witness—look, he is baptizing, and all are going to him" (John 3:25-26, ESV).

Baptism is an *exterior* expression of an *inner* spiritual reality. It

---

[23] Heb. כָּבַס, *kabas, to wash*

[24] Heb. 6:2: Gk. βαπτισμων, *baptismos*, (the act of) a dipping or washing. Strong, James. Strong's Exhaustive Concordance. Abingdon Press, 1890.

symbolizes the washing away of sins and the inner regeneration that takes place in the spirit of the believer. Apostle Paul freely uses this idea of washing in some of his letters:

> And such were some of you. **But you were washed**, you were sanctified, you were justified in the name of the Lord Jesus Christ and by the Spirit of our God" (1 Cor. 6:11, ESV).

> Husbands, love your wives, as Christ loved the church and gave himself up for her, that he might sanctify her, having cleansed her by the **washing of water with the word,** so that he might present the church to himself in splendor, without spot or wrinkle or any such thing, that she might be holy and without blemish (Eph. 5:25-27, ESV).[25]

> "He saved us, not because of works done by us in righteousness, but according to his own mercy, by the **washing of regeneration** and renewal of the Holy Spirit" (Tit. 3:5, ESV).

Water baptism is an integral part of New Testament conversion because it points to a specific time and location where public confession and profession of faith in Jesus Christ were made by the believer. It also expresses our identity with Jesus's death, and that we have embarked on a new life. Nowhere in the Scriptures are we enjoined to be rebaptized every time we confess our sins (If that were the case, many Christians, including this author, would likely die of pneumonia). However, we are to continually purify avail ourselves of the blood of Jesus. In his first letter, the Apostle John writes:

> But if we walk in the light as He is in the light, we have fellowship with one another, **and the blood of Jesus Christ His Son cleanses us from all sin**. If we say that we have no sin, we deceive ourselves, and the truth is not in us**. If we confess our sins**, He is faithful and just to forgive us *our* sins and **to cleanse us** from all unrighteousness (1 John 1:7-9, NKJV).

Moreover, we must actively purify ourselves from anything that would defile us:

---

[25] Some Bible commentaries interpret that the "washing of the water with the word" (Eph. 5:26, ESV), relates to baptism in water. There is, however, another, and perhaps better, interpretation: Paul refers to the ongoing preaching of the word which brings the church to a place of cleansing and renewal.

"Since we have these promises, beloved, **let us cleanse ourselves** from every defilement of body and spirit, bringing holiness to completion in the fear of God" (2 Cor. 7:1, ESV).

"Therefore, **if anyone cleanses himself** from what is dishonorable, he will be a vessel for honorable use, set apart as holy, useful to the master of the house, ready for every good work" (2 Tim. 2:21, ESV).

"Draw near to God, and he will draw near to you. **Cleanse your hands**, you sinners, and **purify your hearts**, you double-minded" (Jas. 4:8, ESV).

Transformation

Jacob lastly instructed his household and the people who were with him: "Change your garments" (Gen. 35:2, ESV). The changing of garments symbolizes a spiritual *transformation* from the common and mundane to the uncommon and lofty exercise of worshipping God. The concept of wearing clean or special garments, when appearing before the Lord, is woven throughout the Scriptures. In Exodus, the Lord commanded the children of Israel to *consecrate themselves* and *wash their clothes*, in preparation of his descent upon Mount Sinai:

The Lord said to Moses, "Go to the people and consecrate them today and tomorrow, and let them wash their garments and be ready for the third day. For on the third day the Lord will come down on Mount Sinai in the sight of all the people (Exod. 19:10-11, ESV).

Washing one's garments was a sign of being consecrated or set apart for God. Whenever Aaron and his fellow priests served in the tabernacle, they were to wash themselves and clothe themselves with holy garments. Their special garments gave them *dignity and honor* as they ministered to the Lord.[26]

"Make sacred garments for your brother Aaron to give him dignity and honor" (Exod. 28:2, NIV).

"For Aaron's sons you shall make tunics, and you shall make sashes for them. And you shall make hats for them, for glory and beauty" (Exod. 28:40, NIV).

---

[26] There are several passages in the Old Testament where God's people are exhorted to worship him in the "beauty of holiness" (1 Chr. 16:29, NKJV). These passages may also be translated, *in holy attire* or *sacred garments*: 1 Chron. 16:29; 2 Chron. 20:21; Ps. 29:2; 96:9. Confront other translations.

Zechariah the prophet reveals the symbolic importance of *clean* priestly garments. In one of his visions, the prophet observes and hears the angel of the Lord, commanding those standing before Joshua the high priest, to change his clothes and dress him appropriately, that he might represent the dignity of his position and fulfill his office. It is significant that Joshua's filthy garments are identified with iniquity:

> Now Joshua was standing before the angel, clothed with filthy garments. And the angel said to those who were standing before him, "Remove the filthy garments from him." And to him he said, "Behold, I have taken your iniquity away from you, and I will clothe you with pure vestments." And I said, "Let them put a clean turban on his head." So they put a clean turban on his head and clothed him with garments. And the angel of the Lord was standing by (Zech. 3:3-5, ESV).

The symbolical importance of special attire or garments continues into the New Testament, conveying different meanings, such as being properly clothed to be admitted into the kingdom of God (Matt. 22:11-12); being clothed in the Father's forgiveness and redemptive love (Luke 15:21-22); describing metaphorically the shabbiness of wealth, gained through fraud and unrighteousness (Jas. 5:1-2); or illustrating that believers should keep themselves clean of sin and carnality (Jude 1:22-23). As we have mentioned elsewhere, Revelation is one of the most prevalent books in the Bible on the subject of worship. It is also significant that it also has more to say about spiritual clothing than any other book of the Bible:

> "Yet you have still a few names in Sardis, people who have not soiled their **garments**, and they will walk with me **in white**, for they are worthy" (Rev. 3:4, ESV).

> "The one who conquers will be clothed thus in **white garments**, and I will never blot his name out of the book of life. I will confess his name before my Father and before his angels" (Rev. 3:5, ESV).

> "I counsel you to buy from me gold refined by fire, so that you may be rich, and **white garments** so that you may clothe yourself and the shame of your nakedness may not be seen, and salve to anoint your eyes, so that you may see" (Rev. 3:18, ESV).

> "Then they were each given **a white robe** and told to rest a little

> longer, until the number of their fellow servants and their brothers should be complete, who were to be killed as they themselves had been" (Rev. 6:11, ESV).
>
> After this I looked, and behold, a great multitude that no one could number, from every nation, from all tribes and peoples and languages, standing before the throne and before the Lamb, clothed in **white robes**, with palm branches in their hands (Rev. 7:9, ESV).
>
> Then one of the elders addressed me, saying, "Who are these, clothed in **white robes**, and from where have they come?" I said to him, "Sir, you know." And he said to me, "These are the ones coming out of the great tribulation. They have washed their **robes** and made them **white** in the blood of the Lamb" (Rev. 7:13-14, ESV).
>
> "Look, I am coming like a thief. The one who is alert and remains **clothed** so that he may not go around naked and people see his shame is blessed" (Rev. 16:15, HCSB).
>
> "Blessed are those who wash their **robes**, so that they may have the right to the tree of life and that they may enter the city by the gates" (Rev. 22:14, ESV).

These Scriptures convey two basic thoughts, concerning spiritual clothing: our personal responsibility in keeping our garments white and spotless, which symbolically relates to spiritual and moral purity; and being clothed by the Lord Jesus, himself, which conveys the idea of being honored by the Lord with dignity. Worshippers in heaven are clothed in white garments. God's people on earth are also spiritually clothed in white garments—garments that may either be spotted by sin, stripped off, or made white in the blood of the Lamb. We make our garments white, that is, pure and spotless, by availing ourselves of the precious blood of Jesus Christ through faith. We also keep our garments by *putting away* of sin, carnality, and separating ourselves from anything that might defile and bring shame upon us. The way one keeps his or her spiritual garments reflects the extent and depth of their devotion to God.

Consecration

Jacob's three-fold injunction, in effect, served to *consecrate* his family and the company of people who were with him, before they embarked upon their journey to Bethel to serve the Lord God. As we discussed earlier, *consecration*[27] is part of the etymological meaning of devotion. Consecration is that which distinguishes and sets apart God's people from all other people and world religions. In fact, the fundamental meaning of consecration is to *set apart, separate*, or *sanctify*.[28] The Scriptures present two aspects of consecration: *First*, it is the Lord God who initiates the process. In the Old Testament, the Lord repeatedly declares he is the one who consecrates or sanctifies[29]:

> "You are to speak to the people of Israel and say, 'Above all you shall keep my Sabbaths, for this is a sign between me and you throughout your generations, that you may know that **I, the Lord, sanctify you**'" (Exod. 31:13, ESV).

The Lord sets his people apart from all other people through his covenantal laws and statutes. He also consecrates a person or thing (e.g., tent, altar, etc.) through his word and the presence of his glory:

> "There I will meet with the people of Israel, **and it shall be sanctified by my glory**. I will consecrate the tent of meeting and the altar. Aaron also and his sons I will consecrate to serve me as priests" (Exod. 29:43-44, ESV).

Second, the people of Israel were to respond to the call of God by separating themselves from the Canaanite people, their idolatrous practices, and anything that was unclean: "**You shall be holy to me**, for I the Lord am holy and have separated you from the peoples, that you should be mine" (Lev. 20:26, ESV). The people of Israel were repeatedly exhorted to consecrate or sanctify themselves to the Lord, because he is holy:

> "Consecrate yourselves, therefore, and be holy, for I am the Lord your God. (Lev. 20:7, ESV).

Like the Old Testament, the New Testament also teaches both of these aspects of consecration. In his letter to the Thessalonians, Apostle Paul writes:

> "Now may the God of peace himself sanctify you completely, and

---

[27] Gk. ἁγιασμός, *hagiasmos*, consecration, sanctification.

[28] Heb. קָדַשׁ, *qadash, to be set apart or consecrated*. The Septuagint uses the Greek word, ἁγιάζω, *hagiazó*, which means, *to make holy, consecrate, sanctify*.

[29] Lev. 21:8, 15, 23; 22:9, 16, 32; Num. 3:13; 8:17; 1 Kgs. 9:3, 7; 2 Chron. 7:16, 20; 36:14; Ez. 36:23; 37:28

may your whole spirit and soul and body be kept blameless at the coming of our Lord Jesus Christ" (1 Thess. 5:23, ESV).

Believers are sanctified through the truth of God's word (John 17:17; Heb. 2:11; Ep. 5:26); through the sacrifice of Jesus Christ and the blood of the covenant (Heb. 10:10, 29; 13:12); and through the working of the Holy Spirit within the believer (Rom. 15:16; 1 Cor. 6:11; 2 Thess. 2:13; 1 Peter 1:2). But believers are also to consecrate (sanctify) themselves to the Lord. Even though they are sanctified through faith in Jesus (Acts 26:18), they must also actively separate themselves from all the vile and unclean practices of the world, putting away those things that lead to defilement:

> "Therefore, come out from among them and **be separate**, says the Lord; do not touch any unclean thing, and I will welcome you" (2 Cor. 6:17, HCSB).

> "Therefore, dear friends, since we have such promises, **let us cleanse ourselves from every impurity of the flesh and spirit**, completing our sanctification in the fear of God" (2 Cor. 7:1, HCSB).

Through the analogy of a large house with service vessels, Apostle Paul affirms that believers are to sanctify themselves for the Master's use:

> Now in a great house there are not only vessels of gold and silver but also of wood and clay, some for honorable use, some for dishonorable. Therefore, if anyone cleanses himself from what is dishonorable, he will be a vessel for honorable use, **set apart as holy**,[30] useful to the master of the house, ready for every good work (2 Tim. 2:20-21, ESV).

Apostle Peter, in his first letter, reiterates the Lord's command in the Old Testament to be holy:

> As obedient children, do not conform to the evil desires you had when you lived in ignorance. But just as he who called you is holy, so be holy in all you do; for it is written: "**Be holy, because I am holy**" (1 Peter 1:14-16, NIV).

Consecration or sanctification is not optional for the believer. We are both exhorted and warned in the letter to the Hebrews: "Pursue peace with

---

[30] Gk. ἁγιάζω, hagiazó, to make holy, consecrate, sanctify.

all men, and the sanctification without which no one will see the Lord" (Heb. 12:14, NASB). It is what sets God's people apart from the world. The present and eternal vocation of God's people is to worship and serve him. But it is impossible to worship and serve the Lord if our heart is divided and bows down before more than one altar. It is also impossible to worship and serve a *holy* God if we allow carnal filth and impurity to rule our lives. Furthermore, it is impossible to worship and serve the Lord if we wear "the garment defiled by the flesh" (Jude 1:23, HCSB). The lack of holiness makes it impossible to possess the mindset and freedom of spirit necessary to biblical worship. For this reason, consecration is such an integral part of biblical devotion.

Devotion and New Testament Discipleship

As we observed earlier, with the coming of the Messiah and the Messianic reformation,[31] the Old Testament laws (or statutes) that governed devotion changed; however, the spirit of devotion continues into the new covenant. It is primarily expressed in New Testament *discipleship*, as taught by Jesus. Because of its unequivocal demands for love and sacrifice, discipleship is, in many ways, tantamount to devotion. In fact, Jesus said: "No one can serve two masters, for either he will hate the one and love the other, or he will be devoted to the one and despise the other. You cannot serve God and money" (Matt. 6:24, ESV). The Lord knew that unless his disciples loved him unconditionally and were totally devoted to him and his mission, for one reason or another, they would eventually stop following him.

The gospel of Luke recounts how at one point in Jesus' ministry, a great number of people were traveling with him. He turned and spoke to them, addressing the issue of discipleship:

> "If anyone comes to Me and does not hate his father and mother, wife and children, brothers and sisters, yes, and his own life also, he cannot be My disciple. And whoever does not bear his cross and come after Me cannot be My disciple. For which of you, intending to build a tower, does not **sit down first and count the cost**, whether he has *enough* to finish *it*—lest, after he has laid the foundation, and is not able to finish, all who see *it* begin to mock him, saying, 'This man began to build and was not able to finish'? Or what king, going to make war against another king, does not **sit**

[31] Heb. 9:10

> **down first and consider** whether he is able with ten thousand to meet him who comes against him with twenty thousand? Or else, while the other is still a great way off, he sends a delegation and asks conditions of peace. So likewise, whoever of you does not forsake all that he has cannot be My disciple. Salt *is* good; but if the salt has lost its flavor, how shall it be seasoned? It is neither fit for the land nor for the dunghill, *but* men throw it out. He who has ears to hear, let him hear!" (Luke 14:26-35, NKJV).

The Lord's teaching speaks volumes, concerning the meaning of devotion. Jesus first addresses the relationship between family and discipleship. He instructed the crowds that if anyone wanted to follow him, they had to *hate* their family members, and even their own life, or they could not be his disciples. At first blush, Jesus' words appear harsh, cruel, and even impossible for those who perhaps enjoy a tight-knit family. The problem lies in our understanding of what Jesus meant by the word, *hate*. The Lord was certainly not teaching the people to loathe, dislike, or repudiate one's family members; this would contradict his other teachings on the law, particularly regarding that of honoring one's father and mother.[32] Instead, Jesus meant the people should love and prefer him above all other relationships, especially the family. That this is meaning is more understandable in the gospel of Matthew, where Jesus taught the same thing, but with an emphasis on the word, *love*:

> **The person who loves father or mother more than Me is not worthy of Me**; the person who loves son or daughter more than Me is not worthy of Me. And whoever doesn't take up his cross and follow Me is not worthy of Me. Anyone finding his life will lose it, and anyone losing his life because of Me will find it" (Matt. 10:37-39, HCSB).

Discipleship is devotion because it requires that we love Jesus with a supreme and undivided love.

Jesus further taught the crowds that if anyone did not carry their cross, they could not be his disciples. The Roman cross was a symbol of public shame and execution. Jesus' disciples were to consider themselves as *dead-men-walking*, that is, men destined for public execution. Luke records that Jesus had previously spoken to his disciples about carrying the cross *daily*:

---

[32] Matt. 15:3-6; 19:18-19

> Then He said to them all, "If anyone wants to come with Me, he must deny himself, take up his cross daily, and follow Me. For whoever wants to save his life will lose it, but whoever loses his life because of Me will save it. What is a man benefited if he gains the whole world, yet loses or forfeits himself? For whoever is ashamed of Me and My words, the Son of Man will be ashamed of him when He comes in His glory and that of the Father and the holy angels" (Luke 9:23-26, HCSB).

Shame is a powerful feeling that can hurt a person's pride. The only way to defeat shame is by denying ourselves and shamelessly embracing our own cross. Discipleship is devotion because it requires that we love Jesus more than the praises and acceptance of the world.

Continuing his teaching on discipleship, the Lord proposed two hypothetical scenarios to the crowd: Jesus asked, which of them would begin to lay the foundation of a tower without first calculating the costs, to see if he had enough fund to complete the project and not become the laughingstock of the people. He then inquired, what king would engage in war against another king without first considering whether or not his army could defeat the other army twice its own size (Luke 14:18-31). The Lord knew that unless those who followed him factored in the cost, they would ultimately fail in their venture. Discipleship is devotion because it requires the cost of total commitment and dedication.

The Lord concluded his teaching on discipleship with a metaphor about good and bad salt:

> "Salt *is* good; but if the salt has lost its flavor, how shall it be seasoned? It is neither fit for the land nor for the dunghill, *but* men throw it out. He who has ears to hear, let him hear!" (Luke 14:34-35, NKJV).

The only way salt can lose its flavor is if it becomes contaminated with other mineral impurities. Total devotion is indeed the flavor and seasoning of discipleship. Those who would attempt to follow Jesus without being *wholly* devoted to him are like contaminated salt that has lost its flavor. Discipleship is devotion because it demands preservation from all spiritual compromise and contamination.

So, how do Jesus' teachings on discipleship specifically relate to worship? Since devotion is an integral part of biblical worship, and in as much as discipleship is an expression of devotion, we cannot truly worship God yet love our family and friends more than Jesus. We cannot worship God yet refuse to daily carry our cross and follow Jesus. More pointedly, we cannot worship God yet be ashamed of his Son, Jesus. We cannot worship God yet offer him a devotion that costs us nothing. And lastly, we cannot worship God yet offer him a devotion that is insipid and compromised. Insipid devotion will only produce insipid worship.[33]

[33] Lev. 2:13; Ezek. 43:24. Salt was an essential ingredient used with grain offerings and animal sacrifices.

CHAPTER 9

The Pillar of the Spirit

(The Intimacy of Biblical Worship)

Then the Lord said to Moses, "Gather for me seventy men of the elders of Israel, whom you know to be the elders of the people and officers over them, and bring them to the tent of meeting, and let them take their stand there with you. And I will come down and talk with you there. And I will take some of the Spirit that is on you and put it on them, and they shall bear the burden of the people with you, so that you may not bear it yourself alone.

Then the Lord came down in the cloud and spoke to him, and took some of the Spirit that was on him and put it on the seventy elders. And as soon as the Spirit rested on them, they prophesied. But they did not continue doing it. Now two men remained in the camp, one named Eldad, and the other named Medad, and the Spirit rested on them. They were among those registered, but they had not gone out to the tent, and so they prophesied in the camp. And a young man ran and told Moses, "Eldad and Medad are prophesying in the camp." And Joshua the son of Nun, the assistant of Moses from his youth, said, "My lord Moses, stop them." But Moses said to him, "Are you jealous for my sake? Would that all the Lord's people were prophets, that the Lord would put his Spirit on them!" (Num. 11:16-17, 25-29, ESV).

In the book of *Genesis*,[1] the Spirit of God is portrayed as hovering over the primordial waters of creation. In the early chronicles of history, it is recorded that, in the days of Noah, the Spirit of God strove with men, before God sent a flood and destroyed the ancient world. In the period of the patriarchs, Pharaoh recognized that the Spirit of God was operating in

[1] Gen. 1:2; 6:3; 41:25-38

Joseph when he interpreted the king's dreams and wisely advised him how the Egyptians could prepare themselves for the coming years of famine. In the book of *Exodus*,[2] God called out Bezalel, son of Uri, by name and filled him with the Spirit so he would possess the necessary wisdom to oversee the making of the tabernacle, the ark of testimony, and all the clothing and objects related to covenant worship and the priestly services. The Spirit also imparted the gift of teaching to Bezalel and his assistant, Oholiab, so they could teach other craftsmen the work (We cannot overstate the important role of God's Spirit in the formation and development of Israel's worship). The book of *Numbers*[3] recounts the story of Balaam, a pagan prophet, who had been hired by Balak, king of Moab, to come and curse Israel. But when Balaam saw a part of Israel's encampment, he could do nothing less than bless the people. When he beheld all the tribes of Israel from the mountain, the Spirit of God came upon him, and he continued to bless the people of God and prophesy against their enemies. We also read in Numbers the Lord instructed Moses to have Joshua son of Nun stand before the high priest and the congregation, and appoint him as the new leader, because he had the Spirit. In *Deuteronomy*,[4] Joshua is described as a man full of the Spirit of wisdom, because Moses had laid hands on him. Briefly surveying the Pentateuch (the five books of Moses), one cannot help but notice the prominent role of God's Spirit in creation, in history, in prophetic utterances, in spiritual authority, and, especially important to our study, in the formation and development of biblical worship, the latter of which is the primary focus of our present study.

Outpouring of the Spirit in the Old Testament

Our study begins with an account, taken from the book of Numbers, of a rather unusual outpouring of the Spirit of God. According to the background of the story, Moses was exceedingly oppressed by the people, due to their complaining and weeping. He said to the Lord that he was no longer able to bear the burden of the people. The Lord, therefore, instructed Moses to choose from among the elders, seventy men who could help him carry the burden. When Moses gathered the congregation, and placed the elders around the tabernacle, the Lord came down in a cloud and took some

[2] Exod. 31:1-11; 35:30-35
[3] Num. 24:2, 10-13; 27:18-23
[4] Deut. 34:9

of the Spirit that was on Moses and placed it to the elders. The elders began to prophesy. For some undisclosed reason, two of the elders, *Eldad* and *Medad*, had not gone to the tabernacle, but remained in camp. When the Spirit came upon the elders, Eldad and Medad also began to prophesy.

> And a young man ran and told Moses, "Eldad and Medad are prophesying in the camp." And Joshua the son of Nun, the assistant of Moses from his youth, said, "My lord Moses, stop them." But Moses said to him, "Are you jealous for my sake? Would that all the Lord's people were prophets, that the Lord would put his Spirit on them!" (Num. 11:27-29, ESV).

Joshua was concerned that by prophesying in the camp without Moses' consent, Eldad and Medad actions, in some way, constituted an affront to Moses' authority. But to his young assistant's concerns, Moses replied, "Are you jealous for my sake? Would that all the Lord's people were prophets, that the Lord would put his Spirit on them!" Moses' response provides an excellent introduction to our study on two accounts: First, it reflects the heart and purpose of God for his people. That purpose is reflected in the words of the prophet Joel, in which the Lord declares:

> "And it shall come to pass afterward, that **I will pour out my Spirit on all flesh**; your sons and your daughters shall prophesy, your old men shall dream dreams, and your young men shall see visions. **Even on the male and female servants in those days I will pour out my Spirit**" (Joel 2:28-29, ESV).[5]

In the Old Testament, the anointing of the Holy Spirit, for different reasons which we will discuss later in our study, was limited to only a few people (For example, only seventy elders received a portion of the Spirit that was on Moses and not all the people). But according to Joel, the day would come when God would pour out his Spirit on all his people without exception. Second, in the Old Testament, the Spirit of God was always the intangible source of inspiration behind praise and worship. The Spirit inspired the people of God to praise and worship God through the prophetic utterances and songs of those who had God's Spirit. For example, both Moses and Miriam (who was also a prophetess) composed renowned songs and led the

---

[5] Joel 2:28-32; Acts 2:17-21. See for the full prophecy.

people in praise and worship.[6] What more could be said of the songs of Deborah and Barak, David, Asaph, the Sons of Korah, Solomon, the prophets, and even Mary, mother of Jesus.[7] Their songs and psalms still have an impact on God's people through the Scriptures and the Spirit. The Spirit is and has always been, as we have already affirmed, the intangible source of inspiration of praise and worship among God's people. Indeed, of all the pillars, we believe the *Pillar of the Spirit* is one of the most important. In fact, the Spirit of God is the heavenly fire that falls on the altar and consumes the *SACRIFICE*[8]; the Spirit of God is the divine anointing of the *PROPHET*[9]; it is the Holy Spirit who makes effectual the new *COVENANT* by placing the laws of God in our minds and writing them on our hearts[10]; the Holy Spirit is the source of divine *REVELATION*[11]; it is the Holy Spirit that makes the word of God become a powerful weapon of *WARFARE* to fight our spiritual enemy[12]; and lastly, it is the Holy Spirit who speaks to us the words of Jesus, challenging us to greater *DEVOTION*.[13] But we would be off-track if we only considered the Holy Spirit to be merely a means to divine end. The Holy Spirit is more than a means; indeed, he is the end—God who dwells in his people.[14] Moreover, when the Holy Spirit makes known his presence, praise and worship become the spontaneous and the immediate outcome. The indwelling presence of the Holy Spirit is one of the seven principles that sets biblical worship apart from all other world religions. While other religions may boast of their sacred rites and rituals, and even mystical experiences, they cannot lay claim (at least truthfully) to the Spirit of God.

Who is the Holy Spirit?

Before we examine the relationship between the Spirit of God and worship, let us briefly survey what the Scriptures teach about the person and identity of the Holy Spirit. In the Old Testament, the Spirit is

---

[6] Exod. 15:1-18, 20-21; Deut. 31:30; 32:1-43; Ps. 90; Rev. 15:3
[7] Judg. 5:1-31; Ps. 42:1; 72:1; 2 Chron. 29:30; Hab. 3:1-19; Luke 1:46-55
[8] 1 Kgs. 18:24, 38-39; 2 Chron. 7:1-3; Matt. 3:11; Luke 3:16; Heb. 12:29; Rev. 4:5
[9] Num. 11:25-29; 1 Sam. 10:10; Joel 2:28-29; Acts 2:16-21
[10] Rom. 8:4; 2 Cor. 3:3, 8; Heb. 8:8-11
[11] Luke 2:26; John 16:13-14; 1 Cor. 2:10; Eph. 1:17
[12] Zech. 4:6; 2 Cor. 10:4; Eph. 6:17
[13] John 14:26; Rev. 2:7, 11, 17, 29; 3:6, 13, 22
[14] John 14:17; Rom. 8:9, 11; 1 Cor. 3:16; Eph. 2:21-22; 2 Tim. 1:14

considered the *Ruach* or *Breath* of God,[15] the divine source of all life.[16] In the New Testament, the Holy Spirit is considered part of the triune God—one with the Father and Son.[17] Regrettably, some people teach and believe the Holy Spirit is nothing more than a power or some sort of invisible force. This, however, does not explain how the Spirit can be both a moral and intellectual power without possessing attributes of morality and intelligence. According to Scripture, the Holy Spirit possesses all the attributes that define a person or personality. Apostle Paul writes:

> But God has **revealed** *them* to us through His Spirit. For the Spirit **searches** all things, yes, the deep things of God. For what man **knows** the things of a man except the spirit of the man which is in him? Even so no one **knows** the things of God except the Spirit of God. These things we also speak, not in words which man's wisdom teaches but which **the Holy Spirit teaches**, comparing spiritual things with spiritual (1 Cor. 2:10-13, NKJV).

According to Paul, the Holy Spirit *reveals*, *searches*, and *knows* the deep things of God. The apostle even compares the Spirit's ability to know the things of God with the ability of man's spirit to know the things of man. Each one of us is conscious of possessing an intellect with moral and cognitive abilities. It would be absurd to affirm that our mental faculties are only a force or power when they are primarily what make us a person. Paul further asserts that the things they had received from God did not come from human wisdom, but from words that were *taught* to them by the Holy Spirit. Jesus also spoke to his disciples of the Holy Spirit's ability to *teach*:

> "When they bring you before the synagogues and the rulers and the authorities, do not worry about how or what you are to speak in your defense, or what you are to say; for **the Holy Spirit will teach you** in that very hour what you ought to say" (Luke 12:11-12, NASB).

> "But the Helper, the Holy Spirit, whom the Father will send in My name, **He will teach you** all things, and bring to your remembrance all things that I said to you" (John 14:26, NKJV).

---

[15] Heb. רוּחַ, ruach, breath, wind, spirit.

[16] Job 33:4; Ps. 104:30

[17] Matt. 3:16-17; 28:19; Luke 3:21-22; 2 Cor. 13:13; Heb. 9:14

The Lord further spoke of the Holy Spirit as the *Spirit of truth*:

> "But when the Helper comes, whom I shall send to you from the Father, **the Spirit of truth** who proceeds from the Father, **He will testify of Me**" (John 15:26, NKJV).

> "However, when He, **the Spirit of truth**, has come, **He will guide you into all truth**; for He will not speak on His own *authority,* but whatever He hears He will speak; and He will tell you things to come" (John 16:13, NKJV).

The Lord also taught his disciples that when the Holy Spirit would come, he would "**convict the world** concerning sin and righteousness and judgment" (John 16:8, ESV). We clearly understand through Jesus' teachings the Holy Spirit possesses all the qualities of personality: He *teaches* all things, *testifies* of Jesus, *guides* in all truth, and *convicts* the world.[18] It simply does not make sense to ascribe such attributes to an impersonal and non-intelligent power or force. This may be quite permissible in poetical literature. For example, the book of Proverbs ascribes personality and gender to *Wisdom* and *Folly*. But Jesus was not speaking in poetical form; he taught emphatically and in a matter-of-fact style. We do not deny that power is also an attribute of the Holy Spirit,[19] but this does not make the Spirit a power or force, any more than the *fruit of the Spirit*[20] make the Spirit, fruit. Besides, if the Holy Spirit were merely a power, those Scriptures that speak of both the Spirit and power would not make any sense:

> "You know the events that took place throughout Judea, beginning from Galilee after the baptism that John preached: how God anointed Jesus of Nazareth **with the Holy Spirit and with power**..." (Acts 10:37- 38, HCSB).

> "And my speech and my preaching *were* not with persuasive words of human wisdom, but in **demonstration of the Spirit and of power**" (1 Cor. 2:4, NKJV).

> "For our gospel did not come to you in word only, **but also in power, and in the Holy Spirit** and in much assurance, as you know what kind of men we were among you for your sake" (1 Thess. 1:5, NKJV).

---

[18] The Holy Spirit can also be *grieved* and *quenched* (Eph. 4:30; 1 Thess. 5:19).
[19] Mic. 3:8; Luke 1:35; 4:14; Acts 1:8; Rom. 15:13, 19
[20] Gal. 5:22

To complicate matters further for those who would deny the personhood of the Holy Spirit, there are also passages of Scriptures that refer to the Holy Spirit, personally speaking to someone[21]:

> "Then **the Spirit said** to Philip, 'Go near and overtake this chariot'" (Acts 8:29, NKJV).
>
> "While Peter thought about the vision, **the Spirit said** to him, 'Behold, three men are seeking you'" (Acts 10:19, NKJV).

The Scriptures not only attribute personality to the Holy Spirit, but they also ascribe to him, *deity and individuality*. In Acts of the Apostles, when Peter had to deal with Ananias' deception, he clearly referred to the Holy Spirit as God[22]:

> Then Peter said, "Ananias, how is it that Satan has so filled your heart that **you have lied to the Holy Spirit** and have kept for yourself some of the money you received for the land? Didn't it belong to you before it was sold? And after it was sold, wasn't the money at your disposal? What made you think of doing such a thing? **You have not lied just to human beings but to God**" (Acts 5:3-4, NIV).

The Holy Spirit is identified with the Father and the Son, yet his individuality is also recognized:

> "Go therefore and make disciples of all the nations, baptizing them in the name of the Father and the Son and the Holy Spirit" (Matt. 28:19, NASB).
>
> "But the Helper, the Holy Spirit, whom the Father will send in my name, he will teach you all things and bring to your remembrance all that I have said to you" (John 14:26, ESV).
>
> "The grace of the Lord Jesus Christ, and the love of God, and the fellowship of the Holy Spirit be with all of you" (2 Cor. 13:14, HCSB).

While we have only gleaned a few of the Scriptures to make our point, there is an overwhelming body of biblical evidence that supports the doctrine of the deity and personality of the Holy Spirit. The only reason anyone would ignore or twist the Scriptural data is because they want to deny the doctrine of the Trinity. And sadly, there are plenty of people and

---

[21] Acts 13:2

[22] 2 Cor. 3:17

religious groups who have this very objective. But to deny the full personality of the Holy Spirit is to undermine one of the most important doctrines of the Holy Writ. In fact, the seventh pillar of our study does not merely represent a function, component, or expression of worship; it is emblematic of the Holy Spirit—the personal presence of God himself.

The Promise of the Father

> "And behold, I am sending the promise of my Father upon you. But stay in the city until you are clothed with power from on high" (Luke 24:49, ESV).

Jesus instructed his disciples to remain in Jerusalem until he sent "the promise of my Father" upon them and they were "clothed with power from on high." The promise of the Father is an important theme in the writings of Luke, especially in Acts of the Apostles, where he specifically relates the baptism of the Holy Spirit to "the Promise of the Father," "the promise of the Holy Spirit," or simply, "the promise" (Acts 1:4; 2:33, 39, NKJV). The gift and outpouring of the Holy Spirit are among the prominent teachings of the New Testament—which prompts us to make several inquiries: *What is the baptism of the Holy Spirit? Why was it imperative that the disciples receive the promise of the Spirit before they began their ministry? Why did the Father have to wait until after the death and resurrection of his Son before he could give the promised Spirit to the disciples? Since worship is the main subject of our study, how does the baptism of the Holy Spirit impact worship? How do we receive the promise of the Spirit; how can we know that we have received it?* There is probably more than one answer to some of these inquiries. Nonetheless, we hope to provide some biblical insight.

What is the baptism or infilling of the Holy Spirit?

The subject and teaching of the baptism of the Holy Spirit is mentioned in all four gospels and in Acts of the Apostles.[23] From the very beginning, it has been an intrinsic part of the gospel message. John the Baptist attested that Jesus was the baptizer in the Holy Spirit:

> John answered them all, "I baptize you with water, but One is coming who is more powerful than I. I am not worthy to untie the strap of His sandals. He will baptize you with the Holy Spirit and fire" (Luke 3:16, HCSB).

The baptism of the Holy Spirit is when the Holy Spirit comes upon a believer

[23] Matt. 3:11; Mk.1:8; John 1:33; Acts 1:4-5

and floods their spirit with divine life of the Spirit.[24] Jesus described the infilling of the Spirit in these terms:

> "He who believes in Me, as the Scripture said, '**From his innermost being will flow rivers of living water**.'" But this He spoke of the Spirit, whom those who believed in Him were to receive; for the Spirit was not yet *given*, because Jesus was not yet glorified (John 7:38-39, NASB).

It is through the baptism of the Holy Spirit that we receive the necessary spiritual power to accomplish the purposes of God. In the gospel of Luke, Jesus spoke to the disciples of being "**clothed with power from on high**" (Luke 24:49, ESV). Acts also records the Lord telling his disciples: "But you will receive **power** when the Holy Spirit has come upon you, and you will be my witnesses in Jerusalem and in all Judea and Samaria, and to the end of the earth" (Acts 1:8, ESV). When the Holy Spirit *clothed* the disciples, they were supernaturally empowered to be Jesus's witnesses. The baptism of the Holy Spirit also empowered the disciples to praise and worship God in an extraordinary way: "And they were all filled with the Holy Spirit and began to speak in other tongues as the Spirit gave them utterance" (Acts 2:4, ESV). In fact, worship and witness go hand in hand. According to the account in Acts, the meeting among the disciples quickly moved from the upper room to the outdoors and in full view of the public. The disciples were suddenly surrounded by those who had heard the sound of rushing wind. Praise and worship continued to flow from the disciples' mouths in the languages of those who had traveled from distant lands to Jerusalem for the *Feast of Weeks*, that is, *Pentecost*.[25]

> And they were amazed and astonished, saying, "Are not all these who are speaking Galileans? And how is it that we hear, each of us in his own native language? Parthians and Medes and Elamites and residents of Mesopotamia, Judea and Cappadocia, Pontus and Asia, Phrygia and Pamphylia, Egypt and the parts of Libya belonging to Cyrene, and visitors from Rome, both Jews and proselytes, Cretans and Arabians—**we hear them telling in our own tongues the mighty works of God**" (Acts 2:7-11, ESV).

---

[24] Rom. 8:2, 6, 10

[25] Deut. 16:9-10

Unleashed praise and worship gave opportunity to Peter and the other apostles to rise up and declare the good news to the crowd. That very day, three thousand souls were converted to Christ and added to the church.[26]

The gospel continued to progress and spread throughout Judah and the surrounding region, until the martyrdom of Stephen and open persecution broke out against the church. Except for the apostles, all the church was scattered throughout the neighboring regions.[27] Philip, one of the seven deacons, "went down to the city of Samaria and proclaimed to them the Christ" (Acts 8:5, ESV). Seeing the amazing signs, deliverances, and healings he performed, and hearing the "good news about the kingdom of God and the name of Jesus Christ, they were baptized, both men and women" (Acts 8:12, ESV). Yet, these new converts still lacked one thing: The baptism of the Holy Spirit.

> Now when the apostles at Jerusalem heard that Samaria had received the word of God, they sent to them Peter and John, who came down and prayed for them that they might receive the Holy Spirit, for he had not yet fallen on any of them, but they had only been baptized in the name of the Lord Jesus. Then they laid their hands on them and they received the Holy Spirit (Acts 8:14-17, ESV).

According to the accounts in Acts, the Gentiles also received the baptism of the Holy Spirit, through the ministries of Peter and Paul. At the urging of the Holy Spirit, Peter received into the house, three Gentile men who had been sent by Cornelius, a centurion. The following day, Peter departed with them for Caesarea. When they arrived, he proclaimed the gospel to Cornelius and to "his relatives and close friends" (Acts 10:24, ESV). But as Peter spoke, something happened that amazed all the Jewish believers who had also travelled with Peter:

> While Peter was still saying these things, the Holy Spirit fell on all who heard the word. And the believers from among the circumcised who had come with Peter were amazed, because the gift of the Holy Spirit was poured out even on the Gentiles. For they were hearing them speaking in tongues and extolling God (Acts 10:44-46, ESV).

During one of Paul's evangelistic journeys, the apostle traveled through Galatia and Phrygia until he came to Ephesus, where he encountered

---

[26] Acts 2:14-41

[27] Acts 8:1

twelve disciples who only knew the baptism of John (i.e., water baptism):

> And Paul said, "John baptized with the baptism of repentance, telling the people to believe in the one who was to come after him, that is, Jesus." On hearing this, they were baptized in the name of the Lord Jesus. **And when Paul had laid his hands on them, the Holy Spirit came on them, and they began speaking in tongues and prophesying** (Acts 19:4-6, ESV).

After baptizing the disciples, Paul laid his hands on them and the Holy Spirit came upon them, and they began to speak in tongues and prophecy. The collective experience of the Jews, Samaritans, Gentiles, and the disciples of Ephesus teach us that the baptism of the Holy Spirit is for all believers. It can happen either as a second experience, or immediately upon hearing the gospel; and it can be received either with or without the laying on of hands. Those who believed the gospel were baptized in both water and in the Holy Spirit, regardless of the order.

The baptism of the Holy Spirit is a present and ongoing experience. In fact, Peter identifies the experience of the Gentiles with the outpouring that took place on the day of Pentecost. When Peter had returned to Jerusalem, he encountered criticism from those of the circumcision for going to the house of a Gentile. Peter, however, related the vision he had received and how the Spirit told him to go with the men who had been sent for him, "doubting nothing" (Acts 11:12, NKJV). He then explained what happened when he entered the house and spoke the good news:

> As I began to speak, the Holy Spirit fell on them just as on us at the beginning. And I remembered the word of the Lord, how he said, '**John baptized with water, but you will be baptized with the Holy Spirit**.' If then God gave **the same gift** to them as he gave to us when we believed in the Lord Jesus Christ, who was I that I could stand in God's way?" (Acts 11:15-17, ESV).

Peter refers to Jesus' words to explain what had transpired among the Gentiles: "John baptized with water, but you will be baptized with the Holy Spirit." The baptism of the Holy Spirit, as a *second experience*, does not call into question the presence and working of the Holy Spirit in salvation. Apostle Paul clearly highlights the Holy Spirit's involvement in the work of redemption: "And such were some of you. But you were washed, you were sanctified, you were justified in the name of the

Lord Jesus Christ and by the Spirit of our God" (1 Cor. 6:11, ESV). Even though we are *justified* in the name of the Lord Jesus Christ and by God's Spirit, we still need to be *filled* with the Holy Spirit.

Why was it imperative the disciples receive the promise of the Spirit before they began their ministry?

The disciples were eyewitnesses of Jesus' ministry and of his death and resurrection. They were to be his witnesses in all the world. But before they could begin their own ministry, Jesus commanded them to *wait* in Jerusalem for the promise of the Holy Spirit. The Lord knew it was imperative they receive the Spirit. On that fateful night, when Jesus was arrested, all his disciples fled and abandoned him in fear. Though Peter followed the Lord and the crowd that had arrested him, he kept himself at a *safe distance* in the courtyard of the high priest. However, when some of the people in the courtyard recognized him as a disciple of Jesus, Peter denied knowing the Lord three times. The disciples obviously needed the power of the Holy Spirit to boldly stand up and be witnesses of Jesus and of all that they had seen. They needed to overcome their *Safe Distance Syndrome*. The Holy Spirit does not necessarily cause fear to just disappear. Paul could candidly write the Corinthians: "And I was with you in weakness, and in fear, and in much trembling" (1 Cor. 2:3, KJV). Instead, the Lord displaces our fear with supernatural boldness. When the early church faced threats and opposition, they came together and prayed: "When they had prayed, the place where they were assembled was shaken, and **they were all filled with the Holy Spirit and began to speak God's message with boldness**" (Acts 4:31, HCSB).

The disciples also needed the Holy Spirit to make their message more affective, through the additional witness and conviction of the Holy Spirit. When the apostles were arrested and brought before the Sanhedrin a second time, they were questioned why they had disobeyed their injunction to stop teaching in the name of this man (the Sanhedrin refused to even pronounce Jesus' name).[28] But Peter and the apostles responded:

> "We ought to obey God rather than men. The God of our fathers raised up Jesus whom you murdered by hanging on a tree. Him God has exalted to His right hand *to be* Prince and Savior, to give

[28] Acts 4:17; 5:28

repentance to Israel and forgiveness of sins. **We are His witnesses to these things, and *so* also *is* the Holy Spirit whom God has given to those who obey Him**" (Acts 5:29-32, NKJV).

The Holy Spirit himself gives witness to the death and resurrection of Jesus Christ. When we testify of Jesus, the Holy Spirit brings conviction and assurance to our witness. This is what the Lord meant when he spoke to his disciples about the Holy Spirit: "When He comes, He will convict the world about sin, righteousness, and judgment:" (John 16:8, HCSB). This is also exactly what happened on the day of Pentecost. When the people heard Peter's message, "**they were pierced to the heart**, and said to Peter and the rest of the apostles, 'Brethren, what shall we do?'" (Acts 2:37, NASB). Even at the distance of more than two millennia, we can still preach the gospel with the convicting power of the Holy Spirit.

Why did the Father have to wait until after the death and resurrection of his Son before he could give the promised Spirit to the disciples?

In the Old Testament, the Spirit dwelt among God's people,[29] but as we mentioned in the introduction of our study, the Spirit only came upon those who held key positions of spiritual authority.[30] This would include patriarchs (in both antediluvian and postdiluvian periods), prophets, elders, judges, and kings.[31] The Lord declared through his prophets that he would

---

[29] Neh. 9:20; Isa. 63:11-14

[30] Spiritual authority and worship are inseparable. One of the many consequences of Adam's transgression was that the spiritual authority God had delegated to him was subverted and destabilized. Throughout biblical history, the Spirit of God would come upon chosen people to reestablish the link of spiritual authority between God and man. It is significant that God always established paradigms of worship among men through divinely delegated spiritual authority. The correlation between spiritual authority and worship is perhaps most clear in the accounts of Jesus' temptation. After the Holy Spirit had come upon Jesus and driven him into the wilderness for a forty day fast, the devil came and tempted him. In one of the three temptations, the devil offered Jesus all the kingdoms of the world in exchange for his worship. The devil was not asking Jesus to adore him for his moral perfections or physical beauty. He simply wanted Jesus to recognize or legitimize his authority. Jesus of course responded, "Go away, Satan! For it is written: Worship the Lord your God, and serve only Him" (Mat. 4:10, HCSB). Those who worship God must also recognize spiritual authority. We could hardly worship God without submitting to the Lordship of Jesus Christ, or to the spiritual authority the Lord has placed in the church.

[31] Exod. 31:1-11; 35:30-35: The Spirit was given to Bezalel for the purpose of building the tabernacle and all that was necessary for its functions and services.

pour out his Spirit on his people (Isa. 32:15; 44:3; Joel 2:28-32). However, before such prophecies could be fulfilled, certain contingencies needed to be fulfilled. In fact, the New Testament links the promise of the Spirit to the death and resurrection of Jesus Christ. On the day of Pentecost, when Peter and the apostles stood up to speak to the crowd, Peter explained that what the crowd was seeing, and hearing was the outpouring of the Holy Spirit—a fulfillment of what the prophet Joel had foretold. Peter boldly continued, declaring that Christ was taken and crucified by wicked hands, but he rose again from the dead and ascended into heaven: "Being therefore exalted at the right hand of God, **and having received from the Father the promise of the Holy Spirit**, he has poured out this that you yourselves are seeing and hearing" (Acts 2:33, ESV). The point is, only *after* Christ had been exalted did he receive the promise from the Father.

John also affirms in his gospel account that the outpouring of the Holy Spirit awaited the resurrection of Christ:

> "He said this about the Spirit. Those who believed in Jesus were going to receive the Spirit, **for the Spirit had not yet been received because Jesus had not yet been glorified**" (John 7:38-39, HCSB).

In his letter to the Galatians, Apostle Paul explains in more detail why the promise of the Spirit was given to Jesus. Like Peter in Acts of the Apostles, he identifies the promise with Christ's death, but he also identifies it with the blessing and offspring of Abraham:

> **Christ redeemed us from the curse of the law by becoming a curse for us**—for it is written, "Cursed is everyone who is hanged on a tree"— so that in Christ Jesus the blessing of Abraham might come to the Gentiles, **so that we might receive the promised Spirit through faith. Now the promises were made to Abraham and to his offspring**. It does not say, "And to offsprings," referring to many, but referring to one, **"And to your offspring," who is Christ**. This is what I mean: the law, which came 430 years afterward, does not annul a covenant previously ratified by God, so as to make the promise void.
>
> But the Scripture imprisoned everything under sin, **so that the promise by faith in Jesus Christ** might be given to those who

---

According to Ex. 35:34, Bezalel and Oholiab were also "inspired" by the Spirit to teach others (ESV).

> believe. Now before faith came, we were held captive under the law, imprisoned until the coming faith would be revealed. So then, the law was our guardian until Christ came, in order that we might be **justified by faith**.
>
> And if you are Christ's, then you are Abraham's offspring, **heirs according to promise** (Gal. 3:13-17, 22-24, 29, ESV).

The promise of the Father is the blessing of Abraham, a promise made to the patriarch's *offspring*, "who is Christ." According to Paul, because of our faith in Jesus Christ, we belong to him, and because we belong to Christ, we are also "Abraham's offspring, heirs of promise." Faith in Christ gives us access to the blessing of Abraham.

Another reason why the Father had to wait for the death and resurrection of Jesus Christ before the promised Spirit could be given to Jesus, and subsequently to his disciples, was the need to be justified by God of all our sins. Within context of Paul's teaching in Galatians, he writes that we are justified, or made righteous, by faith in Jesus (Gal. 3:24). Elsewhere in his writings, Paul further develops the theme of justification, explaining in more detail that we are justified by faith in his atoning blood of Jesus:

> For all have sinned and fall short of the glory of God, **being justified as a gift by His grace through the redemption which is in Christ Jesus**; whom God displayed publicly as **a propitiation in His blood through faith**. *This was* to demonstrate His righteousness, because in the forbearance of God He passed over the sins previously committed; for the demonstration, *I say*, of His righteousness at the present time, so that **He would be just and the justifier of the one who has faith in Jesus** (Rom. 3:23-26, NASB).
>
> Much more then, having now been **justified by His blood**, we shall be saved from the wrath *of God* through Him. For if while we were enemies we were reconciled to God through the death of His Son, much more, having been reconciled, we shall be saved by His life (Rom. 5:9-10, NASB).

Jesus offered himself up as a propitiation for sin so that God could justify (i.e., forgive and make righteous) those who have faith in Christ's blood. Because we are justified and sanctified through the precious blood of Jesus, we may receive the promise of the Holy Spirit. Only sin and unbelief stand in our way. When Peter concluded his first public preaching on the day of Pentecost, the people were convicted of their sin. They asked Peter and the apostles what they should do. Peter's response is significant:

> "Repent," Peter said to them, "and be baptized, each of you, in the name of Jesus Christ for the forgiveness of your sins, **and you will receive the gift of the Holy Spirit**. For the promise is for you and for your children, and for all who are far off, as many as the Lord our God will call" (Acts 2:38-39, HCSB).

How or in what way does the baptism of the Holy Spirit impact worship?

The baptism of the Holy Spirit dynamically impacts and transforms worship in different ways. But to understand these changes, it is necessary we recognize the various expressions that often accompany worship, such as *praise*, *thanksgiving*, *prayer*, and rendering *spiritual service* to God.[32]

Throughout the Scriptures, *praise* and *thanksgiving*, whether articulated in word or song, are often an integral part of worship.[33]

> When all the people of Israel saw the fire come down and the glory of the Lord on the temple, they bowed down with their faces to the ground on the pavement and worshiped and gave thanks to the Lord, saying, "For he is good, for his steadfast love endures forever" (2 Chr. 7:3, ESV).

> "And Hezekiah the king and the officials commanded the Levites to sing praises to the Lord with the words of David and of Asaph the seer. And they sang praises with gladness, and they bowed down and worshiped" (2 Chr. 29:30, ESV).

> "All the earth will worship You and sing praise to You. They will sing praise to Your name. *Selah*" (Ps. 66:4, HCSB).

> "I will worship toward Your holy temple, And praise Your name For Your lovingkindness and Your truth; For You have magnified Your word above all Your name" (Ps. 138:2, NKJV).

> "Then those who were in the boat worshiped him, saying, 'Truly you are the Son of God'" (Matt. 14:33, NIV).

---

[32] Luke 2:37

[33] Ps. 96:1-9

> "And the twenty-four elders and the four living creatures fell down and worshiped God who was seated on the throne, saying, 'Amen. Hallelujah!'" (Rev. 19:4, ESV).

On the day of Pentecost, when the disciples were filled with the Holy Spirit, they prophesied and proclaimed the praises of God in different languages through inspiration of the Holy Spirit (Acts 2:4). The same experience repeated itself when the Holy Spirit came upon the first Gentile believers:

> And those of the circumcision who believed were astonished, as many as came with Peter, because the gift of the Holy Spirit had been poured out on the Gentiles also. **For they heard them speak with tongues and magnify God**" (Acts 10:45-46, NKJV).[34]

In both incidents, the public expressions of praises and worship were bold and given without reserve.

Prayer is another expression of worship,[35] greatly impacted by the baptism of the Holy Spirit. After Jesus ascended into heaven, the disciples returned to the upper room where they "all continued with one accord in prayer and supplication, with the women and Mary the mother of Jesus, and with His brothers" (Acts 1:14, NKJV). They were still meeting together when the Holy Spirit was poured out on them on the day of Pentecost. Their prayer meeting suddenly reached a new level of inspiration and power when the disciples began to prophesy and speak in tongues. Following their experience, the church continued to pray together. Acts provides a brief account: "And they continued steadfastly in the apostles' doctrine and fellowship, in the breaking of bread**, and in prayers**" (Acts 2:42, NKJV). When the church began to encounter strong opposition in its early days, the disciples sought the Lord in prayer:

> "Now, Lord, look on their threats, and grant to Your servants that with all boldness they may speak Your word, by stretching out Your hand to heal, and that signs and wonders may be done through the name of Your holy Servant Jesus." **And when they had prayed,** the place where they were assembled together was shaken; **and they were all filled with the Holy Spirit, and they spoke the word of God with boldness** (Acts 4:29-31, NKJV).

---

[34] Acts 19:5-6

[35] Rev. 5:8

The church asked the Lord to grant them boldness to speak the word, by allowing them to perform divine healings, signs, and wonders in the name of Jesus. God responded by sending them an earthquake and a fresh outpouring of the Spirit. Prayer and the Holy Spirit clearly impacted the church and the preaching of the gospel. Prayer assumes a prominent role in the New Testament. In fact, in the book of Acts alone, the words, *to pray* (προσεύχομαι) appears 16 times; *to pray*, in the sense of *beseeching* or *requesting*, (δέομαι), 4 times; and *prayer* (προσευχή), 9 times. In his letter to the Romans, Apostle Paul explains how the Holy Spirit interacts with our prayers and leads us into deeper intercession:

> In the same way the Spirit also joins to help in our weakness, because we do not know what to pray for as we should, but the Spirit Himself intercedes for us **with unspoken groanings**. And He who searches the hearts knows the Spirit's mind-set, because He intercedes for the saints according to the will of God (Rom. 8:26-27, HCSB).

Paul also exhorts the church in Ephesus to "pray at all times in the Spirit with every prayer and request, and stay alert in this with all perseverance and intercession for all the saints" (Eph. 6:18, HCSB). Though the baptism or infilling of the Spirit is not mentioned in connection with either of these two passages, it would be rather difficult to imagine that believers could intercede with such intensity— "unspoken groanings"—or even pray "in the Spirit" without having first been baptized in the Spirit.

Spiritual service is an extremely important expression of worship. It is written of Anna the prophetess, who encountered Joseph and Mary as they brought their child, Jesus, to the temple, that she "departed not from the temple, but **served** [λατρεύω, *latreuó*] God with fastings and prayers night and day" (Luke 2:37, KJV). When the devil tempted Jesus, offering him all the kingdoms of the world if he would only bow down and worship him, the Lord responded, "Go away, Satan! For it is written: Worship the Lord your God, **and serve** [λατρεύω, *latreuó*] **only Him**" (Matt. 4:10, HCSB). There are different Greek verbs that are translated, *to serve*[36]; however, the words, λατρεύω, *latreuó, to serve*, and λατρεία, *latreia, service*, are particularly related to worship, sacrifices, and priestly services:

---

[36] The other Greek words are: διακονέω, *diakoneó, to serve, to minister* [e.g., Matt. 4:11; 20:28; Luke 10:40; John 12:26; etc.]; δουλεύω, *douleuó, to be a slave, to serve* [e.g., Matt. 6:24; Luke 15:29; Acts 20:19; Rom. 6:6; 7:6; 12:11; etc.]; ὑπηρετέω, *hupéreteó, to serve as a rower, to minister, to serve* [e.g., Acts 13:36; 20:34; 24:23]; θεραπεύω, *therapeuó, to serve, to cure* [e.g., Matt. 4:23-24; 8:7; Luke 14:3; Acts 17:25; etc.].

> "But this I confess to you, that according to the Way which they call a sect, so **I worship** [λατρεύω, *latreuó*] the God of my fathers, believing all things which are written in the Law and in the Prophet" (Acts 24:14, NKJV).

> "They are Israelites, and to them belong the adoption, the glory, the covenants, the giving of the law, the temple **service** [λατρεία, *latreia*], and the promises" (Rom. 9:4, HCSB).

> "Therefore, brothers, by the mercies of God, I urge you to present your bodies as a living sacrifice, holy and pleasing to God; this is your spiritual **worship** [λατρεία, *latreia*]" (Rom. 12:1, HCSB).

> For if He were on earth, He would not be a priest, since there are priests who offer the gifts according to the law; who **serve** [λατρεύω, *latreuó*] the copy and shadow of the heavenly things, as Moses was divinely instructed when he was about to make the tabernacle (Heb. 8:4-5, NKJV).

> "Then indeed, even the first *covenant* had ordinances of divine **service** [λατρεία, *latreia*] and the earthly sanctuary" (Heb. 9:1, NKJV).

Because of the Holy Spirit and the blood of Christ, *serving* God or rendering him *service* takes on a deeper and more spiritual meaning than in the Old Testament:

> "For we are the circumcision, who **worship** [λατρεύω, *latreuó*] God in the Spirit, rejoice in Christ Jesus, and have no confidence in the flesh" (Phil. 3:3, NKJV).

> "How much more will the blood of Christ, who through the eternal Spirit offered himself without blemish to God, purify our conscience from dead works to **serve** [λατρεύω, *latreuó*] the living God" (Heb. 9:14, ESV).

Acts of the Apostles documents a special worship service that took place in Antioch:

> In the church that was at Antioch there were prophets and teachers; Barnabas, Simeon who was called Niger, Lucius the Cyrenian, Manaen, a close friend of Herod the tetrarch, and Saul. As they were **ministering** [λειτουργέω, *leitourgeó*] to the Lord and fasting, the Holy Spirit said, "Set apart for Me Barnabas and Saul for the work I have called them to" (Acts 13:1-2, HCSB).

The Greek word for "ministering," λειτουργέω, *leitourgeó*, means, among other things, *to perform religious service*. The word was used in reference to the priests who ministered and offered daily sacrifices in the tabernacle: "Every priest stands day after day ministering [λειτουργέω, *leitourgeó*] and offering the same sacrifices time after time, which can never take away sins" (Heb. 10:11, HCSB). The prophets and teachers in the church of Antioch were gathered together to minister to the Lord. They prayed, fasted, and most likely, sang hymns, and offered praise and thanksgiving to God. Suddenly, the Holy Spirit spoke and said, "Set apart for Me Barnabas and Saul for the work I have called them to." The Holy Spirit could give such directives because these men had already set themselves apart, as the entire incident would strongly suggest.

How do we receive the promise of the Spirit; and how can we know that we have received it?

Today, God is still baptizing believers in the Holy Spirit. Years ago, a brother and colleague in the ministry showed me an important truth, regarding the baptism of the Spirit: As long as the Lord is calling people to salvation, he will continue to give the promise of the Holy Spirit. When Peter finished proclaiming the gospel, in Acts, chapter two, the crowd asked what they should do:

> "Repent," Peter said to them, "and be baptized, each of you, in the name of Jesus Christ for the forgiveness of your sins, and you will receive the gift of the Holy Spirit. For the promise is for you and for your children, and for all who are far off, **as many as the Lord our God will call**" (Acts 2:38-39, HCSB).

Peter's closing comment is important and should not be overlooked. "For the promise is for you and for your children, and for all who are far off, as many as the Lord our God will call." The only requirements to receive the promise of the Spirit are repentance, faith, and obedience to Jesus (Acts 5:32; Gal. 3:2, 5, 14). Yet, even then, the baptism of the Holy Spirit does not always immediately follow one's conversion, as it did in the case of Cornelius and the Gentile believers. Instead, we must ask God for the infilling of the Spirit, just as Jesus taught his disciples: "If you then, being evil, know how to give good gifts to your children, **how much more will *your* heavenly Father give the Holy Spirit to those who ask Him!**" (Luke11:13, NKJV). The amazing thing about

Jesus' statement is that it reveals the extreme willingness of our heavenly Father to give us the Holy Spirit. Indeed, he is more willing than we are when it comes to giving gifts to our own children.

Some believers perhaps wonder how they might know whether they have already received the baptism of the Holy Spirit. The most common evidence of the baptism of the Holy Spirit is speaking in tongues. In almost every case in Acts of the Apostles where a group of believers received the baptism of the Holy Spirit, there was also the evidence of speaking in tongues. In case of the Samaritans, nothing is explicitly said of them speaking in tongues. However, there must have been some sort of accompanying sign or manifestation that would prompt the warped mind of Simon (he practiced magic among the Samaritans: Acts 8:9), into thinking he could purchase from the apostles, the ability to lay hands on people so they could receive the Holy Spirit. The book of Acts also recounts the story of how the Apostle Paul was filled with the Holy Spirit (Acts 9:17). Though Acts of the Apostles says nothing of Paul, speaking in other tongues, the apostle personally affirms in his letter to the church of Corinth that he indeed spoke in tongues, and not just a little:

> "**I thank my God I speak with tongues more than you all**, yet in the church I would rather speak five words with my understanding, that I may teach others also, than ten thousand words in a tongue" (1 Cor. 14:18-19, NKJV).

It is unfortunate there is much some misunderstanding and even confusion, concerning speaking in tongues. Some teach that tongues and the other gifts of the Spirit ceased after the Apostolic period or with the canonization of the New Testament.[37] Some believe tongues were actually human languages. Regrettably, some even argue that speaking in tongues is of the devil. As we mentioned earlier, as long as God is calling people, the baptism of the Holy Spirit is still readily available. While it is true that on the day of Pentecost, the first disciples spoke in actual human languages, this was only because the Holy Spirit had given them the ability to communicate with those who had come to Jerusalem from foreign countries, to celebrate the Feast of Weeks. Perhaps this, in part, is what Paul means when he writes:

---

[37] We do not accept the doctrine of Cessationism. We believe the gifts and ministries of the Spirit are still present and available to the church (Rom. 1:11; 12:6-8; 1 Cor. 12:4-11; Eph. 4:8-12).

"Tongues, then, are a sign, not for believers but for unbelievers; prophecy, however, is not for unbelievers but for believers" (1 Cor. 14:22, NIV).

Normally, tongues are an *unknown* language—a language of the Spirit. In his first letter to the Corinthians, Paul explains in more detail the nature and purpose of tongues in our private devotions and in public church meetings:

> Follow the way of love and eagerly desire gifts of the Spirit, especially prophecy. For anyone who speaks in a tongue does not speak to people but to God. Indeed, no one understands them; they utter mysteries by the Spirit. But the one who prophesies speaks to people for their strengthening, encouraging and comfort. Anyone who speaks in a tongue edifies themselves, but the one who prophesies edifies the church. I would like every one of you to speak in tongues, but I would rather have you prophesy. The one who prophesies is greater than the one who speaks in tongues, unless someone interprets, so that the church may be edified.
>
> For this reason the one who speaks in a tongue should pray that they may interpret what they say. For if I pray in a tongue, my spirit prays, but my mind is unfruitful. So what shall I do? I will pray with my spirit, but I will also pray with my understanding; I will sing with my spirit, but I will also sing with my understanding. Otherwise when you are praising God in the Spirit, how can someone else, who is now put in the position of an inquirer, say "Amen" to your thanksgiving, since they do not know what you are saying? You are giving thanks well enough, but no one else is edified (1 Cor. 14:1-5, 13-17, NIV).

When we speak in tongues we speak to God and not men. No one understands our heavenly language (unless the Spirit gives us the ability to communicate in human languages, such as that which happened on the day of Pentecost). When we speak in tongues, we express "mysteries by the Spirit." One of the beautiful things about this incomprehensible and ecstatic language is that we may use it in our devotions: "I will pray with my spirit, but I will also pray with my understanding; I will sing with my spirit, but I will also sing with my understanding." Thus, praying and singing in tongues becomes a potential dynamic of praise and worship. According to Paul, tongues are also an important source of *edification.* When we speak in tongues, our spirit is built up or edified through interaction with God's Spirit. Tongues also edify the church, but only if they are *interpreted*.[38] That is why Paul writes: "For this reason the one who speaks in a tongue should pray that they may interpret what they say" (1 Cor. 14:13, NIV). Through edification, believers may also find the needed *inspiration* and *motivation* to worship and serve God. Speaking in tongues, both privately and publicly, clearly assumes an important function in New Testament worship.

Another evidence of the baptism of the Holy Spirit is the *exuberance of divine life*. The Holy Spirit may take us by surprise, but certainly not unaware. He causes divine life to overflow in our spirit. This is not religious hyperbole; it is experiential, something of which we are quite conscious. Among the four gospels, the gospel of John particularly relates Jesus' teachings on the exuberance and overflowing virtue of the Holy Spirit:

> On the last and most important day of the festival, Jesus stood up and cried out, "If anyone is thirsty, he should come to Me and drink! **The one who believes in Me, as the Scripture has said, will have streams of living water flow from deep within him." He said this about the Spirit**. Those who believed in Jesus were going to receive the Spirit, for the Spirit had not yet been received because Jesus had not yet been glorified (John 7:37-39, HCSB).

Flowing "streams of living water" expresses an exceptional experience that takes place when a believer is baptized and filled with the Holy Spirit. When we believe in the death and resurrection of Jesus Christ with all our heart, we should experience God's forgiveness and a sense of peace and joy in our spirit. We have been adopted into the family of God. We should also experience a new desire to worship and serve God and to fellowship with other believers. These are the normal experiences of *conversion*. Even the first disciples worshipped the Lord and continually met together in the temple to praise God before they were baptized in the Holy Spirit:

> "And behold, I am sending the promise of my Father upon you. But stay in the city until you are clothed with power from on high." And he led them out as far as Bethany, and lifting up his hands he blessed them. While he blessed them, he parted from them and was carried up into heaven. And they worshiped him

---

[38]1 Cor. 12:10. Interpretation of tongues is one of the gifts of the Spirit.

> and returned to Jerusalem with great joy, and were continually in the temple blessing God (Luke 24:49-53, ESV).

However, when they were filled with the Holy Spirit, their previous experience of joy and worship paled in comparison. Divine life began to flow from deep within them, like streams of living water. These streams then became ecstatic utterances of the Spirit. Passion and fire for the Lord could no longer be contained in a building, as a result, their praise and adoration overflowed into the street. Streams of living water will freely flow from those who ask the Father for the promise of the Holy Spirit.

ABOUT THE AUTHOR

Wendell grew up in Joliet, Illinois. In his late teenage years, he gave his life to the Lord Jesus and joined the evangelistic tent ministry that had preached the gospel to him. Within a year, he was sent out with a group of missionaries to be part of the ministry's work in Italy. Wendell served twenty years in that evangelistic tent ministry. He also served as worship leader and elder in a local church in Milan. He and his wife, Marilina, concurrently hosted a Bible study in their home in the small town of Sant'Angelo Lodigiano. Wendell and Marilina and their two boys, eventually moved to the city of Taranto in the southern part of Italy. Wendell continued to itinerate as a preacher and Bible teacher. But among all his personal experiences, worship has always had a special place in his heart and ministry. As a musician, composer, and worship leader, Wendell led worship and supported other worship leaders and musicians. He and Marilina also recorded and produced praise and worship music in the Italian language (some of his songs are still used in the Italian evangelical church). Wendell and Marilina presently reside in Claremore, Oklahoma.

For questions and comments about the book, the author may be reached at: **7pillarhouse@gmail.com**

Made in the USA
Columbia, SC
04 January 2022

53383935R00117